MW01615588

SEX AND THE CITIZEN

HOW THE ASSAULT ON MARRIAGE IS DESTROYING DEMOCRACY

CONN CARROLL

BOMBARDIER BOOKS

Published by Bombardier Books
An Imprint of Post Hill Press
ISBN: 978-1-63758-951-9
ISBN (eBook): 978-1-63758-952-6

Sex and the Citizen:
How the Assault on Marriage Is Destroying Democracy

Cover Design by Jim Villaflores

This is a work of nonfiction. All people, locations, events, and situations are portrayed to the best of the author's memory.

Post Hill Press
New York • Nashville
posthillpress.com

Published in the United States of America
1 2 3 4 5 6 7 8 9 10

For my wife, Wendi Conti Carroll

TABLE OF CONTENTS

INTRODUCTION

HOW SEX DRIVES HUMAN HISTORY

AT FIVE A.M. ON DECEMBER 29th, 2022, Romania's Directorate for Investigating Organized Crime and Terrorism invaded a warehouse in the town of Voluntari, just north of Bucharest.

The armed agents arrested two men, brothers Andrew and Tristan Tate, who were held in jail for three months and under house arrest for another three months, before being released on bail. The charges against them for rape and human trafficking are still outstanding, but even assuming they are innocent of those charges, what Andrew Tate has already admitted to doing is troubling enough.

Even before his arrest, Tate had become a household name among teenage boys in the English-speaking world. One 2022 survey of American teens ranked him as the top online influencer ahead of Kanye West, Mr. Beast and Duane Johnson. Before his TikTok account was banned, his videos had been viewed more than 12 billion times. He still has 9 million followers on Twitter.

Not all of Tate's appeal is bad. "My message is traditional masculinity," Tate told Tucker Carlson just weeks before his release. "My message is to stand up and say what you mean and mean what you say."[1]

For a lot of American boys who are constantly told that masculinity is toxic and that "the future is female," Tate's message could be a positive one.

"I basically just say to men: look, it's a very hard life. You're gonna need to get up, work hard, and go to the gym. Get yourself a strong network of brothers. Don't tolerate men who just smoke drugs and play video games or men who are disloyal or dishonest," Tate told Tucker.

This is all great advice. Unfortunately, Tate has a lot more to say, particularly about women, and it is all horrible.

"Females have no innate responsibility or honor," Tate said in one podcast, explaining why women shouldn't be allowed to drive.[2] Women are also "intrinsically lazy," according to Tate, which is why they need a man to tell them what to do.

Only the youngest of women, eighteen- and nineteen-year-olds, are worthy of Tate's time because by age twenty-five, according to Tate, they've slept with too many other men. Tate adamantly denies that he dislikes women. He claims he loves them. They are, according to Tate, "The true currency of ballers. Fuck money. It's women."

As repulsive as Tate may be to feminists here in the United States, however, no movement has done more to make his lifestyle possible.

"The institution of marriage is the chief vehicle for the perpetuation of the oppression of women," Marlene Dixon, founder of the Democratic Workers Party wrote in 1969. "It is through the role of wife that the subjugation of women is maintained."[3]

Taking this argument to its logical conclusion, Simone de Beauvoir, author of *The Second Sex*, told *Feminine Mystique* author Betty Friedan in 1972, "The family must be abolished, with absolute measure."[4]

Feminists have not completely succeeded in destroying the American family...yet. But they have made a lot of progress. From the first census of the United States through 1960, about 80 percent of all households were led by a married couple. That percentage started falling in the 1960s, it dipped below 50 percent in 2010, and has fallen to just 45 percent today.

No one is happier about the declining power of marriage to regulate who gets to sleep with whom than Andrew Tate.

By his own admission, before he was arrested Tate ran a camgirl empire employing dozens of women in multiple countries. On his old website Tate once explained, "My job is to meet a girl, go on a few dates, sleep with her, test if she's quality, get her to fall in love with me to where she'd do anything I say, and then get her on a webcam so we could become rich together."[5]

Getting married to one woman would be a serious detriment to Tate's lifestyle.

"I have beautiful women that are in love with me, and we are all happy and smiling every day," Tate once said, specifically explaining why he would never get married to one woman. "I get to fuck whatever I want. I don't think one woman is capable of completing a man's life."[6]

Feminists abhor this kind of talk. But they fail to recognize how their movement has empowered it.

What Tate understands about monogamous marriage is that as an institution it does far more to control men's lives than it does to control women. It is no accident that Tate comes from a broken home and was raised without a father. Tate is what happens to men in a world without marriage, and marriage is fast disappearing from our world every day.

THE CONVENTIONAL WISDOM ON MARRIAGE

Tate, and his unwitting feminist allies, are not the only ones happy to see humanity evolving past monogamous marriage. America's most popular sex columnist, Dan Savage, has been calling for an end to monogamy for years. "Monogamy is ridiculous," Savage tells his followers. "People aren't any good at it. We aren't wired for it. We didn't evolve to be monogamous. It's not natural."[7]

Savage's comments reflect the established conventional wisdom on monogamy: It isn't natural to humans; it is a learned cultural behavior contrary to our innate desires, and the whole point of the assault on marriage is to throw off its baleful influence and return to a more natural state of affairs in which desire is unfettered.

Savage's understanding of sex dovetails with the feminist view that monogamy is at the heart of a patriarchal order that treats women and children as property and was created specifically to control female sexual activity. Feminists and their libertine allies (like Tate and Savage) are thus united in seeking to overthrow this oppressive "heteronormative" system.

When the narrative gatekeepers at *Vox Media* (the "explanatory journalism" website created by progressive activists Ezra Klein and Matt Yglesias) created their first ever project for Netflix, they turned to Savage and fellow fidelity skeptics Dr. Stephanie Coontz and Chris Ryan to star in a video titled, "Monogamy, explained."[8]

"Anatomically modern human beings have existed for at least 300,000 years," Ryan says in the video. "And for more than 90 percent of that time, we lived as hunter-gatherers. Anthropologists refer to them as fiercely egalitarian. There's no reason to think that our ancestors shared everything except sexual partners."

According to Ryan, author of *Sex at Dawn: How We Mate, Why We Stray, and What It Means for Modern Relationships*, marriage did not exist in hunter-gatherer bands. Everyone had sex with everyone else and no one knew who the biological father of any particular child was. Instead, everyone raised everyone else's children together.

It was not until the spread of agriculture, and the concurrent invention of property that, according to Ryan, marriage was invented. "As the Greeks put it, you don't want a foreign seed introduced into your soil," Dr. Coontz explains. According to Dr. Coontz, author of *Marriage, a History: How Love Conquered Marriage*, marriage continued to be entirely about property until people began marrying for "love" around two hundred years ago.

Love, according to Coontz, is why marriage is declining in the United States today. "As soon as the idea that love should be the central reason for marriage was first raised, observers of the day warned that the same values that increased people's satisfaction with marriage as a relationship had an inherent tendency to undermine the stability of marriage as an institution," Coontz wrote. "The skeptics were right to worry about the dangers of the love match."[9]

Marriage, according to this narrative, isn't really needed for anything. It's just one of many perfectly acceptable options on the menu of life. "Monogamy is like vegetarianism," Ryan says. "You can choose to be a vegetarian. And that can be healthy, it can be ethical, it can be a wonderful decision, but just because you've chosen to be vegetarian, that doesn't mean that bacon stops smelling good."

"It's no longer about what kinds of relationships we should have in the modern world," the *Vox* narrator instructs the audience. "It's about designing the kinds of relationships we want to have."

And more Americans are redesigning their relationships today than ever before.

An extensive lexicon of non-monogamy has developed over the last two decades to help people navigate their bodies' true desires. There's old school polygamy which consists of both polygyny (one man, many wives) and polyandry (one woman, many husbands).

Then there is polyamory where several people are in a continuing relationship at the same time. This can mean one man and two women or one woman and two men, where all three people have romantic sexual relationships with each other. Or it can be where a man has separate sexual relationships with two different men, but the other men don't have a relationship with one another.

Open relationships, which are generally thought of as different than polyamorous ones, usually denote a situation where a couple has an ongoing sexual relationship with each other but are allowed to have short-term relationships with third parties. Representative Katie Hill (D-CA) lost her congressional seat after it was revealed that she was involved in a "throuple" with her husband and a member of her congressional staff.

These non-monogamous relationships are a lot more common than people think. A 2016 YouGov poll found that of those Americans currently in a relationship, more than one quarter said that relationship was non-monogamous.[10]

This is a remarkable increase over a short period of time. Gallup has been asking about the acceptability of polygamy for decades. From a low of just 5 percent approval in 2006, now a quarter of Americans say they find polygamy socially allowable. And the younger a person is, the more likely they are to accept non-monogamy.[11]

With more and more Americans utilizing this newfound freedom to design the relationships they want, without oppressive heteronormative constraints, shouldn't they be having more and better sex than ever before? With all this honesty, communication, and acceptance about our physical needs, shouldn't the number of Americans in healthy sexual relationships be at record levels?

Yet the exact opposite is happening. Americans have never been more alone or unhappy.

Fewer Americans are in relationships now than ever before.[12] Fewer Americans are having sex, and those that are having it are having less of it.[13] Americans have fewer friends than ever before and what friends they do have they spend less time with.[14] Fewer Americans are going to church, fewer are socializing with their neighbors, and fewer are volunteering in their communities.[15] The percentage of Americans living alone has never been higher and the percentage of people who believe others can be trusted has never been lower.[16]

Paradoxically, as our freedom to pursue our most intimate physical and emotional needs has risen, our success in meeting those needs has collapsed. Meanwhile, the social bonds that hold us together are falling apart.

What went wrong?

AN UNCONVENTIONAL VIEW

The research that became this book began when I was communications director for a United States senator who had recently been named chairman of the Joint Economic Committee. Originally established by the Employment Act of 1946, traditionally the JEC issued staid reports on the state of the U.S. economy looking at customary economic indicators like gross domestic product, unemployment, inflation, etc.

My employer at the time, Senator Mike Lee (R-UT) wanted to take the JEC in another direction. He created the Social Capital Project to "investigate the evolving nature, quality, and importance of our associational life—namely, our families, communities, workplaces, and religious congregations."

The idea for Lee's project stemmed from Harvard Professor Robert Putnam's essay, and then book, *Bowling Alone: The Collapse and Revival of American Community*, which noted that instead of bowling on teams in organized leagues, more Americans were choosing to bowl by themselves. This phenomenon mirrored, according to Putnam, similar retreats from participation in churches, labor unions, and other civic organizations like the Boy Scouts. Putnam argued that the loss of these civic engagements threatened to undermine the values and skills necessary for democracy to thrive.

As communications director for the senator, my duties included helping to take all the research and reports the JEC staff were producing, and turn them into speeches, op eds, YouTube videos, and 280-character tweets. The reports the JEC staff produced were fascinating, and I soon found myself tracking down footnotes for the studies I found particularly compelling.

As a conservative, I had a vague understanding that there was a body of research showing marriage was beneficial both to married partners and their children. But I had no idea just how broad and compelling the literature was.

And what I found out is that virtually everything in *Vox*'s "Monogamy, explained" video is wrong.

Our human ancestors did not mate promiscuously, as Ryan claims. Every hunter-gatherer society encountered throughout history has been centered on monogamous marriages (with occasional small-scale polygamy).[17] There are no polyandrous hunter-gatherer societies on record. Ryan is correct that hunter-gatherer bands were highly egalitarian entities with intricate food sharing rules, but they were not the free-love communes Ryan makes them out to be. Families shared food, yes. But husbands did not share their wives with each other or vice versa.

Now, in any primitive society where death can and does come suddenly, and there are no social safety net programs, sometimes one husband would die and if no single men were available, his wife would marry another already married man, most often one of his brothers. Extra pairings did happen. But they were rare. And more importantly, in any society where everyone must carry everything they own on their back, there simply isn't the opportunity for one man to acquire enough wealth to support more than one or two wives. Monogamy was the overwhelming norm.

All that changed with the advent of agriculture. The specialized warrior classes of agriculture societies conquered and enslaved neighboring communities. The high-ranking men of these warrior classes amassed great power, wealth, and harems of wives. So, Ryan is correct that the adoption of agriculture coincided with a change in human sexual relations, but the change was a move away from monogamy, not its first adoption.

For the next ten thousand years polygamous empires dominated the Earth. Whether it is Hammurabi's Babylon, the Maurya Empire in India, the Qin Dynasty in China, the Mali of Africa, the Vikings in Europe, or the

Aztecs in Mexico, on every continent men have settled, large slave-holding polygamous empires were the norm.

Polygamy's reign did not begin to end until the rise of Christianity in the second and third centuries.

The Romans already practiced a form of monogamy that they borrowed from the Greeks. But the monogamy of the Roman world would be unrecognizable to us today. Roman men were not allowed to have sex with the wives of other male citizens, but every other man, woman, and child was fair game. Wealthy Roman men had regular sex with their slaves and concubines of both sexes (especially young boys). Poor Roman men used prostitutes, which were usually slaves owned by other, wealthier men. The entire industry was taxed, regulated, and very much approved by the government.

But the followers of Jesus and their rapidly growing church took a different approach to managing sexual desire. Sex, for Christians, is never just physical. The act, though carnal, is also a transcendent union of two bodies becoming one spirit. Even more revolutionary, this new sexual ethic applied equally to rich and poor, to men and women. The monogamy of a Christian marriage was reciprocal, unlike the monogamy of Greek and Roman marriages, which was only unilaterally enforced on wives.

As the Church fought to impose monogamous norms on powerful men who did not want their sexual options limited, it developed a new regime of laws and customs that also happened to weaken tribe and clan-based patriarchal power structures allowing more independent and egalitarian nuclear families to form, grow, and thrive.[18]

Separated from controlling family patriarchs, nuclear families gathered in cities where new norms of behavior proved crucial to success. Sometimes these polities even elected their own leaders, and those elections served as the first inklings of representative democracy.

Where polygamous clan-based survival depended on conformity, obedience, and in-group loyalty, success in the world of nuclear families rewarded honesty, trust, and creativity. As the power of clan-based institutions dwindled, new civil institutions like guilds, universities, and the Church itself grew to take the patriarchal family's place. These new institutions became crucial to the development of science, capitalism, and eventually democracy.

Better than any other family form, the nuclear family channels the ambition and drive of men into productive and collaborative behaviors. Instead of pushing men to dominate each other and acquire more women, monogamous marriage binds men and women into a long-term project of cooperative care for each other and their children.

This is not to say that the nuclear family guarantees perfect behavior. It does not. We are all still human. But it is better, empirically, than polygamy, polyamory, or any other family type.

In a 2018 essay, University of Oklahoma classics professor Dr. Kyle Harper described the cultural transformation of the Roman Empire outlined above as "The First Sexual Revolution."[19]

But if we step back and look at the history of marriage, we can see an earlier sexual revolution among our promiscuous ape ancestors that first set us on the path to monogamy. Then, with the advent of agriculture, a second sexual revolution delivered a highly unequal and often tyrannical polygamous world. Finally, with the rise of Christianity, humanity experienced a third sexual revolution that pushed us back towards a monogamous and more egalitarian way of life.

Even before the West's unparalleled prosperity convinced many, but not all, nations of the world to abandon their polygamous norms, the seeds of a fourth sexual revolution were already growing.

As reason began to explain and conquer the physical world, some began to believe it could do the same for the ethical world as well. What were once taken as truths from established culture and tradition, began to be seen as corrupting influences that were only holding the individual back from achieving his best and truest self.

This rising individualism was reinforced by young fields of social science like psychology and anthropology. Soon elite thinkers began to question the most basic assumptions of Western civilization. By the late 1960s, these skeptics made up a majority of Supreme Court justices, and in the span of just five years, the Court demolished what had been the American Family Consensus in favor of the nuclear family that had bound the nation together since the nation's founding.

Where once it was the explicit holding of the land's highest court that the married household was the foundational unit of civil society, by 1972 marriage had been completely rejected as the proper regulator of sexual relations. Instead, the individual and his personal right to privacy, completely divorced from any sexual morality beyond consent, reigned supreme.

Where it was once expected that husbands were to provide for mothers, the state now stepped in. But the state's offer of lifetime support for women forced them to choose: marriage or the state. Unfortunately, more and more of them end up choosing the state every year.

The radical individualism embraced by the Court in 1972 would continue to shape culture and policy for decades, first liberalizing pornography in 1973, then decriminalizing sodomy in 2003, then legalizing gay marriage in 2015, and finally affirming trans ideology in 2020. Now all the old sexual identities must be torn down and replaced with an infinite new menu of identities including androsexual, asexual, bisexual, cisgender, genderqueer, non-binary, pansexual, transgender, and many many more.

The impact of this ongoing assault on marriage is clear. Among adults ages eighteen to forty-four, the share who have ever cohabited (59 percent) is now larger than the share who have ever been married (50 percent).[20]

But this fourth sexual revolution isn't affecting us all equally. Among upper-income mothers, 95 percent are married. Among middle-income mothers, 76 percent are married. Among low-income mothers, just 35 percent live in a married household.[21] This fact completely dismantles Dr. Coontz's love-destroyed-marriage thesis.

According to Dr. Coontz, it should be those among us with the most freedom that are the least likely to be married today. Instead, we see the exact opposite: the more power and choice a person has, the wealthier and better educated someone is, the more likely they are to be married.

A DISTURBANCE IN THE FORCE

Some liberals have begun to recognize the damage that the assault on marriage is causing to the fabric of our democracy, but their responses are underwhelming.

In his book, *Of Boys and Men*, Brookings Institution scholar Richard Reeves acknowledges that while more women are thriving in the modern world, some men are suffering.[22] Women, Reeves notes, get better grades in high school than boys, are more likely to go to college, and are more likely to graduate once they get there.

Moving into the working world, while men's wages (adjusted for inflation) have fallen since 1979, women's wages have risen dramatically. Men also have far higher rates of alcoholism, drug abuse, and suicide.

While Reeves argues that the cause of men's woes can be found in an education system that is more friendly to female development, as well as a changing economy that increasingly values emotional intelligence over physical strength, he also allows that missing fathers are a big part of men's struggles.

But instead of lamenting marriage's demise, Reeves celebrates it. "Marriage and motherhood are no longer virtually synonymous," Reeves writes. "About 40% of births in the U.S. now take place outside marriage, up from just 11% in 1970… From a feminist perspective, which to be clear is my perspective, these are marvelous developments."[23]

To help men cope with these "marvelous developments" Reeves calls for giving boys an extra year of government-run pre-K so they can start kindergarten a year later than girls; he calls for parental leave so fathers can have time to bond with their children; and he calls for new scholarship programs to help push men into "HEAL" jobs (health, education, administration, and literacy).

While red-shirting boys will marginally help some academically, it will not repair the damage done by missing a father in the home. Neither will parental leave cause unmarried fathers to spend more time with their sons, many of whom will go on to have more children with other women. The best proven way to ensure boys have an active male role model in the house is marriage. Helping men get and stay employed absolutely could help more men get and stay married, but pushing them into industries they are ill-suited for, and uninterested in, is not an effective corrective.

More provocatively, an avowed feminist from across the Atlantic, Louise Perry, has written an entertaining book making a strong case that the decline of marriage has been a disaster for women. In *The Case Against the*

Sexual Revolution, Perry spends a whole chapter detailing what to most people was common sense just a decade ago: Men and women are different.[24]

After covering why consent is a completely inadequate basis for guiding sexual ethics, and making a persuasive case against the pornography industry, Perry closes with an argument that marriage is the best "technology" we have that "discourages short-termism in male sexual behavior, protects the economic interests of mothers, and creates a stable environment for the raising of children."

All very true. But as amazing a "technology" as marriage is, it is also a technology that is much older than Perry gives it credit for. In fact, it has been around long enough to shape our very DNA. For example, cooking is not natural. It must be taught and learned every generation. But it is a technology that has been around long enough to change how our bodies process food. If humans didn't cook we'd need much larger stomachs to process uncooked foods. And there is plenty of evidence that just as our stomachs grew to depend on cooking, our minds became just as hardwired to thrive in monogamous cultures as well.

In this sense, Perry undersells marriage when she calls it "unnatural since it is not the human norm." But it very much was the human norm for hundreds of thousands of years right up until the spread of agriculture just ten thousand years ago. Polygamy's ten-thousand-year reign as the dominant human mating system may seem impressive compared to monogamy's triumph in just the last 200 years, but monogamy prevailed for many hundreds of thousands of years before that.

When we push for cultural norms and public policy that promote monogamous marriage, we are swimming with, not against, the current of human nature. The emotions that drive our behavior evolved in an environment where monogamy was dominant.

As strong a case as Perry makes for marriage as an essential institution for human flourishing, and she does advise women personally to make marriage a priority in their own lives, Perry stops short of identifying any policy solutions that could reverse marriage's decline. University of Maryland economist Melissa Kearney, however, steps up to that challenge in her book *The Two-Parent Privilege: How Americans Stopped Getting Married and Started Falling Behind*.[25]

Where Perry's book focuses on the harm to women from the sexual revolution, Kearney documents the mountains of empirical research showing that the decline of marriage has been a disaster for everyone: men, women, children, and the communities they live in. Unlike Reeves's contribution, there is no celebration of the decline of marriage in Kearney's book.

On the solution side, Kearney does mention policies that might help reverse the decline of marriage—like more funding for apprenticeship programs and expanded earning supplements like the Earned Income Tax Credit. But Kearney's refusal to acknowledge the role the welfare state has played in weakening the institution of marriage, undermines her case for a "stronger safety net for families, regardless of family structure."

She goes on to explain how the cash benefits given to single mothers through Aid to Families with Dependent Children (AFDC), now Temporary Assistance for Needy Families (TANF), were small throughout the 1980s and have declined since then, but she completely ignores the very real and large marriage penalties that exist in every other means-tested welfare program including, Medicaid, food stamps, Section 8 housing benefits, the Children's Health Insurance Program, Affordable Care Act insurance subsidies, and yes, even the Earned Income Tax Credit.

Until we admit that these programs have played a huge role, and are still playing a huge role, in furthering the assault on marriage, we should probably not talk about expanding them.

TOWARD A LARGER UNDERSTANDING

As helpful as each of these books are (and you should read them), their narrative of marriage as an institution begins in the 1950s at the earliest. Most books about marriage available today suffer from the same presentism.

This book is an effort to backfill that hole in the story. By starting from the dawn of humanity and tracing marriage's key role in the shaping of human civilizations throughout time, this book will explain why marriage works, why marriage is declining, why the decline of marriage matters, why the state cannot replace marriage, and how the decline of marriage can be reversed.

"The central conservative truth is that it is culture, not politics, that determines the success of a society," Senator Daniel Patrick Moynihan once said. "The central liberal truth is that politics can change a culture and save it from itself."[26]

Moynihan is right. We can make changes so that our public policy elevates the family over the individual. Marriage doesn't have to be the new marker of class and privilege. It can be a foundational, egalitarian, and democratizing institution for every American again. We just have to make it a priority. This book will make the case that we should.

CHAPTER ONE

THE DAWN OF HUMANITY

IN BOOK FIVE OF PLATO'S *Republic*, Socrates details an ideal city-state without monogamous households. "Women should be shared among all the men," Socrates tells Glaucon, "so that no individual woman and man should live together, and that the children, too, should be shared, with no parent knowing its own offspring, and no child its parent."[1]

But the modern roots of the revolt against monogamous marriage can be found closer to home. Karl Marx's *Communist Manifesto* explicitly calls for the "abolition of the family" and socialist governments have targeted the family as an enemy of the state ever since.[2]

For Marx and his wealthy patron Friedrich Engels, the foundational sin of capitalism, private property, originated in the family. The husband exploits the wife and the married couple exploit their children together. The family, in the communist view, must therefore be destroyed because it is where children first learn to accept hierarchy. Worse, it perpetuates inequality when wealthy parents pass property on to their children.

In making this argument, Marx and Engels believed they were simply proposing a return to humanity's prehistoric past.

"Monogamy appears as the subjection of one sex by the other," Engels wrote in *The Origin of the Family, Private Property and the State*, "as the proclamation of a conflict between the sexes entirely unknown in prehistoric times."[3]

This view that monogamous marriage is an invention of men used to oppress women is still a foundational belief of the progressive movement today. "The material base upon which patriarchy rests lies most fundamentally in men's control over women's labor power," writes Institute for Women's Policy Research founder Heidi Hartmann.[4]

"Men maintain this control by excluding women from access to some essential productive resources (in capitalist societies, for example, jobs that pay living wages) and by restricting women's sexuality," Hartmann continues. "Monogamous heterosexual marriage is one relatively recent and efficient form that seems to allow men to control both these areas."

Only by eliminating marriage, progressives believe, can true equality be obtained between the sexes. "Marriage as the preferred societal solution has become the problem," Emory University Law School professor Martha Albertson Fineman explains in a 2001 law review article articulating the feminist case against marriage. "The family is the way the state has effectively privatized dependencies that otherwise might become the responsibility of the collective unit or state."[5]

"We must begin to look beyond that institution," Fineman continues, "making demands for transformation in the workplace and the state." When Hillary Clinton says *It Takes a Village*, via the title of her book, and pushes for government run universal childcare, she is seeking to undo the privatization of care created by marriage, and return to an age when children were supposedly raised by everyone.

But is the progressive understanding of history true? Was Engels right? To understand the roots of the modern ideological attack on monogamy, we must go back to the beginning of human history to evaluate the claim that monogamy is unnatural, an imposition on human nature, not an expression of it. If economic and sexual communism could be established as the default mode of human existence, then the utopian social order they sought to create could be viewed not as an imposition from above, but as a form of restoration.

EVERY MAN TO EVERY WOMAN, EVERY WOMAN TO EVERY MAN

Anthropology was in its infancy as a field of study when Marx and Engels were writing, but both men were familiar with the work of an American businessman from upstate New York named Lewis Henry Morgan.

A lawyer by trade who was fascinated by the Seneca Iroquois, Morgan visited their reservation for years before they finally asked for his legal help against a corporation that was trying to evict the tribe from their land. Morgan won the case for the Iroquois who then adopted him into their tribe. Morgan would go on to become one of the first outsiders to document the Iroquois' language, religion, family organization, and political structure.

The Iroquois, Morgan observed, married monogamously, although divorce was common. But Morgan noticed that the words they used to refer to certain family members were different from English norms.

An Iroquois child would refer not only to his biological mother as "mother," but also his mother's sisters. Similarly, a child would refer not only to his biological father as "father," but also his father's brothers. This same child would also call the sons and daughters of his father's brothers "brother" and "sister," as well as the sons and daughters of his mother's sisters.

When Morgan found out that other tribes throughout North America also used this family terminology, as well as communities in Asia and Polynesia, he concluded that these terms must have developed from actual biological relations in a now distant past. In his book, *Ancient Society*, Morgan theorized that man began as a "promiscuous horde" where, in Engels words, "every woman belonged equally to every man and, similarly, every man to every woman." The children from all this promiscuous sex, Engels wrote, "are regarded as being common to them all."[6]

For Marx and Engels this "group marriage" stage was essential to the creation of humanity. A nuclear family stood no chance of defending or providing for itself in nature, Marx and Engels believed. Only the "united strength and joint effort of the horde" could ensure survival. In this context, one man's jealous attachment to a single female threatened the cohesiveness of the larger group.

"Mutual toleration among the adult males, freedom from jealousy, was the first condition for the building of those large and enduring groups in the midst of which alone the transition from animal to man could be achieved," Engels wrote. "If anything is certain," Engels continued, "it is that jealousy is an emotion of comparatively late development."[7]

By abolishing the family and ridding humanity of this "bourgeois" jealousy, Marx and Engels believed a more free and fair communist order could deliver mankind back to its promiscuous natural state.

A REAL PROMISCUOUS HORDE

Seventy-six years after Engels published *The Origin of the Family*, a young primatologist named Jane Goodall observed a chimpanzee not only use a blade of grass to fish termites out of their home, but also strip a branch of its leaves so he could more effectively harvest his prey.

"Now we must redefine tool, redefine man, or accept chimpanzees as humans," Goodall's supervisor, the noted archaeologist Dr. Louis Leakey telegraphed after she reported her findings.[8]

"The reason Louis Leakey sent me to study chimps," Goodall explained years later, "was because he was searching for the fossils of early man and from the fossils you can tell a lot about what a creature looked like and what it ate, but you can't tell about the behavior."[9]

Among the many things Goodall documented in the chimpanzees living in the Gombe Stream National Park in Tanzania, in addition to tool use, was their mating behavior. Turns out, chimpanzees are a promiscuous horde.

Unlike gorillas, which mostly live in single family groups where one alpha male mates with a harem of females, chimpanzees live in multi-male, multi-female groups ranging in size from fifty to 150. And in these large groups the chimpanzee females do have sex with almost every male.

The distribution of sex among male chimpanzees, however, isn't as equal as Marx and Engels probably hoped. Chimpanzees are an aggressive and brutal species. There are rigid social hierarchies among both males and females enforced by violence. Alpha males frequently use force to prevent all but his most trusted allies from mating with the group's most desirable females. These same alpha female chimpanzees are then known to steal infants from lower ranking females, denying these infants care from their mothers, and essentially starving them to death.[10] Male chimpanzees do not help females provide or care for their young, although they will protect them from outside males. Disturbingly, however, when one troop of males conquers another troop of males, the conquering males will then kill the offspring of the females to ensure their sexual availability.

The mate guarding performed by high-ranking males does not leave lower ranking males, usually the youngest chimps, without any options for sex. Unlike human males who usually prefer younger, more recently fertile females, chimpanzees prefer the opposite. The most desirable female chimpanzees are those that are proven successful mothers.

This leaves young childless female chimps largely ignored by mature higher ranked males. It also creates an opening for young males to form consort relationships with these young females where the two chimps leave the group and remain alone for days at a time.

Taking a step back, it becomes apparent that instead of one promiscuous mating behavior, chimpanzees practice a mix of three: 1) promiscuous, non-competitive mating by all males with an obviously fertile female; 2) possessive mate guarding by alpha males and their lieutenants with the most desirable females; and 3) monogamish consortships between younger lower ranking males and females.

Marx and Engels were right about one aspect of our prehistoric ancestors: They needed to be in large social groups to survive. Chimpanzees are highly territorial, with all-male subgroups spending significant time patrolling the boundaries of their territory. Male chimps also organize into raiding parties where they invade enemy territory, kill the resident males, then claim the females in the new territory as their own. A single male protecting a harem of females would never survive this environment dominated by cohesive male bands.

As genetically similar as chimpanzees are to humans, however, their habitat is largely confined to the savannas and tropical forests of equatorial Africa. Humans, on the other hand, have become the dominant predator on all seven continents.

What revolutionary change occurred among our common ancestors with chimpanzees that allowed us to move out of the forests of Africa and conquer the world beyond?

HUMAN SEE, HUMAN DO

Humans are not the strongest animals. A fully grown 400-pound silverback gorilla is six times as strong as the average male human.

Nor are they the fastest. Cheetahs can run up to seventy miles per hour while humans max out at under thirty.

Humans don't even have the biggest brains in the animal kingdom. That honor goes to sperm whales with an average eighteen-pound brain compared to our average three pounds.

But it turns out that when it comes to intelligence, size doesn't matter. Ratio is what is important when trying to estimate the relative intelligence of mammals. And the ratio of human brain mass to the rest of our body shows that we are the brainiest on the planet. Our fifty-to-one body to brain mass ratio is well above the 180-to-one average ratio for other mammals, and far above birds whose average body-to-brain mass ratio is 220-to-one.

It is not just the relative size of your brain that matters, it's what you do with it that counts. And humans excel at a particular kind of intelligence: social intelligence.

Social intelligence is kind of like your ability to cooperate with and, more importantly, learn from others. It includes the ability to communicate so you can influence the behavior of others; it includes social learning, which is the ability to watch how other people perform tasks successfully and then copy their behavior; and it includes the ability to deduce the perspectives of others, so you can understand their goals and how they see the world.

Another kind of intelligence is your ability to understand and anticipate the physical world. This includes skills like the ability to count and add (quantitative reasoning); the ability to remember where things are and be able to rotate them in your mind (spatial reasoning); and to recognize how a simple tool like a stick could be used to help retrieve an object (causal reasoning).

A team of anthropologists from Europe and the United States even developed a series of tests they called the Primate Cognition Test Battery and gave it to 106 chimpanzees from Uganda and the Republic of Congo, thirty-two orangutans from Borneo, and 105 children from Leipzig,

Germany.[11] The researchers chose to test children so they could better capture inherent human intelligence before it was enhanced by formal education.

The average chimpanzee outperformed the average human child on both the causal and quantitative physical intelligence tests with the average human just barely edging out the chimpanzees in spatial reasoning. The orangutans closely trailed both species in all three tests but were almost equal in quantitative reasoning.

The social intelligence results were a different story. The human children were solidly ahead of both chimpanzees and orangutans in the communication and theory of mind tests, but the humans trounced the other apes in the social learning test. That is our real competitive advantage: watching others successfully complete tasks and then copying what they do.

It's not that other animals don't learn from others. They absolutely do. Gibbons, orangutans, gorillas, chimpanzees, and bonobos all must teach their young how to build nests to sleep in at night. Crows learn where to find food by watching other birds. Some species of fish are known to find faster swimming routes by following other swimmers.

Animals do learn to master their surroundings through social learning. But humans are just much better at it. More importantly, as a group we have demonstrated a much stronger capacity for cumulative cultural learning.

Cumulative cultural learning means that we are able to remember, practice, and experiment with existing cultural changes at a high enough rate so that not only are cultural changes preserved for future generations, but those future generations can then create new cultural innovations that build off previous generations' existing tool set.

Through this ongoing process the total number of cultural innovations held by a group of people far exceeds the ability of any single human to invent everything a group knows in just one lifetime.

We can see the power of cumulative cultural learning by taking a closer look at how native peoples survive in some of the world's harshest climates.

Take the Inuit who survive throughout the Arctic, including on King William Island in Canada where the average high temperature in the winter months is minus twenty degrees Fahrenheit. In his book, *The Secret of Our Success*, Harvard University professor Joseph Henrich writes:

> Let's briefly consider just a few of the Inuit cultural adaptations that you would need to figure out to survive on King William Island. To hunt seals, you first have to find their breathing holes in the ice. It's important that the area around the hole be snow covered—otherwise the seals will hear you and vanish. You then open the hole, smell it to verify that it's still in use (what do seals smell like?), and then assess the shape of the hole using a special piece of caribou antler. The hole is then covered with snow, save for a small gap at the top that is capped with a down indicator. If the seal enters the hole, the indicator moves, and you must blindly plunge your harpoon into the hole using all your weight. Your harpoon should be about 1.5 meters (five feet) long, with a detached tip that is tethered with a heavy braid of sinew line. You can get the antler from the previously noted caribou, which you brought down with your driftwood bow. The rear spike of the harpoon is made of extra-hard polar bear bone (yes, you need to know how to kill polar bears; best to catch them napping in their dens). Once you've plunged your harpoon's head into the seal, you're in a wrestling match as you reel him in, onto the ice, where you can finish him off with the aforementioned bear-bone spike.[12]

If all that sounds like a lot for one man to learn in a lifetime, or even a hundred men, it is. Which is why, when Sir John Franklin's expedition went looking for a sea route from the Arctic to the Pacific Ocean and ran aground on King William Island in 1845, his entire crew of about 125 well-armed men eventually died of starvation. They never figured out how to successfully hunt on the frozen island.

Only through generations of cumulative cultural learning can a group of people come up with all the skills and knowledge necessary to survive and thrive in an environment as harsh as King William Island.

But for cultural learning to accumulate in a group over generations, that group must first be made up of individuals with a sufficient capacity to learn existing innovations and adapt successful new ones. This capacity for social learning requires big brains, brains which require big heads that are too wide to pass through the hips of women which must stay relatively skinny to maintain the ability to walk upright.

Humans "solved" this problem by delaying most brain growth and development until after birth. This post-birth development of children is actually a bigger burden on mothers than pregnancy. The energy costs of human lactation are twice those of hosting a growing baby in the womb. Even after weaning, human mothers must still assist in feeding their young for over a decade. In observed hunter-gatherer tribes, children eat more calories than they produce all the way through to their teens. By contrast, once a chimpanzee is weaned from its mother it can feed itself.

Chimpanzees also remain infertile throughout the weaning process, which takes about five years, which means a chimpanzee mother only needs to care for one child at a time. Because of the extended juvenile dependent phase of human development, however, women are responsible for providing for multiple children at once (her infant and other young children) in a way that mother chimpanzees are never required to do.

How did human mothers solve the problem of getting all the extra calories needed to birth, breastfeed, and then provide for her multiple children?

Additionally, given the high costs of developing big brains, how did they come to exist? Remember, dominant male chimps are far more successful in monopolizing fertile females than non-dominant males, and size and strength are the decisive determinators of which chimps are the most dominant.

A close examination of the archaeological, biological, and anthropological record paints a convincing picture of how our chimp-like ancestors became human.

A SHIFT IN MATING STRATEGIES

Sometime around four million years ago our chimp-like ancestors were testing the boundaries of their livable habitats, moving from the branches of the forests to the flatlands of the savanna.

This changed their lives in two ways. First, it freed up their hands to use more complex tools more often. Second, the increased presence of large predators (like lions and other big cats) forced them to live in larger, more compact groups. We see this in baboons who live on the savanna today in large troops of up to 150. Again, Marx and Engels were right about our prehistoric ancestors needing to live in large groups to survive.

More tool use means more opportunities for primates to experiment with new ways to use tools. For example, a primate who sharpened a stick so it fit better down a termite hill might then try and see if he could stab a mole rat hiding in its hole.

A larger group would also mean that there would be more individuals conducting more experiments. And it meant more primates watching and learning from those experiments, adopting the new techniques that worked, and then experimenting with even more complex tool use.

In other words, the more individuals there are in a group, the larger the collective brain it has. And the bigger the collective brain, the more innovations there will be. Another thing we know about primates is that the larger the group, the harder it is for the alpha male to monopolize fertile females. In bigger groups there are just too many females for the alpha male to keep track of, and also a lot more other males to fight off. Add increased tool use into the picture, and the entire dynamic changes.

Many of the new tools our chimp-like ancestors were developing could also be used as weapons. These evolving weapons were a great destabilizer and equalizer for male dominance hierarchies. Before weapons it was pretty easy to tell that the bigger stronger primate was going to win and therefore many actual fights were avoided. But with new and evolving weapons, it is less certain who is going to win a fight between a dominant male who wants to butt in on a smaller male and his female partner. At the very least, the cost of doing so has gone up substantially.

A lady's prerogative also played a role in these changes. It has been observed in multi-male gorilla groups that male gorillas who play with a female's children are more likely to father her next offspring. Primate mothers like males who invest time with their children. These dynamics tend to foster a more stable monogamous pair bond.

Another factor pushing our primate ancestors towards monogamy was their instinctual preference for incest avoidance. Primates without some instinctual method for avoiding incest would have died out millions of years ago from inbreeding. In chimpanzees and gorillas, it is the females that migrate from their natal community to a new community at sexual maturity. This means that when a female begins to reproduce, she is in unfamiliar territory and may not know the best locations and methods for gathering food. A friend willing to show her the ropes would be a huge help. Non-alpha males from her new community looking to increase their breeding chances by forming a consort relationship with a new female would fit this role nicely.

Taking a step back we can begin to see some major changes occurring in the probable payoffs of the three mating strategies for our savanna-transitioning primate ancestors. The old dominant mating strategy was to invest in size and strength hoping to become the alpha male, or at least one of his lieutenants, and then use that relatively brief reign of privilege to monopolize as many females as possible.

But the emerging strategy would be for males and females to choose the consort route, relying on the size of the group and use of tools to defend their burgeoning monogamous bond against larger, violent, more traditionally dominant males. The benefit for a non-alpha male would be guaranteed access to a single female, while the benefits to a female would be increased knowledge about the group's territory, someone to reliably protect, feed, and play with her offspring, and the avoidance of non-consensual sexual contact with more violence-prone males. In short, the scales are beginning to tip away from size and strength as the best use of precious calories, and towards bigger brains and heightened social learning.

A LONG-TERM PROJECT OF COOPERATIVE CARE

But we still need to get primate mothers the help they need for the extra calories that bigger social brains require.

As these monogamous bonds develop further, we begin to see some other advantages for monogamous mothers and their children. Without monogamous pair bonds, sons have no idea who their fathers are and vice versa. But with monogamy, sons can bond with their fathers and learn from them. Fathers are more confident in their sons' paternity and are therefore more willing to teach, protect, and share resources with them.

Additionally, remember that it is the females who change groups at sexual maturity in our closest chimpanzee relatives. This means that mom's mom is not around to help mom with her kids. But you know who is around? Dad's mom. And thanks to monogamy, dad's mom can now recognize her son's children. Just as fathers are more likely to invest in their children when they are more likely to know a child is theirs, a father's mother is more likely to invest in a child when she knows it belongs to her son. Potential grandmothers can't help every child in the group. But if she can tell which specific children are her son's then she is happy to help.

And thus grandparents were invented. No monogamy, no grandparents.

In almost all species on earth, females are capable of reproduction right up until they die. Only in humans, and some species of whales, do females show the propensity for significant lifespans beyond their reproductive years. The ability of grandmothers to offer knowledge to the group, and to increase the chances her genes will spread to further generations by helping her grandchildren, are big reasons why humans are one of the few species to go through menopause.

Monogamy has thereby brought three generations of individuals (siblings, fathers, and grandparents) into a long-term project of cooperative care. We can see this model in modern hunter-gatherer societies where mothers only do about half of all direct childcare. Another quarter is provided by siblings and grandparents, and the last quarter by fathers, aunts and uncles.[13]

CHANGING CULTURE, CHANGING GENES

As monogamy became the dominant mating strategy in these pre-human groups, evolutionary forces acted on our genes to reinforce it.

Mammals already produce hormones that foster tight emotional bonds with other mammals. Oxytocin not only helps mothers give birth but also helps them bond with their breastfeeding baby. With this neural pathway already established, it wouldn't be hard for this hormone to also reinforce bonding behaviors between sexual partners. And, in fact, that is exactly what we see. In humans, oxytocin spikes in both men and women at orgasm, prompting both parties to form strong emotional attachments to their partners.[14]

Another hormone, vasopressin, has been linked to aggressive mate guarding behaviors in monogamous prairie voles as well. Male voles with normal functioning vasopressin systems act aggressively against any male that comes near a female vole they have recently mated with. Voles with this system turned off, don't care who is around their mate.[15]

Turns out jealousy is a little older than Marx and Engels thought.

We often think of jealousy as a "bad" emotion that we should suppress. But like many of our other "bad" emotions, it actually serves a useful evolutionary purpose, one that has not been made obsolete by modern society.

Take depression. In his book, *Good Reasons for Bad Feelings*, Dr. Randolph Nesse explains that feelings of depression are often caused by failing to accept a loss in a status competition.[16] For example, if a reigning-alpha male is defeated in a fight with an upstart-alpha male, he may respond by continuing to fight even though he is no longer the stronger ape. If he does not relent, this could get him killed.

A depressive emotional response, however, can set the former-alpha male on a different path. By pulling back and not engaging with others, a losing ape has the time to regroup and reassess strategies, maybe invest in selected potential allies, or withdraw socially until a better time.

Such an emotional response to setbacks is still valuable to humans today. Instead of manically pursuing the same failed professional strategy over and over again, depression can lower our mood after a failure, so we are forced to reevaluate what we are trying to accomplish and how we are trying to accomplish it.

Similarly, jealousy drives us to guard our mates. In a group of apes, if a male never cared when his partner wandered, he would end up having fewer offspring. Female apes who didn't care if their male partners had other sexual partners would lose out on the care and resources that male gave to his other children.

The same is true of humans today. Anytime a partner bonds sexually with another person there is a good chance that partner will then choose to spend more time with that other person. Mate poaching is common across cultures. Jealousy keeps us vigilant about sharing our partner's affections.

Now like any emotion, jealousy can go too far. Violently beating a spouse because of jealous feelings is never acceptable. But depression, and even positive moods like excitement, can be harmful at extremes too. The challenge is learning to recognize when these emotions have stopped becoming beneficial to us and when they start leading to harmful behavior. Bottom line, however, jealousy still serves a useful purpose.

We can see the value of jealousy in studies of modern human males which show that men with high functioning vasopressin systems were more attached to their current mate and reported more stable marriages.[17] Those men with weaker vasopressin systems were less attached to their mate and reported more marital distress.

The workings of oxytocin and vasopressin in our nervous systems show that we evolved to become hardwired for bonding emotionally with our sex partners.

The culture of our primate ancestors would also begin to change as we became more monogamous. If a father is gentle with his wife and daughters, then his sons will watch that behavior and treat the women in their lives better too.

Members of the group will begin to expect not only that their partner should be loyal and monogamous, but that other individuals in the group should be loyal and monogamous to their partners as well. Over time, those kinder and gentler men will be more successful at reproducing than those that are not. Our human ancestors slowly became more kind, cooperative, and monogamous—at least among their immediate tribe and family.[18] Interactions between unrelated bands of humans have often been violent and deadly. But to be successful in intergroup competition, intragroup cooperation is imperative.

If you doubt that human culture can change human biology I'd like to introduce you to your stomach. As mentioned in the introduction, our stomachs are far too small, only about a third of the size they should be, for a primate of our weight. Without the digestive powers of a larger stomach, our bodies lack the ability to detoxify and digest many of the same foods that our primate cousins eat regularly.

So how do we survive without properly detoxifying or digesting our food? Easy. We predigest it by cooking. Cooking is a completely culturally learned activity. No other animal cooks and no human is born knowing how to cook. It must be taught. Cooking is culture.[19]

And yet because we have been cooking for almost two million years, we have slowly been able to shift the calories and space needed for larger stomachs out of our bodies and into our fires, ovens, pots, and pans. We are stronger, faster, and smarter without all that extra stomach weighing us down. And it all happened slowly through evolution enabled by cultural changes.

Another power of culture is that it can deputize third parties to monitor, reward, and sanction others based on widely shared rules. Culture can transform our baser instincts, which can occasionally stray into anti-social behaviors (like cheating) and channel them into prosocial activities (like providing for your wife and children).

We can also see the power of culture in pushing humans toward productive monogamous behaviors by comparing humans to other monogamous animals without monogamy-reinforcing cultural norms.

For example, an estimated 90 percent of bird species are considered to be monogamous and for decades many biologists just assumed these species were faithfully mating for life (or at least for the duration of a mating cycle). But thanks to DNA tests, scientists now know that while many of these birds do mostly practice monogamy, they also slip out for the not-so-occasional side action. The percentage of extra-paternal offspring in many bird species exceeds 20 percent! Meanwhile, in human societies that have monogamous social norms, extra-paternal births are usually closer to about 2 percent.[20]

Those groups that had stronger monogamy norms would then tend to be more egalitarian and more cohesive overall. Across cultures, those communities with stronger monogamous bonds and increased parent certainty show more male investment in their children.[21] By channeling male effort from fighting each other for control of as many women as possible, and towards investment in child development, a monogamous group could spend more time cooperating and becoming more productive as a unit.

If any new cultural norm gives one group an advantage over another, there is a strong chance that norm will spread. The new norm could make it easier for a group to survive in a hostile habitat, or it could make the group better at reproduction, or it could make them a stronger fighting force.

There used to be some debate about how much intragroup violence there was between our earliest hunter-gatherer ancestors, but the more comprehensive the data is, the more the evidence points to the conclusion that conflict was pervasive. Looking at hunter-gathering bands encountered by anthropologists, 90 percent of these groups practiced warfare "frequently" and a full third were continuously at war with other groups.[22]

Looking back at the archaeological record, burial sites from regions as diverse as Southern California, Egyptian Nubia, British Columbia, the Andes, and Australia show somewhere between 15 percent and 20 percent of all skeletons with violent skeletal trauma. The percentage of violent deaths for adult male skeletons is even higher.

Even low levels of casualties can be disastrous for small bands. As Lawrence Keeley notes in his book *War Before Civilization: The Myth of the Peaceful Savage*, a community with one hundred warriors who fought at least four times a year and would retreat after losing just 5 percent of its force, would lose sixty-four warriors in just five years. That is more than enough churn for cultural norms to impact which groups survived those conflicts and which didn't.[23]

In addition to giving a group a leg up as a fighting force, monogamy also made it more likely that neighboring groups—otherwise natural competitors—would establish more peaceful relations, thus enabling cooperative relationships between groups. When our female primate ancestors left their birth-families at sexual maturity, they found mates in a neighboring group. If relations between these groups went south, brothers in one group would be more likely to recognize and not attack their sisters and her offspring in the other group. Fathers would be less likely to attack their daughters and their husbands. Daughters and their offspring would be more likely to be able to act as peacemakers between these two groups.[24]

With steady peaceful relations, these interbreeding smaller bands could become a larger tribe of people. They would still live separately most of the year in smaller groups, but they would come together regularly to peacefully meet, exchange knowledge, and discover new mates, thus forming more monogamous ties to better sustain peace in the growing tribe. This would only increase the size of the group's collective brain thus making new cumulative cultural learning easier.

THE TRANSITION TO MONOGAMY

To recap, millions of years ago our formerly tree-dwelling primate ancestors began to explore the African savanna. Moving from the trees to flatland allowed them to use more complex tools and forced them into larger groups to protect themselves from predators.

The increased size of the group and the equalizing aspects of more lethal tools made it harder for alpha males to monopolize females and easier for non-alpha males to form and sustain the consort relationships that were already common.

Our female ancestors, who changed groups at sexual maturity, increasingly sought out these monogamish consort relationships so they could better learn how to access food from the males who already knew the group's territory. Females were also more likely to form such relationships with males who spent time with their children.

These deepening monogamous relationships increased bonds between siblings and enabled grandmothers to recognize and help their grandchildren thus providing three generations of help in raising the burgeoning conjugal family's young. Biological changes (increased oxytocin and vasopressin production) then further strengthened these monogamous bonds and at some point these behaviors became social norms which enabled the whole community to reinforce monogamous behaviors.

With more help caring for their young, mothers could now supply the extra calories and care needed to develop larger brains that are built for social learning. As male aggression decreased and child investment increased, groups became more egalitarian and cooperative. Monogamy also made it easier for neighboring groups to maintain peaceful relations, enlarging the collective brain of the growing tribe, and enabling even faster social learning.

This story is supported by the fossil record which shows our human ancestors slowly evolving from higher levels of body-size difference between species (like polygynous gorillas where the males are twice the size of the females) to a more equally sized species like monogamous gibbons and tamarins. Our bodies still show marked differences between the sexes, males are 15 percent heavier on average, but men and women are still far less different than our promiscuous chimpanzee cousins, where males are 30 percent larger.

The sharp dagger-like fangs of gorillas and chimpanzees, best designed for fighting other males for control of females, have also shrunk to small stubby teeth best for grinding away at already cooked food. The smaller differences between the sexes in body size, and the deweaponization of our teeth, show a species moving away from winner-take-all polygamy and promiscuity, and towards a body built for cooperative and egalitarian behavior.[25]

MONOGAMY IN HUNTER-GATHERER TRIBES

The anthropological record also supports this story, with all observed hunter-gatherer tribes demonstrating some type of established marriage norms.[26]

Now the exact rules of these marriages are different. In some hunter-gatherer groups divorce is easier than in others, and with shorter lifespans than we have in the modern world, remarriage is almost universally accepted.

Returning to *Sex at Dawn*, mentioned in the introduction, it seems clear that Christopher Ryan cherry-picked stories from numerous hunter-gatherer tribes to paint a picture of early man living in a blissful world of promiscuous consensual sex. On closer inspection, all these cultures have monogamous pair bonds, just not necessarily as we practice monogamy today. More importantly, what deviations there are from monogamy, aren't exactly the progressive paradise Ryan makes them out to be.

Ryan first introduces us to the Aché of Paraguay who believe in what anthropologists call "partible paternity," which is where it takes semen from multiple men to create one baby. "Far from being enraged at having his genetic legacy called into question, a man in these societies is likely to feel gratitude to other men for pitching in to help create a stronger baby," Ryan writes. "Far from being blinded by jealousy as the standard narrative predicts, men in these societies find themselves bound to one another by shared paternity they have fathered together." Ryan goes on to note that children with more than one father have a better chance of survival than those with just one father.[27]

And it is true, Aché children whose mothers sleep with more than one man do have a greater chance of survival than those with just one father. But this is not because Aché women have sex with as many men as they can and then everyone shares the burden of childcare equally. Quite the opposite. And brutally so.

The Amazon habitat of the Aché is an extremely inhospitable place to eke out an existence. The Aché do have reciprocal meat sharing norms among married couples. But if a father dies, that reciprocity is no longer there. There is no man in the family unit to share meat with. Meat is not shared with widowed children and as a result, an infant Aché child who loses his father is four times as likely to die as an infant with a living father.

An Aché woman will often sleep with a backup husband while she is pregnant as sort of an insurance policy. If her primary husband dies (which is not uncommon when 40 percent of adult males die from violence), then the backup husband can still provide her meat. But this does not mean Aché women are trying to have sex with every guy in camp. If she sleeps with too many men, then none of the secondary fathers will take responsibility for her when her primary husband dies. Mothers of infants who sleep with too many men are just as likely to be abandoned when a primary husband dies as mothers who sleep with no other men.

The optimal number of men a wife sleeps with when pregnant, in Aché society, is two: her husband and one backup husband. Even then, Ache´ wives best not spend too many nights with the backup husband. Aché men are known to beat their wives for spending too much time with other men.[28] So much for the swinging Aché.

Ryan also highlights the Canela people of nearby Brazil. Among the Canela, girls are assigned a husband at the age of thirteen, but the marriage isn't permanent until the girl becomes pregnant. Before young women get pregnant, they are expected to participate in a male bonding festival every summer where they have sex sequentially with as many as twenty-five men at a time. These group sex ceremonies "increase sharing, cooperation, and peaceful stability" Ryan argues.[29]

What Ryan fails to mention is that the Canela are a highly war-like people and the group sex ceremonies they practice are used to help maintain military discipline. These are not a peaceful laid-back group of men. Ryan also fails to mention that if a young girl refuses to participate in the festival, she is gang raped by a smaller group. Unsurprisingly, there is no concept of a female orgasm in Canela culture. All sex is purely for the benefit of men.[30]

Again, the reality of the Canela's extra-monogamous sexual relations aren't quite the progressive paradise Ryan wants his readers to believe.

Ryan also spends a lot of time on the Mosuo people of China, a community of about forty thousand people who live around Lake Lugu in the Yunnan plateau. The Mosuo are a matrilineal society built around the eldest woman in each household.

At sexual maturity, Mosuo girls are given their own bedrooms, which traditionally have easy direct access to the street. The women are then free to choose which men of the village they sleep with each night. Adult men do not live with the women they sleep with; instead, they live with their mothers and help raise the children of their sisters.

"Custom prohibits any talk of love or romantic relationships in the family home," Ryan writes. "Complete discretion is expected from everyone." "Particularly libidinous Mosuo women and men," Ryan continues, "unashamedly report having had hundreds of relationships."[31]

The first thing to note about the Mosuo is that they are not a hunter-gathering people. They are sedentary agriculturists that were dominated by much larger patriarchal feudal lords for centuries. If anything, their feudal rulers would have encouraged a matrilineal system for their subjects since it would make them easier to control.

Also, considering how small the Mosuo villages are, and that the Mosuo male lovers are expected to be gone by morning, there is simply no way that Mosuo women are having relationships with dozens of men at one time. There is just too much distance between villages, and not enough men in each village, for the women to be having that many multiple partners. Finally, considering the Mosuo traditionally didn't have access to birth control, the culture's low fertility rate suggests there isn't much sex going on at all.[32]

Polygamy does sometimes occur in hunter-gatherer bands, where the best hunter may be able to support an additional wife. But the egalitarian nature of observed hunter-gatherer culture makes it rare. In his book, *Hierarchy in the Forest*, Christopher Boehm describes a particularly successful Baruya man from the highlands of Papua, New Guinea who attempted to have sex with the wives of other men in the tribe. Instead of sitting back and letting it happen in a non-jealous communistic fashion, the other men banded together and killed him.[33]

In addition to the social norms that discourage some members of the group from having more than others, there simply isn't a lot of stuff that hunter-gatherer men can accumulate. Everything they own must be small enough to carry to the next food source.

FROM THE JUNGLE TO THE ARCTIC

To summarize: the first sexual revolution, from promiscuity to monogamy, turned us from a promiscuous horde, where males contributed nothing to the care of offspring and females were left to fend from themselves, often fending off attacks on their young from other females, into a band of egalitarian pairs, where men and women were bound together in long-term projects of cooperative care for each other and their offspring.

This monogamous conjugal family, nested into a larger egalitarian band all connected by extended family relations made possible by monogamy, proved to be an immensely successful formula, enabling early humans to develop a culture based on inherited knowledge, to use that knowledge to spread rapidly across the continents, and ultimately to conquer every corner of the Earth.

In sum, it is not a question of when marriage emerged among humans, marriage is what enabled us to become human. Like cooking, it has always been with us. It shapes how our bodies work.

However, about ten thousand years ago, after hundreds of thousands of years with this monogamous norm, things began to change. What were previously nomadic tribes became settled communities, city states, and eventually kingdoms. New technological developments altered the incentive structure of human mating strategies. And an older, less equal form of mating would return to dominate human behavior for millennia to come.

CHAPTER TWO

THE POLYGAMOUS WORLD ORDER

HIGH IN THE SPANISH PYRENEES, just south of the border with France, there is a cave at the base of a mountain rising out of the surrounding plateau. Dubbed the Els Trocs cave site, the remains of nine individuals estimated to have lived more than seven thousand years ago were found among broken ceramics and stone tools.

The five adults and four children did not die a natural death. The skeletons of both the adults and children show traces of blunt force violence to their entire bodies, while the adult skeletons show additional damage consistent with arrow injuries to their skulls. This forensic evidence, along with cave paintings depicting battle scenes between hostile groups in the region, led researchers to believe the individuals in the cave had been the victims of a violent massacre.

"Els Trocs probably documents an early escalation of inter-group violence between people of conceivably different origins and worldviews, between natives and migrants or between economic or social rivals," researchers who analyzed the site wrote. "The type of aggression suggests a clash between enemy groups."[1]

We'll never know who killed the Els Trocs victims, but a genetic analysis of their remains shows that they were relatively recent migrants to the area. They were either the first generation, or a close second generation, of Central Europeans who brought farming and pastoralism into what was then an area dominated by hunter-gatherers.

Similar scenes played out across Europe as Neolithic farmers pushed mobile hunter-gatherers off the most productive lands. These farming peoples settled in one place, investing more time and energy in altering the land so that it produced more food to support denser, larger populations.

This transition from nomadic hunter-gatherer tribes to sedentary city states, then kingdoms, and then empires, ushered in a second sexual revolution.

When the world was populated with nomadic hunter-gatherer tribes, an egalitarian monogamy reigned. But as this chapter will show, the development of agriculture led to more organized conflict carried out by those who could specialize in violence. The result was rising economic inequality, rigidly enforced social hierarchy, and the ruthless acquisition of women who were treated as property and as marks of social status.

This monopolization of most women by a few men, left many men without wives. Keeping these unfortunate men in-line required capricious political tyranny and caused unstable dynastic succession.

This was not a pattern of behavior limited to one region or one continent. It was the way of all major civilizations across all continents throughout most of recorded history.[2] After a brief narrative of how humanity transitioned from nomadic hunting and gathering to a more sedentary agricultural existence, this chapter will offer vignettes of some of the biggest names in history, across time and distance, to demonstrate the brutality and ubiquity of the Polygamous World Order.

THE AGRICULTURAL REVOLUTION

It is hard for us to imagine today, but the nomadic hunter-gatherer life was highly preferable to living in a Neolithic farming settlement. For starters, agriculture is a lot more work. The grains that supported early farming communities started out as wild grass. For the first farming settlements of the Fertile Crescent, in what is now the Middle East, that grass was wheat.

To get wheat to grow productively in a new location, other plants would have to be cleared while rocks and debris had to be removed from the soil. The wheat would then need to be planted and watered. Neolithic farmers had no pesticides or herbicides, so they would have to spend considerable time each day protecting their crops from invasive weeds, insects, and animals. When the crop was ripe, it had to be reaped using a scythe or sickle and then the edible seed had to be threshed from the straw. The grain could then be stored in a granary until it was needed, at which point the seed needed to be winnowed from the chaff and then milled using stone tools. None of this infrastructure constructed itself.

We can't go back and see how much time the hunter-gatherers of the Fertile Crescent spent acquiring food each day, but modern hunter-gatherer tribes, living in harsher environments like the African desert and Amazon jungle, only work three to five hours a day finding and preparing food. A study of hunter-gathering peoples in the Philippines in the midst of moving from hunting to agriculture found that the farming families spent ten hours longer working every week than those families that still foraged.[3]

Hunter-gatherers had better diets too. Where farmers were confined to basically one crop, hunter-gatherers in the Fertile Crescent had access to over one hundred different edible plants. Hunter-gatherers would also eat a wide variety of game and fish while farmers ate meat far less often, and when they did it was the meat of less healthy, often diseased, domesticated animals. As a result of these bad diets, Neolithic farmers were several inches shorter than their hunter-gatherer counterparts, and their bones and teeth were significantly weaker too.

Neolithic farmers did not have our modern immune systems or vaccines either. These first dense population centers often included herds of cattle or flocks of chickens. This mix of people and animals in close quarters, along with all their waste, was a pathogen's dream environment. Nomadic hunters knew urban centers were disease factories and avoided them literally like the plague.[4]

But if adopting a sedentary agricultural life means more work, bad food, and worse health, why did people give up their spears for plows? The answer appears to be that they may not have had much of a choice.

THE RISE OF PRIVATE PROPERTY, SPECIALIZATION, AND WAR

One advantage that farming does have over hunting and gathering is the capacity to store and preserve the food surpluses a set piece of land can produce. A hunter-gatherer group may be able to dry or smoke some meats or other foods, but when you live a mobile lifestyle, the amount of food you can save for later is always limited to what you can carry. Farmers, however, can store far more of their surplus harvest and then use it when and how they see fit. We see this in the archaeological record as granaries and other food storage technologies spread along with the first farming communities.[5]

This shift from gathering food from relatively large geographic areas to producing food from a smaller defined plot of land required new cultural norms. Farming requires intensive work to alter an environment so that it produces more food than the surrounding natural environment. In most hunter-gatherer cultures, it is expected that all resources are unowned until collected; then when they are harvested, they are to be shared with all other families. But this leaves little incentive for any one family to put in the effort to make a plot of land more productive. Researchers once observed two Batek men in Malaysia put in the effort to plant and cultivate rice. But when their fellow tribesmen simply harvested their crop and shared it with everyone, they abandoned future farming efforts.[6]

Only with an understanding of private property, defended by force, can agriculture become a worthwhile pursuit. And once you have private property, inequality begins to grow. A recent study of over fifty ancient farming societies found that those societies which were better able to invest in increasing agricultural production (specifically by harnessing cows and horses for plowing), also had higher rates of income inequality (as measured by the differing sizes of people's houses).[7]

As the land farmed became more productive, it also became more worth defending. The surpluses stored were especially valuable in times of bad weather and famine. This led early farmers to build structures, most often city walls, to better defend their land and granaries from outsiders.

As farming society became wealthier, the individuals, and the tools they used, became more specialized. Instead of a spear which could be used to hunt big game and attack other humans, you begin to see the mass production of arrowheads. Instead of farmers who occasionally fight, you have warriors who train to fight all day. And once you have trained warriors with weapons designed specifically to kill other humans and not just hunt animals, it becomes easier for early farming communities to conquer neighboring non-farming communities, and other smaller farming settlements.

The driving motive for larger farming communities to conquer other peoples was rarely the desire for more land. These societies had more trouble finding enough people to farm the land they already had. Instead, most wars were fought to secure captives that could then be forced to work for the ruling elite.

In 3,000 BC the city state of Uruk had a population of around forty-five thousand, including nine thousand slave laborers in the state-run textile industry alone. Also in Uruk, in 1805 BC we have records of state-run slave houses that would rent out slaves to wealthy families and temples. While these slaves were listed as having professional skills including boatman, gardener, harvest worker, herdsman, weaver, potter, and cook, they were not treated well. Evidence shows they were constantly kept in metal neck collars and were frequently beaten with clubs, sometimes to death. In 2000 BC Egypt, "The demand for shackles was so great that the temples regularly placed orders for their manufacture."[8]

Throughout the civilized agricultural world, the egalitarian hunter-gatherer norms were becoming extinct. With specialized warrior elites, average men could no longer band together to punish a wealthier upstart who appropriated too many wives. Those men that could, used their newfound monopoly on power to satiate their instinctual desire to sexually monopolize as many women as possible, just as our despotic bullying promiscuous ape ancestors did before them. Male slaves did not reproduce and were often worked to death. Female slaves were used as breeders for the wealthy elite that could afford them.[9]

By the end of the Neolithic age, the monogamous world of early man was gone. The polygamous world order was upon us. And the reproductive results were dramatic.

Looking at the diversity of Y chromosomes (which are only passed through men) geneticists have determined that there was a sharp decline in the percentage of men who became fathers during the Neolithic age. Women are always more likely to become parents than men, but in a monogamous society the difference between the sexes is small. For each man that reproduces in a monogamous society, a little more than one woman reproduces.

But during the Neolithic age, there were seventeen women passing their genes onto the next generation for every one man. Only a highly unequal polygamous society could produce that skewed result.[10]

For the first time in human existence, large swaths of the population were being cut out of the continuing project of humanity. Sure, male slaves could live out their hellish existences, but their lives would be the end of their contribution to humanity. Under the polygamous world order, only wealthy and powerful men could project their identities into the future. And it took a lot of violence and coercion to keep this state of affairs stable.

GILGAMESH AND ENKIDU

A testament to the angst of recently urbanized ancient peoples may be found in the oldest surviving literature known to man: the Epic of Gilgamesh.

Gilgamesh was the demigod king of the southern Mesopotamian city of Uruk in what is now Iraq. While Gilgamesh was tall, handsome, and smart, he was also a typical ruler of his era, who used slave labor to build city walls and took whatever woman struck his fancy, whether she was married or not.

The people of Uruk prayed to their gods to end Gilgamesh's oppression, and the gods answered their prayers by sending a large primitive man, named Enkidu, to save them. At first Enkidu lived in the wild with the animals until he was seduced by a temple prostitute who convinced him to live in a shepherd's camp outside the city. There he learned how to eat cooked food and wear clothes.

Enkidu was happy to live out his existence with the shepherd's flock until he met a stranger on the way to Uruk for a wedding. When the stranger told Enkidu that Gilgamesh was going to have sex with the bride after the wedding ceremony, Enkidu became enraged, promising to confront Gilgamesh, and make him change his ways.

When Enkidu appeared in the city, the people rejoiced, shouting, "This is the one who was reared on the milk of wild beasts. His is the greatest strength." Enkidu quickly found his way to the groom's house where he managed to stop Gilgamesh from entering the bride's bedroom. The two fought, shattering doors, and shaking the city's walls. It was Gilgamesh who finally threw Enkidu, but instead of killing him, Gilgamesh recognized him as an equal and the two became fast friends, then setting off on many adventures together.

What is noteworthy from Gilgamesh's story for our purposes are the themes of slavery, oppression, and the sexual liberties those with power exercised over their subjects. Enkidu's rage at the mere mention of a ruler appropriating another man's wife evokes a natural instinct among the common people that those who are selfish and aggressive were once justly met with communal violence. Enkidu, the embodiment of a vanished egalitarian hunter-gathering social order, lives in harmony with nature and is offended by the urban tyrannical behavior of Gilgamesh.

The records we have of Mesopotamian kingdoms from the same time show that Gilgamesh's conduct was typical, with despotic rulers constantly warring among themselves, and taking many women as concubines in the process.

Stone tablets recovered from the ruins of Mari, an ancient city on the Euphrates in what is now Syria, tell such a story.

Zimri-Lim the second oldest son of the king of Mari narrowly escaped the royal palace after a neighboring king to the north invaded. Just two years before, Zimri-Lim's older brother had murdered their own father so he could assume the throne, but the surrounding rulers sensed weakness and took advantage.

Zimri-Lim did not have to wait long to return to his family's palace. After biding his time with the nomadic tribes in the Euphrates Valley, Zimri-Lim waited till the king that conquered his home died, and then he swooped in and reconquered Mari before that king's son could establish order.

According to the tablets found thousands of years later, when Zimri-Lim resumed power, he inherited a harem of 350 women, some of whom were princesses from surrounding kingdoms; others were concubines, and some were slaves. Within just five years Zimri-Lim added another 300 to his harem, proudly noting that many of them were skilled in a variety of musical instruments, in addition to being receptive to his carnal desires, whenever he had them.

Like other early kings, he also found himself constantly at war during his fifteen- year reign.

Besides the more mundane slave raids on smaller communities, the neighboring kingdom of Elam, in what is now Iran, soon invaded the Euphrates Valley. Zimri-Lim responded by entering into a treaty with his rival to the south, Hammurabi of Babylon. Together, Zimri-Lim and Hammurabi repelled the Elamites, but they could never settle on which of them should control the border city of Hit, whose bitumen deposits were used to waterproof boats.

Frustrated by Hammurabi's refusal to renounce his claim, Zimri-Lim sent emissaries to a kingdom north of Babylon seeking an alliance against him. When Hammurabi found out, he sacked Zimri-Lim's palace, enslaved the entire population of Mari, transported them to Babylon, and burned the city to the ground.

Hammurabi would go on to form one of the largest ancient empires of Mesopotamia and author one of the first-known written legal codes in human history. This comprehensive body of law covered all aspects of ancient Mesopotamian life, including detailed rules governing relations between husbands, wives, concubines, slaves, and masters.

Under the Code of Hammurabi, a husband could divorce his wife for any reason at any time, but if the couple had children, the wife was entitled to keep the children and her dowry, and she was given the use of additional property (e.g., an arable field) to support her offspring. If the wife had no children, however, she could be returned to her family with just her dowry.

The code also makes clear that husbands were allowed to take additional wives, if they could afford it, and they could also adopt the children they produced with their female slaves. Those children not adopted were treated the same as any other slave. Helping a slave hide or escape was punishable by death, with slave owners obliged to repay slave captors an exact two shekels for each returned slave.

Hammurabi's kingdom fell apart within a year of his death. The city-states he conquered quickly announced their autonomy. Nevertheless, their freedom was short-lived. A few decades later, the Hittites invaded and conquered the entire region.

While Hammurabi's empire did not last long after his death, the legend of his legal text did. Rediscovered in 1901 on basalt slabs in what is now Iran, the original Hammurabi's Code sits in the Louvre in France with copies on display in the United Nations Headquarters in New York City and Berlin. There is also a portrait of Hammurabi in the United States Capitol.

The Code of Hammurabi is just one of many ancient Near East legal codes that have been recovered by historians. They all have their differences, but each of them also describe a world where slavery and polygamy were common.

One such legal text describes the rights of a daughter sold by her father to become a concubine:

> When a man sells his daughter as a slave, she shall not go out as the male slaves do. If she does not please her master, who designated her for himself, then he shall let her be redeemed; he shall have no right to sell her to a foreign people, since he has dealt unfairly with her. If he takes another wife to himself, he shall not diminish the food, clothing, or marital rights of the first wife. And if he does not do these three things for her, she shall go out without debt, without payment of money.[11]

This passage of the Old Testament comes just one chapter after Moses revealed the Ten Commandments to the Israelites at Mount Sinai. It is a law clearly designed to protect concubines from neglect by their masters. If a wealthy man buys a concubine, he must treat her just as well as a wife. If he fails to provide for her, she is free to go. But it is also a law that clearly condones the taking of multiple women for sexual purposes by wealthy men.

The point to stress here is not that the Babylonians or Israelites were uniquely drawn to polygamy or slavery, but that these two institutions were omnipresent throughout the region and were considered a normal part of everyday life.

As the Epic of Gilgamesh shows, this state of affairs was still thought of as unjust on some level. The egalitarian hunter-gatherer instinct was still there, at least subconsciously. Man was not accustomed to such subjugation. But short of praying to the gods for a savior, there was nothing they could do to change it.

BUDDHA AND THE BEAST

Twelve hundred years after Hammurabi's death and twenty-four hundred miles to the east, a Hindu priest gifted his daughter, Subhadrangi, to the second king of the Mauryan Empire, Bindusara. Bindusara accepted the young woman into his harem where his chief wife, jealous of her good looks, made her a barber.

Barbers were generally considered unworthy of conjugal contact with kings, but Bindusara was taken with Subhadrangi's beauty and asked how she came by her profession. When Subhadrangi explained that she was the daughter of a priest and that it was his chief wife who had put her in her current station, he immediately relieved her of her vocational duties and took her to bed. Subhadrangi named their first child Ashoka, which means "without sorrow," because, in Subhadrangi's words, "When this child was born, I became without sorrow."[12]

Bindusara's harem was large and he had many sons, each of whom were given administrative tasks by the king's bureaucrats to test their capacity to govern. Despite having rough skin and generally unpleasant looks, Ashoka proved himself to be a capable leader and when the city of Takshashila rebelled against the empire, Ashoka was sent to crush the resistance.

After quelling the rebellion with minimal violence, Ashoka was rewarded with the governorship of the much larger city of Ujjain. Along the way, Ashoka stopped in the town of Vedisa where he fell in love with a merchant's daughter named Vedisa-Devi. Ashoka took Devi as his first wife and the two settled in Ujjain, where the couple had two children, Mahinda and Sanghamitta.

While Ashoka was governor of Ujjain, his father, the king, became ill and advisors sent for Ashoka to rush to the capital. Bindusara had named another of his sons, Sushima, as crown prince, but Bindusara's aides thought Sushima to be arrogant and incompetent. They preferred Ashoka instead. So, they arranged for Sushima to be away from the capitol when Bindusara died and installed Ashoka on the throne.

Sushima, however, would not be denied his right to rule so he attacked the capitol. For the next four years civil war raged throughout the Mauryan Empire, with Ashoka killing ninety-nine of his half-brothers, including Sushima, sparing only his maternal brother Vitashoka.

After peace had been secured, Ashoka declined to take his first wife Devi to the capital. This was a common practice of Indian kings who would often maintain palaces with different wives stationed in each province as part of a network of political alliances.

Even with his first wife in a distant city, Ashoka was by no means lonely in the royal palace. He built up a harem of at least 500 women who he took to a park east of the capital one day where he came across an Ashoka tree, his namesake. Excited by the beauty of the tree, Ashoka satiated his needs with his concubines and then fell asleep. The women of his harem did not like touching the king's rough skin, however, so when he was asleep, they chopped all the flowers and branches off the tree.

When Ashoka awoke and saw that his tree had been mutilated, he became enraged and asked his servants who had cut the tree. When the servants said, "Your majesty's concubines," Ashoka then had all 500 concubines burned to death.

Not much is known about Ashoka's second and third chief wives, but according to accounts, his fourth wife Asandshimitta, was the one who converted Ashoka to Buddhism. But while Ashoka's son Mahinda went on to become a celibate monk, credited with spreading the faith to Sri Lanka, Ashoka himself carried on with a plethora of wives and concubines.

Through Ashoka we can see that polygamy was accepted and practiced by both Hindus and Buddhists alike. The Hindu sacred texts, the Dharmasastra, specifically sanctions polygamy, as long as its practice helped fulfill the four goals of life, the Purusarthas. The taking of extra wives was not supposed to be for pleasure, but was a perfectly acceptable practice among the warrior caste and wealthy merchants to secure a family's lineage. It was not until the push for modernization after independence from Britain, that India outlawed polygamy, but it is still practiced occasionally in predominantly Muslim rural areas.

Unlike Hinduism, marriage is not a sacrament for Buddhists. They generally view it as an entirely secular affair left to the powers of the state.

There is, however, nothing in Buddhist scripture that prohibits polygamy. Buddhism does encourage nonattachment in all romantic relationships—the Buddha did abandon his wife and children to pursue enlightenment—but it does not forbid either monogamous or polygamous marriage. Many Buddhist kings, including Ashoka, successfully practiced both Buddhism and polygamy without any complaint.[13]

THE MERCHANT AND HIS CONCUBINE

Just a little over a decade after Ashoka's death in 232 BC, Zhao Zheng became the first emperor of a united China following his victory over Qi, the last of the independent Warring States.

According to the Records of the Grand Historian Siam Qin, when Zhao Zheng's father was rescued from a neighboring Warring State by a wealthy merchant named Lu Buwei, he fell in love with his rescuer's concubine, who was then gifted to him to become his wife.

What Zhao Zheng's father did not know was that his concubine, now known as Lady Zhao, was already pregnant by the merchant Lu Buwei. And when Zhao Zheng's father died three years later, Lu Buwei was named regent to rule in Zhao Zheng's place until he was old enough to be king.

As Zhao Zheng neared maturity, Lu Buwei worried that he would find out about his affair with his mother. So, he recruited a handsome man to become a fake eunuch servant of Lady Zhao. This fake eunuch ended up seducing Lady Zhao, producing two boys of his own. He then mounted a rebellion against Lu Buwei's regency, seeking to install one of his own sons as king.

The eunuch's forces were quickly defeated, and when captured he was tied up to five horses who tore him to pieces as they galloped in opposite directions. The eunuch's entire extended family, including his two sons, were all captured and executed. Only Lady Zhao was spared, as Zhao Zheng's advisers feared the other Warring States would unite against Qin if it was known that Zhao Zheng killed his own mother.

Eight years after becoming king of Qin, Zhao Zheng launched a campaign to conquer the other six Warring States. Nine years after that campaign began, he had defeated all the other kings, and crowned himself as China's first emperor.

In addition to building the Great Wall of China, constructing the Lingqu canal, connecting the Xiang and Li Jiang rivers, and building an entire army of terracotta warriors, Zhao Zheng also constructed over 270 palaces throughout China, filling them with over ten thousand "beautiful women" that he had "taken from feudal rulers." Zhao Zheng never named an empress, but it is estimated that by the time he died he had over twenty-eight hundred children.

As impressive as Zhao Zheng's engineering legacy was, his dynasty lasted only one generation beyond his rule. Obsessed with immortality, he died far from home in search of an elixir of eternal life. His closest advisers hid his death, returned to the capital, and changed his will to select a weak heir who could be easily manipulated. That heir proved too weak, however, and the kingdom quickly descended into chaos.

Confucius died a little over two hundred years before Zhao Zeng, and his teachings were just becoming widespread as Zhao was consolidating power. Zhao did not embrace Confucian thought, however, in fact there is strong evidence he suppressed it.

Confucianism did survive Zhao's crackdown and would go on to become the dominant tradition in China. Confucianism is a deeply patriarchal system of thought that places the utmost importance on the subordination of the individual, both men and women, to legitimate authority. Under Confucian thought, women are to be obedient to their father before marriage, obedient to her husband during marriage, and obedient to her son after her husband's death.

Men could only marry one wife, but they could and did take as many concubines from lower social strata as they could afford to maintain, all the better to assure a male heir to continue the family line. As the story of Zhao Zhen and Lu Buwei shows, the taking of concubines was not limited to kings or even the nobility. Any wealthy man could have a concubine, and many did.

The Empress Guo of Wei did prohibit her relatives from taking concubines because she wanted to ensure that her soldiers could find wives for themselves. But the ban did not survive her death, and the functional polygamy of concubinage has long since been a pillar of Chinese society. It was not until the 20th century that the communists outlawed concubinage since it was considered a bourgeois decadence.[14]

SINGLE VIKING RAIDERS

A little over one thousand years after Zhao Zheng died, a Norse chieftain named Reginherus sacked the city of Paris.

Many people believe that this Reginherus is the famed Danish raider featured in The History Channel's *Vikings* television series, Ragnar Lothbrok. But the actual written accounts we have of the Saga of Ragnar Lothbrok, weren't written down until the 13th century, hundreds of years after Ragnar supposedly lived. These tales also begin with Ragnar slaying a dragon. For some reason, The History Channel chose to leave that part out of its "historical" drama.

This doesn't mean we know nothing of Viking life. The Vikings were a major geopolitical force from about 750 AD to 1050 AD. They established colonies as far north as Greenland, and as far south as Tunisia. They consistently raided an even larger geographical footprint stretching as far west as Portugal and as far east as the Caspian Sea. These incursions drew attention from both Christian and Muslim scholars, and it is their contemporaneous written accounts that give us the best remembrance of Viking life.

The secret to the Vikings' military success was their longboats. These light and shallow draft ships were highly maneuverable. They navigated shallow rivers as easily as the high seas, giving their occupants access to both coastal communities and inland targets (like Paris). This allowed the Vikings to amass large fighting forces in unprotected areas, attack, and then quickly disappear before their foes could muster an effective counterattack.

Monasteries were a favorite Viking target as they were usually undefended and located far away from larger settlements that might have fighting men. These religious orders were generally comparatively wealthy for the time, and often willing to pay a ransom for high-ranking clergy who had been taken hostage.

Captives not ransomed were usually sold as slaves in what became a vast commercial network of human bondage. One Irish captive reported being sold three times soon after he was captured by Vikings in a 9th-century raid. The city of Dublin was founded as a major slave-trading center at the height of the Viking Age.[15]

The Islamic explorer Ahmad Ibn Fadlan described a Viking chieftain who had forty slave girls that "were destined for his bed." His 400 warriors were also given two slave girls each. And these were just their concubines.[16] An 11th-century German missionary noted that Swedish men often had two or three wives at a time, with the wealthier men having more.

But if a Viking chief had forty-plus concubines and wives, and his favored warriors had an additional four or five women as well, where did that leave the vast majority of Viking men who wanted a mate?

It left them on a longship headed towards an unsuspecting village to capture a woman and sell her husband into slavery.

According to Viking custom, for a woman to be legally considered a wife, her family had to receive a bride price. If a suitor and his family didn't have the money to pay a bride price, a man couldn't get married. But he could join a raiding party, potentially capture a woman, and maybe carry off enough treasure to purchase a legitimate wife.

This is why mass graves of defeated Viking raiders are filled with young men between the ages of eighteen and twenty-five. These warriors were seeking to obtain the wealth necessary to build and sustain their own households.[17]

The genetic evidence of the less than consensual nature of the Viking mating practices can still be seen today. A recent analysis of DNA from modern Icelanders found that, while 80 percent of the men who founded Iceland were Scandinavian, over half of the women were Celtic.[18]

Now it's theoretically possible that hundreds of handsome and persuasive Viking men all simultaneously convinced hundreds of Irish women to voluntarily sail with them to a cold and distant island. It's much more likely Viking raiders conquered Irish villages, murdered their husbands or sold them into slavery, and carried their wives off to be their mates.

What the young male crews of the Viking longships teach us is that even in polygamous societies where most marriages are monogamous, even a moderate amount of polygamy can end up having an outsized impact on the rest of society. A little math shows why.

Consider a hypothetical community of 200 adults with an even split of one hundred men and one hundred women. The sixty wealthiest men each take one wife. Of those sixty, the top twenty-five take a second wife, leaving thirty-five monogamous marriages. Then the top ten of those men take a third wife and the top five take a fourth. Now all one hundred women have a husband. And of the married men in this society, a majority are married monogamously. This is a typical distribution of mates in a real-world polygamous society.[19]

But this simple thought experiment also leaves 40 percent of men unmarried. And that assumes there is an even mix of men and women to begin with. In many patriarchal societies there are often more men than women since families favor male children.

This means that any polygamous society will be teeming with young unmarried men desperate to attain the means necessary to secure a wife. It is these desperate unpartnered men that filled Viking longships throughout medieval Europe, and it is these same desperate unpartnered men that continue to destabilize polygamous societies today.

THE FATHER OF CENTRAL ASIA

A few hundred years after the first written accounts of Ragnar Lothbrok were being recorded in Scandinavia, a Mongolian herder named Temujin was born some five thousand miles away in the Khentii Mountains.

Temujin, who would later become known as Genghis Khan, was born to the youngest wife of a Borjigin chief in the western regions of the Mongolian steppe. When he was nine, Temujin was betrothed to a girl from the neighboring Olkhunut tribe, and he was sent to serve the Olkhunut as bride price until he became an adult, which was the Mongolian custom. But when Temujin's father was murdered in a raid by a different tribe, the Olkhunut released him from his service so he could go back and help his family.

By the time he got back, however, he found that the Borjigin had completely abandoned his father's wives and children, taking their horses and sheep, leaving them with nothing but their clothes and weapons on the cold Mongolian steppe.

In addition to the challenge of surviving in the wild on small fruits and game, Temujin and his full brothers faced another problem. By Mongolian custom, their older half-brother was now the assumed leader of the family, giving him the right to claim Temujin's mother as his wife. Temujin and his brothers chose to kill their half-brother before this could happen. Temujin was now head of the family.

Upon reaching adulthood, Temujin returned to the Olkhunut to claim his bride, only to find that she had been kidnapped by yet another rival tribe. The alliances he formed to recapture her set him on the path to not only uniting Mongolia but conquering the known world.

Temujin knew that Mongolia would never be secure if Mongols continued to orient their lives around clans. So, he broke down tribal loyalties by organizing the Mongols into regiments, with the leader of each chosen by Temujin personally. Temujin gave these leadership spots to the best fighters, not those of noblest birth.

When Temujin conquered a rival clan, instead of sparing the noblemen, thus affording them a chance to seek revenge, he simply executed them. He then distributed the noblewomen and children to his followers, thereby integrating the Mongol nobility into one coherent whole.

After uniting the Mongolian steppe, Temujin turned to dominating first China, then Central Asia, then the Middle East, before finally pushing into Europe, making it as far west as what is now Ukraine. While creating the largest contiguous empire in the history of the world, Genghis Khan killed millions of men, and took thousands of concubines along the way.

The Mongols did not leave much in the way of art, literature, or architecture, but the results of their polygamy can still be seen today. An estimated 8 percent of Central Asian men are descended directly from Genghis Khan and the many women he forced into sexual service.[20]

The success of the Mongols shows that the excess man problem of polygamy can be solved, but only by devising a rapacious war machine that can never stop conquering.

THE RICHEST MAN IN THE WORLD

A little over one hundred years after Genghis Khan's death, a caravan including sixty thousand people, one hundred elephants, and one hundred camels, each carrying one hundred pounds of gold, arrived in Cairo. The leader of the travelers was taken to Al-Nasir Muhammad, the sultan of the Mamluk caliphate that stretched from modern day Turkey in the east to Libya in the west.

Custom dictated that the leader of an arriving caravan kiss the ground before the sultan, but this caravan commander refused, and a tense standoff began. Eventually it was agreed that the traveler, who happened to be the Emperor of Mali, Mansa Musa, would join the sultan in prayer to Allah. The two Muslim rulers made peace on the spot and became friends.

Musa would stay in Cairo for three months to rest and resupply, before continuing his pilgrimage to Mecca. In the meantime, he became famous for his generosity.

"The man flooded Cairo with his benefactions," the historian Ibn Fadl Allah al-Umari recorded. "He left no court emir…no holder of a royal office without the gift of a load of gold. The Cairenes made incalculable profits out of him and his suite in buying and selling and giving and taking. They exchanged gold until they depressed its value in Egypt and caused its price to fall."[21]

Musa's display of wealth put him on the map, literally. Legends of his wealth led medieval Spanish mapmakers to include the likeness of Musa in their works, sitting atop a golden throne with a golden crown and scepter, offering a gold nugget to a passing merchant.

At its height, the Mali empire stretched from the Atlantic Ocean in the west to modern-day Niger in the east, an area about twice the size of France.

The secret to Mali's power was control of the trans-Saharan salt and gold trade. Gold was desirable, but salt was essential. It was needed not only as an additive to preserve food, but also to replace the copious amounts of salt people sweated out of their bodies when working the gold mines of southern West Africa.

By controlling the production and trade of salt and taxing the sale of gold, Musa was able to build the largest army in the region, including a ten thousand–strong, chain-mail-armored cavalry that he used to conquer surrounding city-states like Timbuktu. But Musa was far more than a conqueror. He invested significant resources in conquered cities to build mosques, schools, and universities, turning them into internationally renowned destinations.

Inspired by Musa's famous pilgrimage, the scholar and explorer Ibn Battuta traveled to Niani, Musa's imperial capital. In his journal, he recounted the desolate salt-mine settlement of Taoudenni he passed through on the way.

"It is a village with no attractions," he wrote. "A strange thing about it is that its houses and mosques are built out of blocks of salt and roofed with camel skins. There are no trees, only sand in which there is a salt mine. They dig the ground and thick slabs are found in it, lying on each other as if they had been cut and stacked under the ground. A camel carries two slabs. The only people living there are the *slaves* of the Massufa who dig for salt."[22]

Soon after Musa died, the Mali Empire disintegrated into civil war. On becoming king his older brother, Suleyman, took a new commoner wife which did not sit well with his existing noble wife Kassi. Kassi then launched an armed revolt with much of the court supporting her, but Suleyman eventually prevailed. Still, Mali was permanently weakened, and the Sudan-based Songhai Empire to the west eventually overshadowed it.

Musa's empire—built on the backs of slaves—reminds us how intertwined slavery and polygamy have been throughout history. Both are still practiced in Mali today, with as many as two hundred thousand people held in direct servitude to a master.[23]

THE HUNGER GAMES

Almost one hundred years after Musa's death, a man named Obsidian Snake led the Aztec people to become the preeminent power of the Valley of Mexico.

While his father had been chief of the Aztecs for decades, his mother had been a concubine slave girl, making Obsidian Snake an unlikely candidate to become king. In fact, it was one of his half-brothers, Hummingbird Feather, who first assumed the throne when their father died.

Hummingbird Feather was a successful ruler of the Aztec people, who themselves had only recently settled the island of Tenochtitlan in the middle of Lake Texcoco. Archaeological evidence shows that the Aztecs, like the Toltecs before them, had been wandering nomads from the modern-day United States who first came to the valley as raiders and mercenaries before finding an abandoned island to call their own.[24]

These nomads had a big advantage over the natives of the Valley of Mexico: the bow and arrow. When men first crossed the Bering Strait into North America, the bow and arrow was not in wide use. But it had since been introduced to Alaska and was slowly spreading south. The Aztecs were just one wave of such bow-and-arrow-wielding peoples to establish themselves in the valley.

The other city-states surrounding the five lakes of the Central Mexican Plateau had only recently recognized Tenochtitlan as a viable political entity. Hummingbird Feather had managed to form a close alliance with the strongest community in the region, the city of Azcapotzalco, and the combined forces of these two peoples conquered many small towns.

Shortly after Hummingbird Feather died, his eldest son, Smoking Shield, took the throne. But political turmoil brewed nearby. When Tezozomoc, the long-time chief of Azcapotzalco, died it was not clear which of his many sons would take his place.

As the chief of the most powerful city state in the Valley of Mexico, Tezozomoc had many wives, each of whom came from a high-ranking noble family from another of the valley's many city-states. Every son knew that if he made a bid for the throne of Azcapotzalco, their respective mother's hometown would likely support their cause.

But every one of them also knew that their half-brothers were thinking the same thing, meaning they were all potential threats. One of these half-brothers, Maxtla, calculated that the Aztecs were likely to side with one his rivals who was related to Smoking Shield's mother, so he had Smoking Shield killed.

Smoking Shield's sons were too young to lead when their father died, so the Aztec people were in desperate need for a leader now that the valley was slipping into civil war. They had little choice but to turn to Obsidian Snake who had loyally served Smoking Shield's father for twenty-four years.

Obsidian Snake assumed control of Tenochtitlan and immediately made a huge bet. Instead of making peace with Maxtla and returning to a subservient status under Azcapotzalco, he sought out alliances with two neighboring city-states that had their own reasons for opposing Maxtla's rule.

Together, these three city-states—Tenochtitlan, Texcoco, and Tlacopan—would first defeat Maxtla, making Azcapotzalco their client state, and then go on to conquer the rest of the Valley of Mexico.

The Aztecs were not micromanagers. They did not seek to change the culture of the people they conquered. They only asked that taxes (paid in beans, chocolate, cotton, and slaves) be paid on time.

A few towns did fight back, and the Aztecs were ruthless in response. One villager recounted, "The soldiers from all the allied provinces took many captives, both men and women, for they and the Mexica entered the city, burned the temple, sacked and robbed the place."[25]

Most prisoners were equally distributed to noble families, though those that had been captured by a warrior through an individual act could be sent to his home as a reward. The remaining prisoners were set aside either for human sacrifice or sale at slave markets.

One city-state, Tlaxcala, was able to resist Tenochtitlan's power, striking somewhat of a lasting truce. Instead of paying taxes every year, Tenochtitlan and Tlaxcala would both select a number of warriors who would then battle each other until all of one city state's warriors had been killed. These "flower wars"—which were not unlike *The Hunger Games* of modern imagination—allowed both sides to save face—Tlaxcala didn't have to formally submit, and Tenochtitlan was still able to exact some price from a powerful rival.

Just four generations after Obsidian Snake died, when the Aztecs conquered the city-state of Coatzacoalcos (now a major port just southwest of Veracruz), they took as booty the young daughter of a nobleman who would eventually be known as Malinche.

Malinche was then taken to the coastal town of Xicallanco where she was sold as a slave to some neighboring Mayans from the town of Potonchan, which is still further west of Coatzacoalcos in the current Mexican state of Tabasco.

Malinche was with these Mayans in Potonchan when ten ships larger than any canoe she had ever seen, each with giant cloths that appeared to catch the wind, landed near the village. After a brief battle in which the Mayans stone-tipped arrows proved no match for Spanish steel armor, Malinche and nineteen other women were given to the bearded men as a peace offering. The Mayans were able to convince the leader of the strangers, a man named Hernando Cortez, that the wealthy nation he sought lay toward the west.

Cortez, his ten ships, and his twenty slave women sailed in that direction, past Malinche's hometown of Coatzacoalcos, to modern day Veracruz. There they were met by canoes carrying emissaries from the Aztec king, Montezuma.

Cortez demanded an audience with this king, but his Spanish translator was unable to convey the message. He spoke only Mayan and Spanish, not the Nahuan of the Aztecs. Cortez was furious. But Malinche knew Mayan and she had never forgotten her native Nahuan language.

When Cortez realized the Spanish translator he had invested so much money in was essentially worthless, Malinche stepped forward and volunteered to explain what the Aztecs were saying. Just beginning to realize her immense value, Cortez offered to give her "more than her liberty" if she helped him find and speak to Montezuma. Malinche agreed. And she would go on to be far more than just a translator.

Not only did Malinche speak both Nahuan and Mayan (and soon Spanish too), but as the daughter of a nobleman she also knew the politics of the Valley of Mexico. She knew the Aztecs had enemies, powerful enemies, who would be eager to ally with anyone who did not demand annual slave tributes for human sacrifice. And many of these possibly rebellious city-states were on the way to the Aztec capital, Tenochtitlan. Malinche would help Cortez navigate and exploit this web of domestic intrigue. And on the way she became his lover.

Within two years, Cortez and his Tlaxcalan allies (the "flower wars" tribe mentioned previously) had killed Montezuma, conquered Tenochtitlan, and renamed it Mexico City.

The rapid fall of the Aztec empire demonstrates how the high stakes nature of polygamous rule can make a political system highly unstable thanks to divided elites. The ruthless nature of Aztec dominance left many city states eager to form an alliance with a foreign power to rid themselves of the Aztecs brutal slave taxation.

The polygamous world order may seem alien to us in the West, but the reality is that for almost all of recorded history—since the invention of writing itself—until just within the last hundred years, most people lived in polygamous societies.

This second sexual revolution, from egalitarian monogamous nomadic hunter-gathering tribes to highly stratified sedentary polygamous empires, profoundly changed human relations. Before the second sexual revolution almost every man had a wife and could start his own family.

But after the second sexual revolution, huge swaths of the male population were left with no wife, no possibility of children, and therefore no connection to the future of humanity. It was an inherently unstable situation, one which was about to be replaced by the model that first gave humanity dominion over Earth.

CHAPTER THREE

MONOGAMY'S RETURN

THE GREECE OF HOMER'S *ILIAD* was not that much different than the Euphrates Valley of Hammurabi. Powerful families fought for control of city-states, with the larger states often conquering and raiding their smaller rivals. Along the way, this wealthy warrior class made slaves of any men they did not kill in battle and took their wives and daughters as concubines. The Trojan War was famously started by the theft of the Spartan queen Helen by a visiting Trojan prince. And the rift between Agamemnon and his greatest warrior, Achilles, was sparked by a dispute over a concubine.

That all began to change in 595 BC when an aristocrat named Solon was put in charge of the Athenian army during a war with the rival city-state of Megara. After defeating the Megarians, Solon was named archon of Athens and he swiftly enacted wide-ranging reforms that would set Athens on the path to becoming the world's first democracy.

On the political front, Solon expanded membership in the citizen assembly, known as the Ekklesia, to all but the poorest citizens. The Ekklesia had the power to declare war, select military leaders, pass general legislation, and hold public officials accountable at public trials. Under Salon's new rules, the small farmers who equipped themselves as hoplites for war could now be part of this ruling body regardless of family ancestry. Solon further weakened the aristocracy by ending the practice of debt slavery and canceling all mortgages. This allowed many small farmers to avoid losing their land to wealthy families.

But the most important of Solon's reforms had to do with marriage. Previously, wealthy aristocrats could keep as many concubines as they wanted and adopt the offspring from those women as they pleased. Solon did not make sex outside of marriage illegal, but he did attach real penalties to fathering children with women other than a citizen's wife.

Under Solon's law, only legitimate children produced within marriage could become citizens. This prevented wealthy men from adopting their own illegitimate children from their concubines. The size of the inheritance a bastard could receive was also capped at one thousand drachmas (the daily wage of a free laborer was one drachma per day). The change wasn't all bad for illegitimate offspring though. Under Greek law, legitimate children were charged with the duty of taking care of their parents in old age. Solon exempted bastards from this responsibility. However, while they were still free residents of Athens, they were not afforded the privileges of citizenship.

Feminists often claim that the labeling of some children as illegitimate was a tool of patriarchy used to control women's sexual behavior. Solon's reforms show why this isn't true. Limiting citizenship to only legitimate children was designed to constrain men's sexual behavior, not women's.

Solon also limited men's control over the sexual lives of women. Under Greek law before Solon, a man had the right to kill any other man he found sleeping with his wife, mother, daughter, or concubine. Solon kept most of this framework but removed concubines from the list. This change took away a man's legal authority to police the sexual behavior of women not directly related to him by marriage.

"By attaching legal disabilities to bastardy, Solon's laws effectively discouraged aristocrats and the wealthy from producing excessively large families," University of Southern California classics professor Susan Lape writes. "In so doing, the legislation foreclosed a source of elite power. It was no longer possible to convert material resources or economic power into reproductive power and hence into political power."[1]

More important than the limitations on the power of wealthy men, Solon's reforms created a new spirit of equality among all citizens that paved the way for democracy. "By attaching privileges to legitimacy and disabilities to bastards, Solon's laws put every citizen on the same reproductive footing. Every man, no matter how wealthy or how poor, could only father legitimate children with one woman, his legitimate wife," Lape writes. "For this reason, the norms of family membership can be correlated to an egalitarian ethos for citizen men."[2]

Before Solon's laws, people in Athens didn't think of themselves as belonging to a political entity, they thought of themselves as being part of a lineage or family dynasty. By strengthening the conjugal family and creating a clear line between citizens and non-citizens, Solon furthered the emergence of a new Athenian political identity that transcended family ties.

Unlike Sparta, which was dominated by a professional warrior class, the Athenian army was anchored by yeoman farmers who were responsible for providing their own body armor, shield, and spear. What the Athenians lacked in professional training, they made up for in numbers and a shared sense of fate. "If the countryside was to be a patchwork of roughly similar farms worked by leather-clad yeomen, the phalanx was an analogous grid of identically bronze-clothed fighters," historian Victor Davis Hanson writes in *The Other Greeks*. "Whether a farmer looked over at his neighbor's plot, or over at the man next to him in battle, or over at the agriculturalist seated next to him in the assembly, the unique egalitarianism of the agrarian polis was continually reemphasized and enhanced."[3]

These Athenian hoplites led the Delian League to victory over the much larger invading Persian army, taking the fight to Asia Minor, and establishing Greek dominance of the eastern Mediterranean.

We shouldn't romanticize Athenian democracy too much. Slaves made up a clear majority of the populace, and in Sparta the percentage was even higher. Athenian democracy also proved highly unstable with a series of coups that installed oligarchic rule, which is probably why Plato said that "tyranny naturally arises out of democracy."[4]

Nonetheless, Athenian democracy was a substantial advancement in human governance, inspiring future attempts at egalitarian participatory government for thousands of years. As inspirational as Athenian democracy was, however, it proved no match for the Roman war machine, which conquered Athens in 86 BC.

THE FAMILY FARM POWERED WAR MACHINE

According to legend, Rome was founded around 750 BC by Romulus, the son of a vestal virgin from a nearby city who was forced to abandon him in the Tiber River because his uncle had just deposed his father as king and saw him as a threat to his rule. Romulus, and his twin brother Remus, were supposedly saved by the god Tiberinus, who sent a she-wolf to suckle them until a kindly shepherd took them in.

When they came of age, Romulus and Remus returned to their home city, overthrew their uncle, reinstated their father, and then set off to start their own city. There was a dispute between the brothers about where the city was to be founded; the two fought, Romulus won, and Rome was created. Archaeologists generally agree, however, that Rome was founded long before 750 BC by migrants who first came to the peninsula from across the Alps at the end of the second millennium BC.[5] Where myth turns into history is unclear, but it is generally accepted that the Latin people of Rome were ruled for some centuries by Etruscan kings before the wealthiest families rebelled, overthrew the king, and formed a Republic.

At first, the Roman city-state was bitterly divided along class lines between the patrician landowners and the plebian class of small farmers, artisans, and tradesmen. From the beginning, the plebeians were considered citizens and could own property, but they could not hold public office (including military titles) and were not allowed to marry into patrician families. Patrician families monopolized the consulate and controlled the senate. Rome was not a democracy where every man had an equal vote. As a result, the early Republic was fairly turbulent, with frequent underclass rebellions.

During these early Republic years. Rome routinely found itself at war with its Sabine and Etruscan neighbors. These wars required significant manpower and the patrician class realized they were not going to be successful if they fought these wars on their own. They needed the plebeians to fight with them if they were going to succeed on the battlefield. A series of reforms were passed around 450 BC erasing some of the legal distinctions between patricians and plebeians, including new protections from debt for those who served in the military. Plebeians were allowed to hold some public offices, including the new title of tribune who spoke for the plebeians in the Senate. Most importantly, the ban on intermarriage between the classes was removed, creating one unified people.

With this newfound unity, the Roman Republic became an efficient war machine. All property-owning citizens owed annual military service to the state and were required (like Greek hoplites) to provide their own armor and weapons. The wealthiest Roman citizens additionally provided their own horses and served in the calvary.

Military service was, without a doubt, a financial burden and a mortal risk, but it was also considered an honor to perform one's duty for the state, and culturally Romans placed a high value on martial virtues like courage and strength. It was considered a great honor to fight for the patria. The taking of slaves and plunder after a victory also softened the financial load.

THE FALL OF THE ROMAN FAMILY

But as the list of the Republic's victories grew, its power and wealth were not equally distributed. The patrician class had always been wealthier than the plebeian masses, but as Rome conquered Sicily and then Iberia and then Carthage, the gap between the wealthy and middle-class started to grow.

Like Greece, Rome had always been a slave state, but Roman military success overseas supercharged the slave economy. Over one hundred thousand slaves were captured and brought to Rome in the First Punic War, and by 225 BC about 15 percent of the Italian peninsula's population were slaves.[6] By the end of the first century it was 35 percent.[7] As it turned out, the growth of Rome's slave population would have unanticipated consequences for the stability of Roman families.

For smaller family farms, extended campaigning was an economic hardship because the labor of the owners was needed to make them productive. This wasn't the case for wealthy families with large estates who could afford enough slaves to do the labor for them. As Rome's constant state of war financially stretched family farms, the wealthy began buying up surrounding property, turning the Roman countryside into a series of sprawling plantations.

With the small family farms disappearing, an insufficient number of citizens were able to afford the equipment needed to outfit themselves as legionnaires. In 100 BC, general Gaius Marius began hiring unemployed Roman citizens as professional soldiers. It is no accident that Julius Caesar was able to successfully cross the Rubicon, ending the Republic just fifty years later. Roman armies made up of farm-owning citizen-soldiers were loyal to the Republic. Armies made up of professional soldiers were loyal only to the general that paid them. Rome was becoming an empire.

After ruling for just five years, Caesar was assassinated in 44 BC. His nephew Octavian prevailed in the ensuing civil war, naming himself Emperor Augustus, and then methodically set about reforming the empire to induce greater stability. In addition to making it easier for wealthy plebeians to serve in higher office (often at the expense of disloyal patrician families), Augustus reorganized how the army was paid, making it an official professional standing force, while also substantially reducing its size.

But Augustus was also concerned with what he saw as the decline of the Roman family and their traditional moral values, particularly among the patrician class. While the population of slaves in Rome was growing dramatically during the first century, the population of Roman elites was shrinking. There was far too much decadence, too little marriage, too much adultery, and too few children. Rome's elite was in need of revival.

To address this problem, in 18 BC, Augustus passed the *Lex Julia de maritandis ordinibus*, a law designed to promote the ideal Roman household. The purpose of the law was not to encourage any coupling that could produce children, but to foster the right kinds of marriages that would strengthen and grow the patrician class as a whole.

To this end, Augustus banned marriages between senators and freed slaves. He taxed unmarried patrician women over the age of twenty, granting only a twelve-month exception for the widowed and a six-month exception for the divorced. Unmarried men above the age of twenty-five were banned from certain public events and also forbidden from receiving inheritances—a strong incentive if ever there was one. Conversely, men whose legitimate wives had multiple children were given preference for public office, which was often quite lucrative.

Yet these reforms did not manage to sweeten the pot. Roman men, by and large, continued to choose bachelorhood over married life.

Why were elite Roman men so marriage-phobic?

For starters, Roman men did not need marriage to have sex. Roman men, particularly wealthy Roman men, were encouraged to have sex with whomever they wanted, whenever they wanted, so long as they didn't do it with another man's wife. Slaves remained a common outlet for sexual cravings and men who couldn't afford slaves could always go to prostitutes, who Romans believed were essential for the maintenance of public order. Without such an outlet for male sexual energy, it was thought, chaos was certain. The capital alone had no fewer than forty-five government regulated brothels.[8]

"In the ancient world, the flesh trade was a dominant institution, flourishing in the light of day," classicist Kyle Harper writes. "Slaves played something like the part that masturbation has played in most modern cultures."[9]

While sex was easily obtained for Roman men, marriage was a bit of a hassle. A rich Roman man did not simply marry whatever woman caught his fancy. Marriages were intricately planned family affairs designed to maximize power and wealth.

The foundation of Roman society was the household (*familia*). The head of the household (*pater familias*) had absolute control (*patria potestas*) over all the family's persons and property. Not only did the pater familias control who married whom, but the Twelve Tables—the foundation of Roman law—explicitly gave him the power to decide which babies lived and which died. Roman women did have access to both contraceptives and abortifacients, but these two methods of managing family makeup did not give the pater familias the ability to select for sex. Infant exposure was widely practiced in ancient Rome, with girls being the primary victims.

Though Roman brides came with dowries, ownership of that property ultimately stayed with the bride's family. So, for example, if the pater familias of the bride's family agreed to give a farm as dowry to the husband's family, the husband's family would control the farm and enjoy its profits while the marriage lasted. But they did not own the farm and could not sell the land. Additionally, if the couple were to divorce, the wife's family would get the property back.

Roman families did need successors to continue the family dynasty, but marriage was not the only way to create legitimate heirs. Adoption was common among the senatorial class of Rome as a way for men without legitimate offspring to secure an heir. Like marriage, there was usually a transfer of property involved, though in this case the adopting family gave property to the party giving up a child for adoption. Additionally, under Roman law, the full social status of the adopting family was immediately transferred to the adopted child. This meant any adopted child could legally inherit everything from the pater familias, thus seamlessly continuing the family name.

A wife, on the other hand, might give birth to multiple children, which would only divide a powerful family's fortune. And a father might not like his biological sons or might not trust them to preserve the family legacy. With adoption, however, a wealthy Roman man could handpick his singular beneficiary, and, hence, limit the number of his successors. This practice stretched to the ultimate heights of Roman power. The emperors Trajan, Hadrian, Lucius Aelius Caesar, Titus, and Augustus himself were all adoptees.

In addition to trying to increase the number of marriages, Augustus criminalized adultery for the first time in Roman history. Before his reign, adultery was a purely private matter to be handled by the pater familias. Augustus's *Lex Julia de Adulteriis Coercendis*, enacted in 17 BC, created a legal duty for the husband to prosecute his adulterous wife and her lover in open court. A third party could also prosecute the wife and lover if the husband refused.

A successful prosecution for adultery required the husband to divorce his wife, who lost half the claim to her dowry. The lover also lost half his property. The father of the adulterous wife was also entitled to kill his own daughter and her lover, but he could also choose to allow their exiles to separate islands instead.

Like the Greeks, the Roman definition of what constitutes adultery was a little different than ours. It was technically impossible for a husband to commit adultery except by having sex with another man's wife. Roman law also permitted, and even expected, husbands to have as much sex as they wanted with concubines, prostitutes, and slaves. Wives, however, were only allowed to have sex with their husbands.

Augustus's "moral" reforms largely proved fruitless—literally. Neither his laws to promote the Roman family nor those that criminalized adultery managed to stop, let alone reverse, the demographic decline of Rome's ruling elite.

Yet a revolution involving the relationship between men and women was just around the corner.

THE TWO SHALL BECOME ONE FLESH

Less than two decades after Augustus died, a Jewish prophet from Galilee was crucified in Judea for treason. His followers would go on to fundamentally change the nature of marriage and, in turn, the world. In fact, without the influence of the Church, democracy as we know it today would likely not have emerged.

It's not that sex had no ethical consequences in Roman society. Wives were supposed to be faithful to their husbands, and a man could be punished for raping another man's slave. But the crime in both these cases arose from the harm done to the pater familias, not to the wife or slave. Raping someone else's slave wasn't considered wrong because the slave did not consent. Slave owners could rape their own non-consenting slaves whenever they wanted. The harm in raping another man's slave was more of a property crime, like stealing a sheep.

But there was no notion in Roman society that sex itself was sinful. In fact, they had no concept of sin whatsoever. Women were supposed to remain pure "maidens" until marriage, but there was no equivalent word for a virgin man. Not that a man couldn't be dishonored in a sexual act. Roman men were expected to be the active, penetrative partner in sex. A passive man who had been violated was simply no longer a man.

For the followers of Jesus of Nazareth, however, sex was not just a bodily act, for they believed that the spirit was not so easily separated from the flesh. This was a monumental shift in perspective. "Have you not read," Jesus explains in the Gospel of Matthew, "that the one who made them at the beginning 'made them male and female,' and said, 'For this reason a man shall leave his father and mother and be joined to his wife and the two shall become one flesh?' So they are no longer two, but one flesh."[10]

The apostle Paul harnessed this sentiment, writing in his First Epistle to the Corinthians, "Do you not know that whoever is united to a prostitute becomes one body with her? ... Every sin that a person commits is outside the body; but the fornicator sins against the body itself."[11]

The Christian message was clear: Sex is never just physical. The act, though carnal, is a transcendent union of two bodies becoming one spirit. According to Christian teaching, God gave us our bodies so that we could wholly unite through the intimacy and commitment of marriage. When we have sex outside of the sacrament of marriage, we are not committing a simple property crime, but betraying a sacred and holy gift.

This sexual ethic applied equally to both slaves and slave-owners. At least in theory, both the rich and the poor had equal sexual integrity for the first time in human history.

This spirit of equal human dignity extended to both men and women. "But because of the temptation to immorality, each man should have his own wife and each woman her own husband," continues Paul's First Epistle. "The husband should give to his wife her conjugal rights, and likewise the wife to her husband. For the wife does not have authority over her own body, but the husband does; likewise *the husband does not have authority over his own body, but the wife does* (emphasis added)."[12]

A husband ruling over his wife's body was common throughout the ancient world, not just in Rome. The idea that a wife should concurrently rule over her husband's body was a truly radical one.

Feminists today may view Christianity as one of the world's greatest sources of patriarchal power, but in reality the new religion was a source of female empowerment.

Almost as radical were the leadership positions entrusted to women in the early Church. In his Epistle to the Romans, Paul commends "our sister Phoebe," who he identifies as a "deacon of the church of Cenchrea."[13] Additionally in his Epistle to Timothy, he points out that women can serve as deacons as long as they are "serious, not slanderers, but temperate and faithful in all things."[14]

Deacons were an integral part of the initial success of the Church. They oversaw administering the congregation's charitable functions, which set Christianity apart from the other religions in the Roman empire.

The Church's care for the sick and poor, often carried out by the women of the congregation, was so successful at bringing converts to the faith that, in 362 AD, Emperor Julian wrote a letter to a pagan priest in Galatia instructing him to emulate the Church's charitable efforts. Julian blamed the growth of Christianity in the empire on the "moral character, even if pretended," of the Christians best evidenced by their "benevolence toward strangers and care for the graves of the dead."[15]

Charitable works were not the only source of the Church's stunning popularity. The Church's sustained commitment to the equal dignity of all human life, and the resulting decrease in female infanticide, also helped the faith spread through intermarriage.

Imperial Rome had a massive gender imbalance problem. The misogyny of Roman society, typified by the common practice of exposing unwanted female infants, meant that Rome had far more men than women. A study of one ancient Roman city found that only six of about 600 wealthy families raised more than one daughter. Broadly, this preference for male children resulted in a skewed ratio of an estimated 140 men per one hundred women.[16]

Christians did not have this gender imbalance problem. For them, leaving infants outside to die, no matter their sex, was as terrible a crime as murder. In addition to producing equal numbers of male and female children, Christianity's comparatively equal treatment of women also meant the new faith attracted more female converts than male ones. Wealthy widowed aristocratic women looking for an opportunity to participate in public life were common converts to the young Church.

This left a significant number of Christian women unable to find a Christian man to marry. Many would go on to marry pagan men, few of whom became faithful Christians. But these Christian mothers would then raise the children from their unions with pagan men in the Christian faith. Through intermarriage and a commitment to the equal dignity of all human life, whether it was male or female, Christian families began to outgrow their declining pagan counterparts.

As popular as Christianity became in Roman urban centers, the rural landowning aristocracy rarely signed up. Although Emperor Constantine issued the Edict of Milan in 313 AD, giving Christians the freedom to worship, Constantine himself was not baptized until he was on his deathbed in 337 AD.

Constantine did, however, become a major benefactor to the Church, building basilicas, exempting clergy from taxation, and perhaps most importantly, allowing the Church to own property as its own separate legal entity. It is worth noting that Constantine was first introduced to Christianity by his Christian mother Helena, who was not of noble birth.

With Rome's now mercenary—and increasingly foreign-born—army loyal only to the generals who paid them, the sway of Rome's central government continued to diminish. This widening power vacuum allowed aristocratic families that controlled rural plantations to progressively assert more police powers over surrounding towns. They even formed private armies to repel barbarian attacks, which had been mounting in frequency. Some succeeded in holding off the mostly Germanic invaders. Many did not.

Rome itself was eventually sacked by a string of Visigoth, Vandal, and Ostrogoth tribes starting in 410 AD. It's hard to say which of these sackings definitively marked the end of the western Roman empire, as it was already weak and unable to control provinces away from the capital. It may be more accurate to say that Rome ended not with a bang, but with a whimper.

THE MARRIAGE AND FAMILY PROGRAM

The mostly Germanic tribes that overwhelmed the Romans were not unlike the polygamous Viking societies discussed in the last chapter. Wealthy and influential males had many wives, and even more concubines, usually captured in war. The more concubines a powerful man could capture in war, the more children he could have, and the more potent his clan.

At the same time, Christianity continued to spread throughout the former empire through intermarriage, as it did when the pagan ruler of a northern Frankish family, Clovis of the Salian Franks, saw an opportunity to forge an alliance with a key southern Frankish family. His Catholic Burgundian bride tried to convert him before they married, but Clovis did not come to the faith easily. He resisted Clotilde's efforts until he won a key victory over a rival Germanic kingdom, finally converting to Christianity on Christmas Day in 508 AD.

Clovis went on to found the Merovingian Dynasty, which unified almost all of modern-day France while also stretching into what today consists of Switzerland, Austria, Belgium, the Netherlands, and Germany. The Merovingian kings, along with their Carolingian successors, formed an alliance with the Church that not only helped establish a unifying Christian identity for the kingdom, but also happened to undermine the power of rival aristocratic families.

A fledgling religion looking for new converts has no interest in reaffirming the absolute control of old men looking to preserve their family traditions. Hence Jesus's recitation of Genesis in the Gospel of Matthew: "For this reason *a man shall leave his father and mother* and be joined to his wife, and the two shall become one flesh (emphasis added)." The Christian Church had a vested interest in Christian households turning away from pagan extended clans and towards the chosen community of the Church.

To this end, the Church developed a number of policies that undermined patriarchal family power including a ban on polygamy, a ban on inheritance to illegitimate offspring, a ban on arranged marriages (which undermined consent), and a ban on cousin marriages (which were often arranged as a means of keeping inherited property within the family).

This "Marriage and Family Program"—so coined by evolutionary biologist Joseph Henrich—weakened the family-based patriarchal power structure, instead allowing more independent conjugal families to form, grow, and thrive.[17]

A recent study led by Henrich compared communities throughout Europe according to their length of exposure to the Church's teachings on sexual ethics. The researchers found that communities with longer exposure to the Church's family policies exhibited more individualism, less conformity, and a greater likelihood to trust non-family members. Communities with less exposure were associated with greater conformity, obedience, nepotism, deference to elders, and in-group loyalty. Each additional 500 years of Church influence was associated with a 91 percent decrease in cousin-marriage rates.

"It was consent, not coercion, that constituted the only proper foundation of marriage," Tom Holland writes in *Dominion: How the Christian Revolution Remade the World.* "The Church, in its determination to place married couples, and not ambitious patriarchs, at the heart of a proper Christian society had tamed the instinct of grasping dynasts to pair off cousins with cousins… The hold of the clans, as a result, had begun to slip."[18]

Wealthy and powerful men, of course, resisted the Church's push towards monogamy. The examples of powerful European men taking mistresses beyond their wife are legion. But under the influence of Christianity, these extra-marital unions were increasingly seen as sinful and not part of the natural order. Slowly it became expected for noble men not to have sex outside of marriage, although this wasn't a widely held convention until around the eleventh century.[19]

By promoting equality and consent in marriage, the Church set the stage for the creation and growth of non-clan based mediating institutions that would prove crucial to the emergence and development of democracy. Guilds, universities, and charter cities, all gave people new opportunities to cooperate and learn from each other in a setting not dominated by patriarchal interests. The dynastic family power of monarchy was being transformed into a democratic civil society.

DEMOCRACY RISING

The Church, not coincidentally, profited greatly from the demise of many aristocratic lines. As the Church's policies restricting inheritance to only legitimate heirs made it harder for noble families to maintain their wealth across generations, its equal commitment to aid the sick and dying meant that priests were often with heirless aristocrats right as they were finalizing their wills. Huge gifts of land from dying members of Europe's upper classes were quite common in the Middle Ages. It's estimated that, by 900 AD, the Church owned about one-third of all cultivated land in Western Europe.[20]

As great an ally as the Church was to kings in limiting the power of rival noble families, it would also become key to limiting the power of kings as well.

Take the Magna Carta Libertatum, one of the first major steps toward representative government in England. Often thought of as an agreement between King John and rebellious nobles, the Magna Carta is actually a document binding three parties, with the Church being mentioned even before the nobility.

"We have granted to God that the Church in England is to be free," the Magna Carta begins. The "we" was the king. And what the document meant by "free" was that the Church was understood to have its own laws and leadership apart from the crown, and, further, that the crown had no right to interfere in Church affairs.[21]

The Magna Carta featured many other limits on royal power, including how and when the king could raise taxes. Arguably though, the most important limits on the king were the protections granted to the Church. It was the Church, after all, that published, preserved, and popularized the document.

A number of written agreements had been made between the crown and the nobility before King John, but these were often forgotten within a generation. Not the Magna Carta. Because protection of the Church was written into it, the Church actively copied and distributed the document throughout all of England. And, thus, the power and the independence of the Church as a mediating institution helped set the West on the path to democracy.

THE FOUNDATIONS OF AMERICA'S NATIONAL MORALITY

As much as the Church broke down the patriarchal family structures in Europe, the Europeans that fled to America took the revolution even further, prompting Alexis de Tocqueville to write in 1840, "In America, the family, taking this word in its Roman and aristocratic sense, does not exist."[22]

By this Tocqueville meant that Americans did not define themselves by what their fathers and forefathers owned or had accomplished. Instead, they looked forward to their own future, to what they could create with their own wives and children.

The result, according to Tocqueville was that "of the world's countries, America is surely the one where the bond of marriage is most respected and where they have conceived the highest and most just idea of conjugal happiness."[23]

Marriage was not just another option on the menu of life for the Founding Fathers. The family was an essential building block of the republic, one charged with educating and preparing the next generation of republicans for self-rule.

The second President of the United States, John Adams, explained the importance of family in his diary. "The foundations of national morality must be laid in private families. In vain are schools, academies, and universities instituted if loose principles and licentious habits are impressed upon children in their earliest years."

Like the Church, the Founders stressed that any happy marriage had to begin with the true informed consent of both parties. In his lectures on American law, Declaration of Independence signer James Wilson stressed, "To this marriage contract the agreement of the parties, the essence of every rational contract, is indispensably required."[24]

Not every marriage was perfect, however, and sometimes divorce was needed. But rarely so. "Of causes which are slight or trivial," Wilson wrote, "a divorce should, by no means, be permitted lest the most tender of human connections be degraded to a transient society of profit or pleasure."[25]

Wilson's mention of "slight or trivial" causes not meriting divorce echoes the Declaration of Independence's language suggesting that revolutions should not be undertaken for "light and transient" reasons. Divorce could be a proper course of action, the Founders believed, but it should be saved as a last resort, just as the Founders had exhausted all other options before rebelling against England.

Like their own revolution that balanced the need for independence and freedom with the necessities of law and order, the Founders saw monogamous marriage as the perfect balance between individual liberty and the obligations all of us have as members of a larger society.

In the *Encyclopedia Americana*, Joseph Story, an associate justice of the Supreme Court, summed up the Founder's vision of family, "Marriage is an institution, which may properly be deemed to arise from the law of nature. It promotes the private comfort of both parties, and especially of the female sex. It tends to the procreation of the greatest number of healthy citizens, and to their proper maintenance and education. It secures the peace of society, by cutting off a great source of contention, by assigning to one man the exclusive right to one woman. It promotes the cause of sound morals, by cultivating domestic affections and virtues. It distributes the whole of society into families, and creates a permanent union of interests, and a mutual guardianship of the same. It binds children by indissoluble ties and adds new securities to the good order of society, by connecting the happiness of the whole family with the good behavior of all. It furnishes additional motives for honest industry and economy in private life, and for a deeper love of the country of our birth."[26]

FIGHTING TO MAKE THE AMERICAN MARRIAGE WORK

The Founders were also well aware that their fledgling Republic was surrounded on all sides by polygamous native communities. But a growing number of Americans also believed that there was a polygamous stain on the country coming from within.

By the 1860s, many abolitionists had rhetorically tied the twin barbarisms of slavery and polygamy together. It was common in the North to note how readily Southern slave owners used and abused the women they owned. Just ask Sally Hemings, the slave concubine of Thomas Jefferson.

"There are many disgusting elements in slavery which are not present in polygamy, while the single disgusting element of polygamy is more than present in slavery," Republican Senator Charles Sumner said on the Senate floor in 1860. "By license of polygamy, one man may have many wives, all bound to him by marriage tie, and in other respects protected by law. By the license of slavery, a whole race is delivered over to prostitution and concubinage, without the protection of any law."[27]

Eventually the Southern states decided the issue of slavery was worth getting a divorce over, but the Northern states wanted them to stay and make the relationship work. After a messy separation, the North eventually prevailed in keeping the union together.

Even before the war was over, the Union began to assimilate ex-slaves into their new lives of freedom. Across the South, General Grant's troops organized "contraband camps" with camp officials directed to "lay the foundations of society" among ex-slaves by establishing public schools, providing opportunities for religious worship, and "enforcing the laws of marriage."[28]

By 1864, the Union Army had authorized all military clergy to perform marriages among ex-slave soldiers and the chaplains reported that the freedmen eagerly embraced the institution. An officer in Mississippi reported that he saw a "very decided improvement in the social and domestic feelings of those married by the authority and protection of the law. It caused them to feel that they are beginning to be regarded and treated as human beings."[29]

Two years later, on the third anniversary of the Emancipation Proclamation, the Reverend Henry McNeal Turner of the African Methodist Episcopal Church, said, "This is a day of gratitude for the freedom of matrimony. Formerly there was not security for domestic happiness. Our ladies were insulted and degraded with or without their consent. Our wives were sold, and husbands bought, children were begotten and enslaved by their fathers."

"We therefore were polygamists by virtue of our condition," Reverend Turner, who was also the first black chaplain in the Union Army, continued. "But now we can marry and live together till we die and raise our children and teach them to fear God."[30]

African Americans eagerly adopted the institution of monogamous marriage after they were freed from their polygamous slave existence, and the black family survived both the Jim Crow South and the Great Depression intact. Divorce has always been more likely in communities facing discrimination and economic stress, and the divorce rates in the black community throughout their time in the United States reflect that. But before the 1960s it was young black men and women, not young whites, who were more likely to be married. If anything, the pressure to get married used to be stronger in the black community than in the white community.

REDEFINING FAMILY

In sum, contrary to the claims of feminists, monogamous marriage is not an institution invented by powerful men to control women's sexual behavior. In fact, it is the opposite. It is an institution created to protect the most vulnerable among us by controlling the sexual behavior of the most powerful.

By limiting each man, regardless of his wealth, to just one mate, marriage redirected the energies of men from aggression and domination to cooperation and mutual development. Studies have found that in a monogamous society getting married lowers the amount of testosterone a man's body produces. Getting married does not have the same effect in polygamous societies.[31] In monogamous societies, a married man's efforts are devoted to protecting and providing for his wife and children. In a polygamous society, a married man is just out trying to add one more wife to his harem.

Today we live in such a Christianized world that it is easy to take for granted the conjugal family as the foundational unit of society. It is hard to reorient our minds to a reality where monogamous family households were not the norm. To help understand just how different the ancient world was from our reality, it is worth considering that neither Greek nor Latin had a word for "family" as we use it today.

The Greeks thought of themselves as belonging to an "oikos" which is best translated as "household." This "household," according to Aristotle, included all those persons subject to the authority of its chief, including slaves and servants. Likewise, the Latin word "familia" referred to all persons subject to the authority of the pater familias, again including slaves and servants. There was no word in either language that specifically referred to the genetic relations of the husband and wife of the house as a distinct and separate unit. It was not until about the mid 7th century that European writers used the word "familia" to refer specifically to the biological offspring of the married unit in a household.[32]

This third sexual revolution, which saw the transition from large, patriarchal, fundamentally polygamous households where one man dominated the economic and sexual lives of everyone beneath him, to smaller conjugal households where one, monogamously married couple could codetermine their own destinies, transformed first the West, and then the world.

CHAPTER FOUR

THE AMERICAN FAMILY CONSENSUS

THE TRANSFORMATION OF THE UNITED States from a nation of small family farms to an industrial international power accelerated after the Civil War, but even by 1850 a majority of the workforce had already moved off the family farm.

This evolution was bound to encourage experiments in family formation, and by some accident of history, a trio of notable movements began in just a twenty-year span—all in upstate New York.

THE MORMON MARRIAGE REVOLUTION

Published by Joseph Smith in Palmyra in 1830, the Book of Mormon actually forbids polygamy. "For there shall not any man among you, have save it be one wife," Jacob 2:27 reads, "and concubines he shall have none."[1]

It wasn't until thirteen years later, in 1843, when Smith dictated the Doctrine and Covenants 132 in Nauvoo, Illinois, that polygamy became the accepted practice of the Church of Jesus Christ Latter Day Saints. While Smith, Brigham Young, and other wealthy Mormons practiced polygamy for the next nine years, however, they did so mostly in secret. It was not until 1852 that Elder Orson Pratt publicly taught the principle of plural marriage in Salt Lake City, Utah.

The Mormons had already been chased out of New York, Ohio, Illinois, and Missouri by the time they announced their polygamous beliefs, but this new revelation made them a national target for scorn, including ridicule in popular novels with titles such as *Mormonism Unveiled* and *Female Life Among the Mormons.*

By 1856, the Mormons had become a national political issue, with the Republican Party platform condemning the "twin relics of barbarism"—polygamy and slavery. Just one year after the South seceded in 1861, the Republican Congress passed the Morrill Act of 1862, making bigamy a federal crime punishable by up to five years in prison.[2]

Understandably distracted by the Civil War, the United States government made little progress against the practice of polygamy in Utah through the 1860s. Indictments were made, and men were brought to trial, but Mormon juries simply would not convict.

When the war finally did end, Congress revisited the problem by passing the Poland Act in 1874. This legislation gave federal courts in the Utah territory the power to empanel juries made up of half Mormons and half non-Mormons.

Convictions for bigamy were still few and far between, after passage of the Poland Act, but enough men were sentenced to jail that a test case arguing that the Morrill Act's ban on plural marriage violated the Mormons' First Amendment right to the free exercise of religion, did make it to the Supreme Court. In *Reynolds v. United States,* the Court sided decisively with the monogamous vision of the Founders.

"It is impossible to believe that the constitutional guarantee of religious freedom was intended to prohibit legislation in respect to this most important feature of social life," Chief Justice Morrison Waite wrote for the majority opinion. "Polygamy leads to the patriarchal principle, and when applied to large communities, fetters the people in stationary despotism, while that principle cannot long exist in connection with monogamy."[3]

"It is within the legitimate scope of the power of every civil government," Justice Waite continued, "to determine whether polygamy or monogamy shall be the law of social life under its dominion."

Despite the successful prosecution of some bigamists, the Mormons stubbornly continued their polygamous ways, so Congress upped the ante, passing the Edmunds Act in 1882, which not only made cohabitation between a man and more than one woman a misdemeanor, but also made it illegal for such cohabitors to vote. The thinking was that it was far easier to prove people were currently living together than it was to prove they had married.

Mormons who were subsequently denied the right to vote challenged this law too, but the Supreme Court again affirmed congressional power to enforce monogamy. "No legislation can be supposed more wholesome and necessary in the founding of a free, self-governing commonwealth... than that which seeks to establish it on the basis of the idea of the family as consisting of in, and springing from, the union for life of one man and woman in the holy state of matrimony," Justice Stanley Matthews wrote for the majority.[4]

Over a thousand men were convicted of unlawful cohabitation in Utah under the Edmunds Act, but the Mormon church continued to deny the authority of Congress to mandate monogamy. In response, Congress passed the Edmunds-Tucker Act of 1887 which both repealed the church's incorporation and seized the church's property. This law was also challenged all the way to the Supreme Court and again the Mormons' First Amendment claims were denied.

"The organization of a community for the spread and practice of polygamy is, in measure, a return to barbarism," Justice Joseph Bradley wrote. "It is contrary to the spirit of Christianity, and of the civilization which Christianity has produced in the western world."[5]

"The state has a perfect right to prohibit polygamy and all other open offenses against the enlightened sentiment of mankind," Justice Bradley continued, "notwithstanding the pretense of religious conviction by which they may be advocated and practiced."

Faced with the imminent confiscation of all church property, the Mormon leadership finally relented. Just months after the Supreme Court's decision in May of 1890, President Wilford Woodruff issued Official Declaration 1 in September, forever ending the practice of polygamy by members of the church. There are still, to this day, some splinter communities that are polygamous, but any Mormon caught in a plural marriage is excommunicated from the church.

Six years after the Mormons finally abandoned polygamy, the Utah territory was admitted to the Union as the 45th state. Today there is no religious community whose members more eagerly embrace monogamous marriage than the Church of Jesus Christ of Latter-Day Saints.[6]

WHEN MONOGAMY IS CONSIDERED A SIN

Just seventy miles to the east from where the angel Moroni revealed the golden plates to Joseph Smith in 1823, the Yale-educated John Humphrey Noyes founded the Oneida Community in 1848.

A minister by trade, Noyes believed Jesus Christ had already returned in 70 AD and it was every Christian's duty to realize the Kingdom of Heaven here on Earth through socialism. Noyes eventually recruited around 300 people to come live with him and his wife in one big "complex marriage."[7]

Noyes believed monogamy was a sin because it allowed people to develop a selfish interest in other people. God, Noyes believed, wanted men and women to enjoy sexual variety, and monogamy denied them that sexual freedom.

Unfortunately, it quickly became apparent that not everyone wanted to have sex with everyone else. Turns out that the men wanted to have sex with the youngest and most beautiful women while the most desirable women were only interested in a few men.

Noyes solved this problem by creating a committee that decided who could have sex with whom and when. When someone wanted to have sex with someone else, they would inform the committee who they wanted to have sex with, and then the committee would arrange a time and place for the two members to copulate. This process worked…to an extent. It is reported that any member of the community that wanted sex, could have it two or three times a week, just not necessarily with the person they wanted or when they wanted it.

True to the dreams of socialists and feminists, women in the Oneida Community were purposefully liberated from all childcare duties. After one year of weaning, children were ushered off to separate living quarters away from the adults. The commune maintained two schools, one for older and one for younger children, both run by men and women specifically trained to educate children.

Noyes also took care to make sure that the older children transitioning into the sexual maturity of adulthood were paired with more experienced partners who could properly introduce them to the holy pleasures of sex. And guess who assigned himself the role as "first husband" to almost every adolescent girl in the community? Yup, Noyes picked himself for this important duty.

The surrounding community of Oneida was always skeptical of the Oneida commune, but since none of the members of the community were officially married to more than one person, Noyes could not be charged with bigamy. But as word of Noyes' role as "first husband" spread, the locals took the opportunity to charge Noyes with statutory rape. Noyes was warned of his coming arrest, however, and he fled to Ontario, Canada where he stayed till his death, afraid to return to the United States for fear of prosecution.

Noyes' son Theodore carried the commune on for a little while, but when the committee assigned his favorite lover to another man for an evening, his lover instead chose to leave the commune entirely by running off with a completely separate man. Distraught, Theodore also left Oneida and the experiment in complex marriage fell apart.

TOWARDS A MORE EQUAL UNION

That same year that Noyes formed his first "complex marriage" in Oneida, Elizabeth Cady Stanton hosted the first Women's Rights Convention just seventy miles southwest in Seneca Falls.

Elizabeth Cady was the seventh of eleven children, six of whom—all the boys—died before reaching adulthood. While Elizabeth's father paid for her to have an excellent education at Johnstown Academy in upstate New York, when the last of his surviving male children died, he told her, "Oh my daughter, I wish you were a boy."[8]

Eight years after graduating from the Troy Female Seminary, Elizabeth met abolitionist Henry Brewster Stanton while visiting her cousin Gerrit Smith in Peterboro, New York (Smith, but not Stanton, would later go on to finance John Brown's raid of Harper's Ferry). The couple honeymooned in London where Henry attended the World Anti-Slavery Convention.

Elizabeth, however, was denied entry to the convention because she was a woman.

Already a firm believer in women's rights—Elizabeth had insisted the word "obey" was stricken from her wedding vows entirely—Stanton turned her exclusion from the Anti-Slavery Convention into the inspiration for the Women's Rights Convention, which took place eight years later.[9]

Over 300 people from around the country attended the Seneca Falls Convention and one hundred signed the event's Declaration of Sentiments which evoked the Declaration of Independence, beginning "When, in the course of human events..." but then went on to tweak the wording, "We hold these truths to be self-evident: that all men and women are created equal."[10]

After listing sixteen "sentiments," including, "he has not ever permitted her to exercise her inalienable right to the elective franchise," and "he has taken from her all right in property, even to the wages she earns," the document concludes with a call for women to receive "immediate admission to all the rights and privileges which belong to them as citizens of these United States."[11]

It would take over seventy years after the Seneca Falls Convention before the 19th Amendment gave women the right to vote in federal elections, but Stanton and her allies had more immediate victories on other issues at the state level.

At common law in most states during the 1800s, when a woman married a man, the woman ceased being her own legal entity. She could own no property and earn no wages that did not automatically belong to her husband.

Stanton was instrumental in New York state passing the Married Women's Property Act in 1848, allowing women to retain ownership in property they owned before they got married, and again in 1860 when the Married Women's Earnings Act gave women the right to keep wages earned during the marriage. Both laws became models for other states and by 1900 every state protected woman's equal property rights.

Stanton fought particularly hard against another common law doctrine that precluded a man from being found guilty of raping his wife. Stanton's friend and fellow suffragist Lucy Stone even placed this protection above the right to vote, writing that voting meant very little "if I may not keep my body, and its uses, in my absolute right. Not one wife in a thousand can do that now, and so as long as she suffers this bondage, all other rights will not help her to her true position."[12]

But while Stanton, a mother of seven, was a strong critic of how marriage was then practiced—she wanted it to be a more equal union—she still believed marriage should be the foundation of family life.

"When marriage results from a true union of intellect and spirit," Stanton said in a lecture in 1871, "when mothers and fathers give to their holy offices even the preparation of soul and body that the artist gives to the conception of his poem, statue or landscape, then will marriage, maternity and paternity acquire a new sacredness and dignity, and a nobler type of manhood and womanhood will glorify the nation."[13]

TEDDY'S PARTNERSHIP OF THE SOUL

Stanton and her fellow women's rights advocates would find an unlikely ally in a Republican politician also from the state of New York. Theodore Roosevelt, who promoted the sport of football because its rough nature helped shape the character of young men, also happened to write his senior thesis at Harvard on "The Practicality of Giving Men and Women Equal Rights."

"A cripple or a consumptive in the eye of the law is equal to the strongest athlete or deepest thinker," Roosevelt's thesis reads, "and the same justice should be shown to a woman whether she is or is not the equal of a man. As regards the laws relating to marriage there should be the most absolute equality between the sexes."[14]

Indeed, just like Stanton, Roosevelt's thesis went on to argue that the word "obey" should be dropped from all wedding vows. Later, as a member of the New York State Assembly, Roosevelt even introduced legislation that would have required a public flogging for men convicted of beating their wives.

Roosevelt was also a firm believer that women should be given every opportunity to succeed professionally. "There is a real need for a certain number of women doctors and lawyers," Roosevelt wrote in support of women pursuing work outside the home. He would often praise Dr. Laura Bassi, an Italian physicist, who held three professorships at the University of Bologna.[15]

His choice of Dr. Bassi was deliberate, however, as she managed to raise twelve children while also pursuing her professional interests. "She never permitted her extraordinary scientific and literary work to conflict with her domestic duties," Roosevelt wrote. "I believe in women's rights. I believe even more earnestly in the performance of duty by both men and women."[16]

And for Roosevelt, the highest duty of both men and women was to get married and start a family. "No other success in life," Roosevelt wrote, "not being president, or being wealthy, or going to college, or anything else, comes up to the success of the man and woman who can feel that they have done their duty and that their children and grandchildren rise up to call them blessed."[17]

Like Stanton, Roosevelt also saw marriage as an equal collaboration where "each partner is honor bound to think of the rights of the other as well as of his or her own." Marriage should be a "partnership of the soul, the spirit and the mind, no less of the body," Roosevelt wrote, and the ideal family would be one where "the father and mother stand to each other as lovers and friends."[18]

For Roosevelt, however, marriage was about more than just personal happiness and fulfillment. The continued existence of the entire American project depended on it. "It is in the life of the family, upon which in the last analysis the whole welfare of the nation rests," Roosevelt told the New York State Agricultural Association in 1903.[19] And Roosevelt saw some troubling signs in the health of the American family.

According to the U.S. Census, which Roosevelt studiously pored over, the number of divorced Americans tripled between 1890 and 1910, while fertility fell 20 percent.[20] "Easy divorce is now, as it ever has been, a bane to any nation, a curse to society, a menace to the home, an incitement to married unhappiness, and to immorality," Roosevelt told the National Congress of Mothers.[21]

Divorce laws vary by state, and after the Civil War western states had become somewhat infamous for their easy divorce rules. Where New York required a judge to find that one spouse committed adultery or desertion, states like Nevada allowed judges to grant a divorce whenever they found it appropriate. These western states also loosened their residency requirements so that someone only had to live in the state for a short period of time—sixty days in Nevada—for a court to gain jurisdiction over a marriage.

It was not uncommon for a wealthy New York husband to move to Reno for sixty days, get a divorce, and then return to New York to surprise his wife with the end of their marriage. Roosevelt not only condemned this practice, but he also pushed for a constitutional amendment that would have federalized the regulation of marriage nationwide.

"I am well aware of how difficult it is to pass a constitutional amendment," Roosevelt said in his 1906 State of the Union. "Nevertheless, in my judgment the whole question of marriage and divorce should be relegated to the authority of the national Congress...and surely there is nothing so vitally essential to the welfare of the nation, nothing around which the nation should so bend itself to throw every safeguard, as the home life of the average citizen. The change would be good from every standpoint."[22]

Roosevelt's push for a constitutional amendment protecting marriage failed, but his "Square Deal" legislative agenda that did advance, was designed to strengthen the American family against what Roosevelt saw as a dangerous "uncontrolled industrialism."[23]

His Newlands Reclamation Act invested in irrigation infrastructure for rural agricultural communities. His Elkins Anti-Rebate Act and Hepburn Act protected small family farms from railroad price discrimination. His Chinese Exclusion Act and Immigration Act of 1907 protected men's wages by restricting low-skilled immigration. And his prosecution of the Northern Securities Company for violating the Sherman Antitrust Act protected communities from Seattle to Chicago from what would have been the largest railroad monopoly in the country.

Roosevelt had plenty of other pro-family ideas that, like his marriage amendment, failed to become law. He called for progressive taxation that would have forced large landowners to sell off their holdings, turning small tenant family farmers into landowners. He wanted both an income tax and an inheritance tax that would "be immensely heavier on the childless and on families with one or two children." Families with three or more children would receive tax benefits instead.[24]

This plan included a $500 tax exemption for a married couple's first two children (worth $10,000 today) and $1000 for every child after that (worth $20,000 today). The federal tax code would eventually provide a similar but less generous child tax exemption, but no bonus was given for large families.

Whether or not Roosevelt's policies deserve credit, some important family indicators did improve after his time in office. Divorce peaked in 1920, one year after women were given the right to vote, then fell steadily until the beginning of the Great Depression.

A FATHER FULLY ABLE TO PROVIDE

Teddy Roosevelt's fifth cousin, Franklin Roosevelt, didn't have Teddy's rhetorical flourish for explaining why the married family ought to be the center of American life, but like Teddy's Square Deal, Franklin's New Deal was very much built to ensure a male wage earner could support a nuclear family.

Almost all of the 2.5 million jobs created by the New Deal's Civilian Conservation Corps went to men. It wasn't until First Lady Eleanor Roosevelt intervened that eighty-six camps employing just 6,400 women were created. And even then, men were paid one dollar a week for the work, while women were paid just fifty cents.

The Works Progress Administration was more open to the participation of women, but the law also specifically limited enrollment to one person per household. About 12 percent of WPA jobs went to women, but only to single women, mostly mothers with minor children. Those mothers that did participate, however, were given the extra benefit of free childcare.[25]

Private employers and local governments were also encouraged to hire men over women, particularly married women, and the sentiment was widely accepted. A 1936 Gallup poll asked if wives should work if their husbands already had jobs, and 82 percent of respondents said "no."[26]

For federal government jobs, the Economy Act of 1932—like the WPA—prohibited two people of the same family from holding federal employment at the time. The language of the law was gender neutral, but in practice families always chose to sacrifice the lower paid wife's job and keep the higher paid husband's job. It was socially acceptable for single women and widows to support themselves, but married women were very much expected not to work outside the home.

Roosevelt's biggest legislative accomplishment, the Social Security Act of 1935, again, did not explicitly preference male wage earners, but the specifics of how the legislation worked did so in practice.

From the beginning, married women were technically allowed pay into and benefit from Social Security's retirement and unemployment insurance programs. But not all sectors of workers were allowed to participate in these programs. It was not an accident that those workers left unprotected by Social Security (part-time, seasonal, domestic, and state government workers) were predominantly women.

Abraham Epstein, an economist and founder of the American Association for Old Age Insurance, wrote in favor of Social Security in 1933: "It must be remembered that the American standard assumes a normal family of man, wife, and two or three children, with the father fully able to provide for them out of his own income."[27]

Where the original 1935 legislation only implicitly favored married men, the 1939 amendments to the Social Security program explicitly targeted support for nuclear families. A "survivor benefit" was created for the wives and minor children of men, who died before the age of sixty-five. Both wife and children would lose the benefit if the wife remarried (it was not until the Supreme Court's 1975 *Weinberger v. Wiesenfeld* decision that this benefit was extended to widowers).

The 1939 amendments also increased a married man's retirement benefit by 50 percent once his wife reached retirement age too, but only if they were still married. A wife could choose instead to take her own earned Social Security retirement benefit instead, but most often the wife's covered employment history (which didn't cover part-time work) meant the husband's 50 percent bonus was bigger.

The Social Security Act of 1935 also created the Aid to Dependent Children (ADC) program which would later become the Aid to Families with Dependent Children (AFDC) and then later still renamed again the Temporary Assistance for Needy Families (TANF). Importantly, as we will cover in detail in the next chapter, ADC was originally intended to help only those children where the father was "deceased, absent, or unable to work." States were given wide latitude to disqualify mothers who were having intimate relationships with men outside of the confines of marriage. A 1939 report found that these state efforts were highly effective. According to the government report, only 2 percent of children receiving benefits through the program were living with never-married mothers.

While marriage rates fell throughout the Great Depression, and the average age of first marriage rose, that is to be expected when jobs paying wages high enough to support a family are hard to come by. As the economy picked up with the beginning of World War II, so did marriage rates. But the stress of war also caused divorce rates to keep rising.

It wasn't until after the war ended that a "golden age of wage labor for young men" began thanks to a booming economy and a tight labor market created by two decades of the country's most restrictive immigration laws.[28]

Median income for full-time employed young men more than doubled in the postwar era, to a peak of $48,500 in 1973. This "Baby Boom" era also saw fertility spike from a Great Depression low of 2.06 children per woman in 1940 to a 3.58 children per woman high in 1960. It was truly a golden age for the American family.

THE NUCLEAR FAMILY NORM

For some historians of the American family, the 1950s are portrayed as a departure from traditional American norms. "The family of the 1950s is not a model we should try to recreate," Evergreen State history professor Stephanie Coontz writes in her book, *The Way We Never Were: American Families and the Nostalgia Trap*, "but a historical aberration that we should try to understand."[29]

In a narrow sense, Coontz is right. There are some elements to the typical 1950s married family that are slightly different from what came before. Prior to the industrial revolution, most men were either self-employed farmers, proprietors of small family businesses (such as butchers, blacksmiths, or bakers), or the unpaid sons of farmers and small business owners. The wives and daughters of these farmers and business owners also worked with their husbands and brothers. University of Minnesota history professor Steven Ruggles calls this family structure the "corporate family" since the family operated as one economic unit.[30]

It took time for the male children of these families to either save up enough money to start their own farms or family businesses or wait until their father died so they could inherit the family property. Because of this delay the average age of first marriage before the industrial revolution was comparatively high. Young couples usually waited till they could form their own household before tying the knot. In these pre-Industrial Revolution times, the average first-time groom was about twenty-six while the average first-time bride was about twenty-two.

This began to change as the Industrial Revolution created manufacturing jobs in America's rapidly growing cities. Young men taking these high paying manufacturing jobs could afford to rent an apartment in the city much earlier than they could afford to buy their own farm. By the end of the 1950s, the average ages of newlywed couples had fallen to a little over twenty-two for men and just under twenty for women.

So, on two points, Coontz is correct: the average family of the 1950s was slightly different from the average American family of the generation before. First, instead of husband and wife working together as self-employed farmers or small business owners, now husbands worked outside the home for wages while the wives worked part-time at most and maintained the family home. Second, because of tight labor markets, these families were slightly younger since the availability of good wages enabled men and women to establish new households earlier.

But those two slight deviations hardly make the typical family of the 1950s "a historical aberration." From the founding of the Republic through the 1960s, the married household was the foundational unit of society. Numbers from before the Civil War are spotty, but from Census of 1860 through 1960, 80 percent of all American households included a married couple. As we will cover in the next chapter, that is no longer true today.[31]

New York Times columnist David Brooks, like Coontz, has also argued that the family of the 1950s was a departure from a healthier past, one which he believes was not based on married couples establishing their own households. In his *Atlantic* article, "The Nuclear Family Was a Mistake,"

Brooks writes, "According to Ruggles, in 1800, 90 percent of American families were corporate families. Until 1850, roughly three quarters of Americans older than 65 lived with their kids and grandkids. Nuclear families existed, but they were surrounded by extended or corporate families."[32]

The mistake Brooks makes here is failing to recognize that corporate families were nuclear families. Yes, 75 percent of adults older than sixty-five lived with their children and grandchildren, but that does not mean that a majority of households had grandparents in them.

It is true that there were no retirement homes to ship grandma and grandpa off to in the 1800s, but there were two factors limiting the number of households with three generations. First, people died a lot earlier in the 1800s, the average life expectancy was just forty years old in 1800 compared to eighty today. So, there weren't a ton of grandparents to go around. Second, people had more children in the 1800s. The average woman had seven children in 1800, compared to just two today. So, there were a lot more households for mom and dad to move into.

Looking at Ruggles own data, we see that for most of American history less than 10 percent of households contained three generations. Now, that percentage did double between 1750 and 1900, rising all the way to 20 percent, but it has since fallen steadily back down to below 10 percent today.[33]

So, Brooks is dead wrong. Extended families living under one roof have always been the exception to the nuclear family norm. And, as this chapter has shown, that was by conscious design.

MONOGAMY CONQUERS ALL

The almost hundred years between the end of the Civil War and the beginning of the 1960s were a tremendously volatile time: The transition between an agricultural economy to an industrial one. Two world wars. A Great Depression. All of this put immense strain on the American people.

But throughout all of it, the monogamously married family served ably as the institution responsible for producing and raising the next generation. To be sure, there were changes—for the better. Wives gained financial independence from their husbands, and women earned the right to vote. But what changes were made to the institution of marriage, were made to improve it, to make it more equal and more conducive to human flourishing. Elizabeth Cady Stanton and her fellow suffragists, as well as their Republican ally Teddy Roosevelt, sought to solidify marriage as the basis of American family life, not supplant it.

And throughout the entire century, the government was there to help monogamous marriage continue as the cornerstone of American civilization. From using the power of the federal government to suppress alternative lifestyles like polygamy, to supporting family farms through infrastructure investments and antitrust prosecutions, to centering the social safety net squarely around the married household, at every step of the way there was an American Family Consensus to support the nuclear family form.

And the nation thrived because of it, becoming the preeminent world power. Other countries not only took notice of our success, but they copied it. Between 1869 and 1960, polygamy was outlawed first in Japan in 1880, then Russia in 1920, then Thailand in 1935, then China in 1950, and India in 1955. Today just 25 percent of the world's population lives in countries where polygamy is legal.[34]

But whatever political consensus there once was around the nuclear family as the preferred family form, has now completely fallen apart. The next chapter will detail how that unity dissolved, and the chapter after that will examine what the effect has been on the nation.

CHAPTER FIVE

THE ASSAULT ON MARRIAGE

SOMETHING HAPPENED TO AMERICAN SEXUAL behavior during the 1970s.

When the National Opinion Research Center asked Americans in 1963 if sex between a man and a woman was acceptable before marriage, fewer than 20 percent said yes. A similar 21 percent told Gallup in 1969 that it was "not wrong" for a man and women to have sex before marriage.[1]

By 1985, a majority of Americans (52 percent) told Gallup that sex between a man and woman outside marriage was fine. Today, 76 percent say the same thing.[2]

While American beliefs about sex outside of marriage have been changing, so has their behavior. In 1960, fewer than 5 percent of American children were born without married parents. By 1980, that number had grown to 20 percent. Today it stands at 40 percent.[3]

There is no doubt that technology played a role in these changes. Various contraceptive methods existed for decades before the 1970s, but the ease and ubiquity of the pill made birth control more affordable and reliable. Additionally, advances in home appliances freed women from hours of cleaning and cooking giving them more time to pursue paid work outside the home. And at the workplace, more office jobs like clerk and secretary were being created that did not require a man's physical strength.

Each of these technological developments narrowed gender differences between men and women, making marriage less essential for women in particular. With easy and affordable birth control, a woman was far less likely to become dependent through a single sexual encounter. Changes in technology, both in the home and at the workplace, meant women could more easily form a household without a man.

But as big as these technological factors were, a strong ideological component also drove the transformation. The word "liberty" has always appeared in our founding documents, but the meaning of the word has changed over time. Instead of a liberty that emanated from natural law and was channeled through marriage into "the happiness of the whole family" (as understood by the Founders), liberty in America was coming to mean the fulfillment of individual desires, no matter how antithetical those desires were to the good of the family.

Instead of being the bedrock of liberty, marriage was recast as just one acceptable lifestyle choice among many. If anything, the pressure to get married is now considered an impediment on the path to individual discovery.

This new focus on individual actualization over family obligations proved popular enough in elite circles that the Supreme Court managed to completely rewrite federal family policy in the span of just five years.

SAVAGE SELF LOVE

Often credited with inspiring the French Revolution, Jean-Jacques Rousseau is also a source of our current sexual revolution as well.

Raised a Calvinist in Geneva, Rousseau was one of the first in the Christian world to reject the idea of original sin. Where John Calvin believed that people were so warped by sin that "everything which our mind conceives, meditates, plans, and resolves, is always evil," Rousseau believed that "there is no original perversity in the human heart." Where Rousseau's predecessor Thomas Hobbes envisioned pre-civilization man in a state of nature that was "nasty, brutish, and short," Rousseau described a peaceful condition where men lived solitary lives without "obligations to one another."[4]

In Rousseau's state of nature individuals acted according to their most basic urges, which were driven by the instinct for "amour de soi"—which can be translated as "self-love." This self-love was not selfish, however, because it was tempered by an equally natural "pitie"—which is best understood as a compassion for one's fellow man.[5]

Men happily pursued their simple desires in this state of nature until, "The first man who, having fenced in a piece of land, said 'This is mine,' and found people naive enough to believe him. That man was the true founder of civil society."[6]

With the advent of property, according to Rousseau, men began to exploit and compete with one another. "Everyone began to look at everyone else and to wish to be looked at himself, and public esteem acquired a price," Rousseau wrote. "The one who sang or danced the best, the handsomest, the strongest, the most skillful, or the most eloquent came to be the most highly regarded, and this was the first step toward inequality and vice."[7]

This drive for vanity, which Rousseau called "amour propre," did not exist in the state of nature, only in society. And unlike the "amour de soi" which drove man's behavior before civilization, this "amour propre" was not tempered by compassion. It made man "two-faced and crooked with some, imperious and harsh with others," and it put man "in the position of having to abuse everyone he needs when he cannot make them fear him and does not find it in his interests to be useful to them."[8]

In the state of nature, Rousseau believed, "the savage lives in himself," but "the man accustomed to the ways of society" is "always outside himself and knows how to live only in the opinion of others." Thus for Rousseau, it is society that is the source of falsehood and inauthenticity in people. Men and women are essentially born good and true to themselves but are then corrupted by the institutions of civilization that surround them.[9]

The key to a good society, therefore, was to teach children to ignore both "custom" and "habit" and instead follow their instinct for self-love. "A man's sole duty," Rousseau wrote, "lies in following in everything the inclinations of his own heart."[10]

This belief that man should ignore the customs of civil society and instead pursue his deepest desires, is the foundational creed of the assault on marriage.

EXPERIMENTS IN LIVING

Writing some seventy-seven years after Rousseau's last work was published, England's John Stuart Mill also saw the institutions of civil society as a threat to the attainment of individual potential. "The despotism of custom is everywhere the standing hindrance to human advancement," Mill writes in *On Liberty.*[11]

For Mill, cultural expectations, like monogamous marriage, threatened not just the growth of the individual, but societal progress. A just society needs a variety of "experiments in living" and a "diversity of character and culture" to produce the creativity needed to drive a nation forward.[12]

Every individual's "experiment in living" should be tolerated, Mill argued, as long as it does not harm another person. "The only purpose for which power can be rightfully exercised over any member of a civilized community, against his will, is to prevent harm to others," Mill wrote.[13]

Like Rousseau, the logic of Mill's reasoning pointed to the conclusion that if fulfilling our hearts' desire is the highest goal in life, then everything conducive to its expression counts as progress, while everything that hinders it is repression by the dead hand of habit and custom.

Writing in the late 1850s, Mill was no stranger to the Mormon experiment in the United States. But while Mill did not personally approve of the Mormons polygamous lifestyle, putting his harm principle to use, he came to the opposite conclusion that the United States Supreme Court did about the use of state power to enforce monogamous marriage norms.

"The article of the Mormonite doctrine which is the chief provocative to the antipathy which thus breaks through the ordinary restraints of religious tolerance, is its sanction of polygamy," Mill wrote. "No one has a deeper disapprobation than I have of this Mormon institution."[14]

But then Mill continued, "Still, it must be remembered that this relation is as much voluntary on the part of the women concerned in it, and who may be deemed the sufferers by it, as is the case with any other form of the marriage institution."

"I cannot admit," Mill reasoned, "that persons entirely unconnected with them ought to step in and require that a condition of things with which all who are directly interested appear to be satisfied, should be put an end to because it is a scandal to persons some thousands of miles distant, who have no part or concern in it."[15]

In other words, for Mill, monogamous marriage was every bit as oppressive to women as polygamy, so who was the Supreme Court to pass judgment on how many wives a Mormon man had some two thousand miles away from Washington, D.C.?

Mills' tolerance for Mormon polygamy wasn't popular in elite circles at the time, but by 1946 similar sentiments were already appearing in the Supreme Court, although admittedly in dissenting opinions.

In 1910, Congress passed the Mann Act which made it a crime to transport "any woman or girl" across state lines "for the purpose of prostitution or debauchery, or for any other immoral purpose." Federal prosecutors began to use this law to arrest fundamentalist Mormons who had left their church to practice polygamy. The defendants in these cases argued that the Mann Act should not apply to them because the wives they were transporting into and out of Utah were not prostitutes.

The majority of the Court held that while the Mann Act was designed to combat prostitution, it also included the clause "for any other immoral purpose" and as the line of Mormon cases discussed last chapter clearly demonstrated, the Court had long considered polygamy to be immoral.

Writing in dissent however, Justice Frank Murphy, a Democrat appointed by President Franklin Roosevelt, defended polygamy as "one of the basic forms of marriage" alongside monogamy, polyandry and group marriage. "We must recognize, then," Murphy wrote, "that polygyny, like other forms of marriage, is basically a cultural institution rooted deeply in the religious beliefs and social mores of those societies in which it appears."[16]

Elite opinion on the primacy of monogamous marriage was changing.

A GIRL WITH NO RESPONSIBILITY

This newfound refusal to condemn the sexual practices of other cultures had been growing in elite circles for decades. In 1928, a young PhD student from Columbia University published a book titled, *Coming of Age in Samoa: A Psychological Study of Primitive Youth for Western Civilization.*

The book's 1966 cover featured a topless young woman dancing. It was a bestseller.[17]

That young student, Margaret Mead, and her mentor, anthropologist Franz Boas—considered the father of cultural relativism—made their agenda clear in the book's forward: "Courtesy, modesty, good manners, conformity to definite ethical standards are universal, but what constitutes courtesy, modesty, good manners, and definite ethical standards is not universal. It is instructive to know that standards differ in the most unexpected ways."[18]

Boas and his followers rejected the idea that cultures evolved. For Boasian anthropologists, there was no such thing as a progression from "primitive" to "civilized" culture. No culture was better than another. All cultures were morally equal. If some cultures mated polygamously or promiscuously, instead of monogamously, that was not something to be judged, it was just an accident of history. This Boasian anthropology became a weapon used by progressives to undermine the consensus cultural norms of Western society.

Mead portrayed Samoa as a peaceful, laid-back paradise where promiscuity, especially among young girls, was the norm. "The seventeen-year-old girl does not wish to marry—not yet" Mead wrote. "It is better to live as a girl with no responsibility, and a rich variety of experience. This is the best period of her life."[19]

According to Mead, the entire idea of Western monogamy was repellent to Samoans. "Samoans rate romantic fidelity in terms of days or weeks at most, and are inclined to scoff at tales of life-long devotion," she wrote. "They greeted the story of Romeo and Juliet with incredulous contempt."[120]

Mead's portrait of a harmonious sexually liberated culture where young women were free to sleep with whoever they wanted whenever they wanted was immensely popular in elite progressive circles. She had a monthly column in *Redbook* magazine which ran for sixteen years, she testified before Congress multiple times, she appeared on Johnny Carson's *Tonight Show*, she had her face on a U.S. postage stamp, and she was awarded the Presidential Medal of Freedom by President Jimmy Carter.

There was just one problem. Her portrayal of the promiscuous Samoan culture turned out to be mostly fiction. In 1983, five years after Mead died, an anthropologist from New Zealand named Derek Freeman published a book titled *Margaret Mead and Samoa: The Making and Unmaking of an Anthropological Myth*, in which he attacked the veracity of Mead's work.[121]

Books have since been written both defending and attacking both Mead and Freeman.[122] And Many of Freeman's claims about Mead's work are unfair. But even Mead's most fervent defenders have been forced to admit key aspects of her portrayal of Samoan life were wrong.

Like the rest of the world discussed in Chapter Two, Samoa was a polygamous society until European contact in 1722. Samoan chiefs were no more likely to let their many wives sleep with other men than high status men in any other polygamous society throughout the world. Nor did the Samoan converts to Christianity develop any new norms of promiscuous sexual behavior.

"A review of the recent ethnographic literature on Samoa from the 1960s through the present, including Freeman's own data, confirms the existence of a restrictive public morality concerning sexual conduct and sexual restrictions on girls and young women," Mead defender and anthropologist Paul Shankman writes.[123]

Shankman then compared data on American female adolescent behavior to what data was available on Samoan female adolescent behavior and concluded that "Samoan girls were somewhat more sexually active than their American counterparts."

"Somewhat more sexually active" is not the claim that drove *Coming of Age in Samoa* to the top of the bestseller list.

But doubts about Mead's portrayal of free love in Samoa did not come until her ideas had long been accepted in elite circles. In what must be considered a triumph for Boasian cultural relativism, Mead's argument that Western monogamous norms were unduly oppressing young women here in America became widely accepted. Our culture has never recovered its traditional view of adolescence as a time of innocence, or of courtship as a process that involves the restraint of sexual impulses.

ACCORDING TO THE LATEST REPORT

Twenty years after Mead published *Coming of Age in Samoa*, another scientist, this time a Zoology professor at Indiana University, published an explosive study of American sexual norms that also had a huge impact on American culture.

Alfred Kinsey was studying gall wasps when the Association of Women Students petitioned the administration for a course on marriage. Already popular with the student body, Kinsey volunteered to teach the new course, titled "Marriage and Family," which, since sexual intercourse was still such a taboo topic at the time, was restricted to seniors and married students.

In addition to delivering lectures based on what little empirical data there was on human sexual behavior, Kinsey began interviewing his own students and recording their sexual histories. This work was noticed by the Rockefeller Foundation who in 1941 gave him a generous grant to expand his research.

Seven years and more than five thousand interviews later, Kinsey published *Sexual Behavior in the Human Male* in 1948, which despite its eight hundred–page length, quickly became, like Mead's book, a bestseller. Among Kinsey's headline- grabbing findings were the claims that: 1) 37 percent of men had at least one homosexual experience; 2) 50 percent of married men cheat at least once; 3) 10 percent of men were exclusively homosexual; and 4) that male sexuality existed on a spectrum, with only small minorities on either end having exclusively hetero or homosexual desires (this became known as the Kinsey Scale). Five years later Kinsey published *Sexual Behavior in the Human Female* which also became a bestseller.[124]

The impact of Kinsey's work was possibly greater than Mead's. It was regularly mentioned in popular songs and movies throughout the 1950s. The American Law Institute specifically cited Kinsey when they rewrote their Model Penal Code in 1955, recommending that states legalize homosexual sex. And Justice William Douglas invoked the Kinsey Report by name in his 1967 dissent in *Boutilier v. Immigration and Naturalization Service*, where the majority of the Court affirmed the deportation of a Canadian citizen who had been convicted of sodomy in New York. (It was not until 1990 that U.S. immigration law was changed to remove sexual orientation as a grounds for deportation.)

As was the case with Mead, however, much of Kinsey's research would later be criticized as shoddy. Kinsey's biggest critic was author Judith Reisman who accused Kinsey of employing pedophiles for his research on child sexuality and even of sexually abusing children himself.[25] Kinsey died in 1956 and couldn't defend himself, but the Kinsey Institute did respond claiming that Kinsey was not a pedophile, nor did he employ pedophiles. Instead, the Institute said that most of the data on child sexuality in Kinsey's research came from one man's journal and that Kinsey lied to make it seem like the data came from more than one source.[26]

While exonerating Kinsey from the pedophilia charges, this defense significantly undermines the integrity of his scientific conclusions.

Kinsey's research methods on adult sexuality had major problems too. Instead of recruiting a random sample of people to interview, Kinsey recruited a disproportionate number of prison inmates and college students. The Kinsey Institute even admits on its own website that, "Kinsey's method of obtaining a sample of Americans would not meet today's standards of nationally representative survey sampling."[27]

Worse, it is now clear that Kinsey had a radical agenda. According to his most respected biographer James H. Jones, "Kinsey decreed that within the inner circle [of research assistants] men could have sex with each other; wives would be swapped freely, and wives too, would be free to embrace whichever sexual partners they liked." Kinsey himself had multiple heterosexual and homosexual affairs with his employees and even filmed his sexual exploits.[28]

Considering the alternative lifestyles Kinsey pressed on his subordinates, it shouldn't be surprising that his findings have not been replicated. Later, actual scientific research has found that at most 6 percent of men have experienced same-sex sexual contact in adulthood, just 4 percent of them consider themselves homosexual,[29] and only between 20 (in some studies) and 25 percent (in other studies) of married men cheat on their wives.[30] The Kinsey Scale itself is no longer used by researchers.

NO POWER ON EARTH WILL STOP IT

Mead and Kinsey were not the only popular pseudoscientists who were pushing for the rejection of monogamous marriage.

Before writing *The Sexual Revolution* in 1936, the first known coining of the phrase, Wilhelm Reich had been a student of Sigmund Freud.[31]

Freud has sometimes been considered one of the intellectual fathers of the sexual revolution since he claimed that the repression of sexual desire was the root of neurosis in many adults. But unlike Mill and Rousseau, Freud believed primitive man ultimately benefited from the limitations "culture" placed on individual behavior.

"Civilized man has exchanged some part of his chances of happiness for a measure of security," Freud wrote in *Civilization and its Discontents*. "We will not forget, however, that in the primal family only the head of it enjoyed this instinctual freedom; the other members lived in slavish thraldom."[32]

Unlike many in the West, Freud had not yet forgotten what life was like outside of the Christian world. "The antithesis between a minority enjoying cultural advantages and a majority who are robbed of them was therefore most extreme in that primeval period of culture," Freud concluded. "With regard to the primitive human types living at the present time, careful investigation has revealed that their instinctual life is by no means to be envied on account of its freedom; it is subject to restrictions of a different kind but perhaps even more rigorous than is that of modern civilized man."[33]

Where Reich departed from Freud was on the efficacy of communism to relieve man of his desire to dominate others. For Freud, man's aggression preceded private property. "This instinct did not arise as the result of property; it reigned almost supreme in primitive times when possessions were still extremely scanty," Freud wrote.[34]

For Reich, communism was man's salvation. Reich believed capitalism brutally turned people into commodities, alienating them from their natural needs and desires. Reich became convinced that working one-on-one with patients like Freud was fruitless since it was society itself that was sick.

In his book *The Sexual Revolution*, Reich argued that the very existence of private property corrupts the sexual relationship between men and women. "The most immediate consequence of private property," Reich wrote, "is the interest in chastity before marriage and marital fidelity to the husband."[35]

An atheist like his mentor Freud, Reich saw the church as just a tool for the ruling class to enforce their "bourgeois morality." Only by breaking down the most fundamental institution of bourgeois society, marriage, could people be freed from guilt and empowered to fulfill their natural sexual desires. Reich's earlier 1933 book, *The Mass Psychology of Fascism*, had argued that the patriarchal family was the key unit of indoctrination that trained children to submit to authority.

True political revolution, Reich claimed, would only be possible once the sexual repression of the family was overthrown. Then people, both men and women, would be free to seek out the orgasms that Reich believed were so essential to mental health. Towards this end, Reich opened free sex clinics throughout Vienna where his like-minded doctors distributed sex-education pamphlets, Marxist indoctrination, and free contraceptives. "A sexual revolution is in progress and no power on earth will stop it," Reich wrote.[36]

A known communist, Reich was forced to flee Europe after the Nazis annexed Austria in 1938, but his ideas on sexual revolution found fertile ground in his adopted home of New York City.

Upon coming to the United States, instead of setting up sex clinics that passed out Marxist propaganda, Reich accepted a position as Assistant Professor at the New School for Social Research where he preached free love while perfecting his theory of "orgone energy."

Orgone, according to Reich, was a universal energy that animates all life and can be harnessed to cure disease and achieve better orgasms. Reich even built an "orgone accumulator" that he claimed could concentrate orgone in the human body. About the size of a telephone booth, patients would sit in these boxes made of wood and sheet iron soaking up concentrated doses of orgone energy.

The accumulators, and Reich's message that orgasms could change the world, were a huge hit in New York's literary community of the 1950s and

1960s. Allen Ginsberg, Jack Kerouac, Norman Mailer, and JD Salinger all used orgone accumulators as did Sean Connery at the height of his James Bond fame. The boxes soon came to be a symbol of the rapidly sexualized culture. A January 1964 edition of *Time* magazine even declared Reich a "prophet" arguing that it "sometimes seems that all America is one big orgone box."

"With today's model, it is no longer necessary to sit in cramped quarters for a specific time," *Time* wrote. "Improved and enlarged to encompass the continent, the big machine works on its subjects continuously, day and night. From innumerable screens and stages, posters and pages, it flashes larger-than-life-sized images of sex. From countless racks and shelves, it pushes the books that a few years ago were considered pornography. From myriad loudspeakers, it broadcasts the words and rhythms of pop-music erotica. And constantly, over the intellectual Muzak, comes the message that sex will save you and libido makes you free."[37]

WHAT IS A WOMAN?

The year before *Time* magazine compared 1960s America to an orgone accumulator, Betty Friedan's *The Feminine Mystique* sold over a million copies.

Friedan, who would go on to co-found the National Organization for Women, was never the average housewife that she claimed to be in her bestselling book. In addition to living in a huge house with plenty of domestic help that allowed her to travel and write, Friedan also had a history of supporting socialist causes that she intentionally kept from the public eye.

After graduating from Smith College in 1942, Friedan studied psychology at the University of California at Berkeley where she tried to become a member of the Communist Party but was turned away because "there were already too many intellectuals in the labor movement." While Friedan excelled academically at Cal, she decided to abandon academia to become more active in politics.[38]

Friedan moved back east to Manhattan, landing her first job at the Federated Press, a left-wing news service associated with the Communist Party of America. After four years covering labor issues, Friedan moved to *UE News*, which was the official publication of the United Electrical,

Radio, and Machine Workers of America, one of the more radical unions of the 1940s. Friedan was with *UE News* from 1946 through 1952, during which time she met her husband and had their first child.

It wasn't until Friedan was pregnant with her second child, however, that *UE News* fired her because the union failed to honor its maternity leave policy. "It's your fault for getting pregnant," a union official told her.[39]

A year after that forced departure, Friedan came across a book, *The Second Sex*, that, in Friedan's own telling, changed her life.

The author of that book, Simone de Beauvoir, was a French existentialist who met her lover and fellow existentialist Jean-Paul Sartre while studying for the French civil service exam in Paris. Her most famous work begins with a question that will sound familiar to those who follow today's transgender debate:

"What is a woman?"

Beauvoir eventually answers, "One is not born, but rather becomes, a woman. No biological, psychological, or economic fate determines the figure that the human female presents in society; it is civilization as a whole that produced this creature, intermediate between male and eunuch, which is described as feminine."[40]

Like Rousseau before her, Beauvoir claimed that it is civilization which corrupts what would otherwise be a naturally happy person. The chief tool of the patriarchy in oppressing women, according to Beauvoir, was, of course, marriage.

"Marriage incites man to capricious imperialism," Beauvoir wrote, "the temptation to dominate is the most truly universal, the most irresistible one there is: to surrender the child to its mother, the wife to her husband, is to promote tyranny in the world."[41]

Instead of marriage, Beauvoir encouraged women to seek open relationships that allowed them to be sexually adventurous and independent. Beauvoir practiced such a "soul partnership" with Sartre, pursuing her own side lovers while never complaining when he stepped out on her, as he frequently did. In fact, Beauvoir actively enabled Sartre's other sexual conquests.

Sartre apparently had a taste for virgins, and Beauvoir evidently had no moral qualms about helping him acquire them, using her position as a teacher to seduce vulnerable young women and pass them on to Sartre. After violating one sixteen-year-old student procured by Beauvoir in a hotel, Sartre told her that the maid would be surprised to see him again so soon since he had just taken a different girl's virginity that same day. Another of Beauvoir's students began harming herself after Beauvoir fed her to Sartre.[42] Today, Beauvoir's arrangement with Sartre would be called an "alternative lifestyle."

Friedan most likely did not know the extent of Beauvoir's complicity in Sartre's exploitation of women when she read *The Second Sex*, but she definitely agreed with Beauvoir's conclusion that marriage was a tool of oppression. Friedan devoted an entire chapter of *The Feminist Mystique* to comparing marriage to, literally, the Holocaust. "Thousands of women, reduced to biological living by their environment, lulled into a false sense of anonymous security in their comfortable concentration camps," Friedan judged, "have made a wrong choice."[43]

By the mid-1960s, the moral consensus that had informed family policy in the United States for almost 200 years was breaking apart. Where once monogamous marriage was understood to be an institution essential to human flourishing, now thanks to the philosophy of Rousseau and Mill, the science of Mead, Kinsey, and Reich, and the feminism of Beauvoir and Friedan, marriage was seen as one of the biggest barriers to individual happiness. And in the span of just five years, the Supreme Court ensured that family policy was changed to reflect the new elite consensus

AN INDEPENDENT ENTITY NO MORE

Conservatives often lament *Griswold v. Connecticut* as a precursor to *Roe v. Wade*, which created a federal right to abortion during the first twenty-six weeks of pregnancy. And it is true that *Griswold* was the first case to find a right to privacy in the Constitution, specifically a right for a married couple to use contraceptives.

But the right to privacy found in *Griswold* was completely consistent with the family policy consensus of the nation's first 200 years. *Griswold* did not find an individual right to privacy emanating from the 14th

Amendment as *Roe* later would. Instead, *Griswold* found a right to "marital privacy" derived from the First, Fourth, and Fifth Amendments.[44]

This puts *Griswold* in line with a well-established series of cases that affirmed the nuclear family as the foundational unit of civil society, including the Mormon cases discussed in the last chapter, but also *Meyer v Nebraska* (where the Court held that the state of Nebraska could not forbid families from teaching their children German) and *Pierce v. Society of Sisters* (where the Court held that the state of Oregon could not interfere with a family's right to send their children to Catholic school).

"Marriage," Justice William Douglas wrote for the majority in *Griswold*, "is a coming together for better or for worse, hopefully enduring, and intimate to the degree of being sacred. It is an association that promotes a way of life, not causes; a harmony in living, not political faiths; a bilateral loyalty, not commercial or social projects. It is an association for as noble a purpose as any involved in our prior decisions."[45]

So, in 1965, when *Griswold* was decided, Chief Justice Earl Warren's Supreme Court still considered marriage a "sacred" institution that promoted "harmony" and "loyalty" in the United States. Just seven years later, however, Chief Justice Warren Burger's Supreme Court coldly tossed marriage aside, elevating the individual's wants and desires over the sanctity of the family unit.

When Massachusetts Supreme Judicial Court Chief Justice Arthur Prentice Rugg ruled in favor of the Bay State's contraceptive regulations in 1917, he said the "plain purpose" of the statute was "to protect purity, preserve chastity, to encourage continence and self-restraint, to defend the sanctity of the home and thus engender in the state and nation a virile and virtuous race of men and women."[46]

For the Burger Court, however, the Massachusetts law designed to channel sexual desires through the institution of marriage by limiting contraception to married couples was "plainly unreasonable." Where the Warren Court had found a marital right to privacy in the First, Fourth and Fifth Amendments, the Burger Court found an individual right to privacy divorced entirely from marriage in the Fourteenth Amendment.

"It is true that in *Griswold* the right of privacy in question inhered in the marital relationship," Justice William Brennan wrote for the majority in

Eisenstadt v Baird. "Yet the marital couple is not an independent entity with a mind and heart of its own, but an association of two individuals each with a separate intellectual and emotional makeup."[47]

"If the right to privacy means anything," Brennan continued, "it is the right of the individual, married or single, to be free from unwarranted governmental intrusion into matters so fundamentally affecting a person as the decision whether to bear or beget a child."[48]

With Brennan's majority opinion in *Eisenstadt,* the Court fully embraced the primacy of individual desires expounded by Rousseau and Mill. Freed from the "custom" and "habit" of marriage, the Burger Court empowered individuals to follow everything in the inclinations of their own heart. Liberated from the "despotism of custom" individuals could pursue the "experiments in living" necessary for progress.

Eisenstadt was then followed by a string of cases that completely dismantled state authority to channel individual sexual desires through the institution of marriage. In *Weber v. Aetna Casualty & Surety Co.*, the court overturned a state statute that guaranteed workmen's compensation to the legitimate, but not illegitimate, children of a deceased father. Similarly in *Richardson v. Davis*, the Court held that the illegitimate children of a worker covered by Social Security had an equal claim to Social Security survivors benefits as the workers legitimate children.

The impulse not to punish illegitimate children for the behavior of their parents is understandable, but the Court never even acknowledges that these distinctions were first created by the Greeks and continued by the Catholic Church as a means of controlling men's sexual behavior, not punishing children. One can cast off these rules as antiquated and cruel, but one should not then be surprised when the very behavior they were designed to limit—sex outside of marriage—explodes.

MEN IN THE HOUSE

As big a blow to marriage as *Eisenstadt* was in 1972, an arguably bigger blow had been delivered four years earlier in 1968.

As we discussed in the last chapter, our modern welfare state began with the Social Security Act of 1935, which provided financing to states for direct payments to mothers through a new Aid to Dependent Children program. Administration of these programs was left up to state governments.

The ADC statute explicitly allowed states to impose eligibility requirements relating to the "moral character" of applicants, which many states used to deny benefits to children born outside of marriage. Many states also adopted "man in the house" rules which allowed caseworkers to deny a mother eligibility if an unrelated adult male was found to be living in her home. These rules were unfortunately enforced on a discriminatory basis with far more black mothers denied payments from the program than white mothers.

All that changed in 1968, however, when a black mother of four challenged Dallas County Alabama's decision to deny her AFDC payments (Congress changed the name of the program to Aid to Families with Dependent Children in 1962). Mrs. Sylvester Smith had three children with her since-deceased husband and a fourth child with a man who later abandoned them. Mrs. Smith's sexual history aside, her four children clearly qualified for payments through Alabama's AFDC program.

Dallas County caseworkers had concluded, however, that Mrs. Smith was carrying on an affair with a Mr. Williams who "came to her home on weekends and had sexual relations with her." Mr. Williams was not the father of any of Mrs. Smith's children and, in fact, was married to another woman who he had nine children with. It was on the basis of this one ongoing sexual relationship with Mr. Williams, that Mrs. Smith was denied AFDC payments.[49]

Alabama argued before the Court that if they were not allowed to disqualify mothers who were having relationships with men outside of marriage, then those families that did get married would be discriminated against because they would no longer qualify for the program, while couples who lived together but did not marry could continue receiving benefits.

In *King v. Smith*, the Court held that Alabama's state interest in protecting poor married couples from discrimination was overruled by Congressional changes made to the AFDC program when it was renamed in 1962.

"Alabama's argument based on its interests in discouraging immorality and illegitimacy would have been quite relevant at one time in the history of the AFDC program," wrote Chief Justice Earl Warren. "However, subsequent developments clearly establish that these state interests are not presently legitimate justifications for AFDC disqualification."[50]

When Congress reauthorized the AFDC program in 1962, they still allowed states to disqualify mothers whose homes the state determined were "unsuitable," but Congress then required states that disqualified mothers on this basis to also provide a "rehabilitative program" to help make their homes suitable. Alabama had no such program.

"In sum," Warren concluded, "Congress has determined that immorality and illegitimacy should be dealt with through rehabilitative measures, rather than measures that punish dependent children, and that protection of such children is the paramount goal of AFDC."[51]

No mention was made of how to protect married families from discriminatory federal welfare policies.

Additionally, just a year after *Eisenstadt*, the Burger Court then cut off any possibility that a state, or Congress, could keep their man "in the house" rule by offering a "rehabilitative program." In 1973, in *New Jersey Welfare Rights Organization v. Cahill*, the Court held that the Equal Protection clause made any differential treatment between children born into or out of wedlock, unconstitutional.

Welfare state marriage penalties were here to stay.

SHE NEVER SEEMS EXPLOITED

The same year that the Burger Court decided *New Jersey Welfare Rights Organization*, extinguishing state efforts to regulate sexual behavior through welfare policy, the Court also significantly hindered the state's ability to limit sexual content consumed by the general public.

A Jewish immigrant from what is now Ukraine, Samuel Roth started out publishing the works of Ernest Hemingway and D.H. Lawrence before he had a falling out with James Joyce over a reprinting of *Ulysses* and was shunned by the literary community. At that point, Roth turned to publishing illustrated editions of erotic novels like *Fanny Hill* and *Lady Chatterley's Lovers*.

Roth eventually graduated to selling an illustrated catalog called "Beautiful Sinners of New York," which included photographs of naked prostitutes describing their services. When Roth was arrested on obscenity charges, his lawyer argued that Roth had a First Amendment right to sell information about sex, just as Alfred Kinsey had a right to sell *Sexual Behavior in the Human Male.* The jury found Roth not guilty.

Roth then expanded his business into other magazines which included both erotic stories and naked pictures of women. Roth was arrested again, this time by the federal government, and that jury did not buy Roth's First Amendment defense.

Roth appealed his conviction all the way to the Supreme Court but lost in 1957 when the Court held in *Roth v United States* that the First Amendment did not protect the sale of obscene materials, which could be defined as "whether, to the average person, applying contemporary community standards, the dominant theme of the material, taken as a whole, appeals to prurient interest."[52]

The *Roth* decision proved to be a valuable weapon used by prosecutors against pornographers until a man named Marvin Miller accidently sent one of his brochures advertising sexually explicit films to a restaurant owner in Newport Beach, California, who reported Miller to the police. Miller was convicted by a California jury who was instructed to apply the community standards of California. Miller then appealed, calling for a national standard, and the Supreme Court took the case.

Writing for the majority in *Miller v California,* Justice Brennan (who also authored *Eisenstadt*) cast *Roth* aside, identifying a new much looser standard that allowed obscenity as long as the obscene content in question also contained "literary, artistic, political, or scientific value."[53]

Armed with this new loophole, America entered the Golden Age of Porn. *Deep Throat* had already come out a year earlier in 1972, but it was quickly followed by *Behind the Green Door,* and the *Devil in Miss Jones.* After *Miller,* hardcore pornography was considered so mainstream that Roger Ebert even reviewed *The Devil in Miss Jones* for the *Chicago Sun-Times,* calling it "the best hard-core porno film I've seen."

Ebert went on to describe the film's star, Georgina Spelvin, as "something of a legend" who "alone among porn stars...never seems exploited."[54]

"Georgina Spelvin" was, of course, a stage name for Shelley Graham who was only meeting with the producers of the movie for a catering job when she was asked to read for one of the actors auditioning for the film. She did so well they hired her as the lead...and the caterer. While Graham knew the film involved sex, she thought it was just peripheral to the part. "I took the role very seriously," she told *Time*. "The fact that there was hard-core sex involved was incidental as far as I was concerned. I was totally deluded."[55]

Graham had been an aspiring actress who performed in Broadway productions of "Cabaret" and "Guys and Dolls." But not after *The Devil in Miss Jones*. Her mainstream acting career was over after that. After a year of failure in New York City, where *The Devil in Miss Jones* was filmed, she packed up and moved to Los Angeles where she would go on to perform in over seventy pornographic productions.

Just four years after Brennan's *Miller* decision made big budget pornos available in most major cities, technology brought pornographic films into everyone's homes in the form of the Video Home System, or VHS tapes. By 1985, 30 percent of American homes had a VCR, and by 1992, it was 75 percent. Throughout the 1980s the pornography industry saturated this market with literally hundreds of thousands of new pornographic movies.

President Ronald Reagan's Attorney General Ed Meese tried to push back against the growing pornography industry by selectively prosecuting cases in the most conservative jurisdictions.[56] He won a string of cases, slowing its spread in the mid-1980s, but then in 1987 the Supreme Court intervened again, this time ruling in *Pope v. Illinois* that juries should be instructed to use a more lenient "reasonable person" standard when determining if obscene material contained "literary, artistic, political, or scientific value," instead of their potentially more conservative "community standards."[57] Conviction rates promptly fell, and then when President Bill Clinton was elected, obscenity prosecutions fell by 70 percent.[58]

"Nobody had gotten popped for a long time, so people were pushing and pushing and pushing," porn producer Max Hardcore told the Villanova Sports & Entertainment Law Journal in 2007. "More gangbangs, more harder content, more teen-themed videos, and people felt pretty safe in doing just about anything they wanted to do. Clinton was good for the industry."[59]

Thanks to the internet and smartphones, an infinite amount of the most hardcore pornography is now available to everyone with just the touch of a button. Approximately 98 percent of pornography is consumed via the internet, including 68 percent who access it with a cell phone.[60] Almost 60 percent of Americans report having ever watched pornography, with the youngest generations most likely to report use. Men are the most likely to watch pornography with 44 percent reporting porn usage within the last month.[61]

Like any vice, the damage porn does depends on how often it is consumed. Viewed in moderate amounts, porn has little impact on behavior. But the more pornography a man consumes, the more detrimental it can be.

Research on college males shows the more porn a man watches, the more likely he is to be unhappy with his own body and the less likely he is to be satisfied with his own personal sex life.[62] Other research has found that men often use porn as a low-cost substitute for real female intimacy, with high frequency users much less likely to get married than those that abstain or use infrequently.[63]

More troubling is the effect pornography can have on the partners of those who watch it. Across the country, college counselors have reported a steep rise in a new form of sexual violence.[64] Not an increase in rapes, but an increase in choking during sex. One randomized study of college students found that almost half of all women reported they had been choked by their partner during sex.[65] A separate survey of American women between the ages of 18 and 60 found that 24 percent reported "scary sexual situations" including choking and anal sex.[66] And it has been established that the more pornography a man consumes, the more likely he is to have an interest in choking behaviors.[67]

With choking as a risk, no wonder so many young women are uninterested in intimate relationships with young men these days.

FIRST DO NO HARM

In 2003 when the Supreme Court extended the logic of *Eisenstadt* to Texas's sodomy law, holding that it violated the Due Process Clause of the Fourteenth Amendment, Justice Antonin Scalia said the decision, "effectively decrees the end of all morals legislation."[68]

"State laws against bigamy, same-sex marriage, adult incest, prostitution, masturbation, adultery, fornication, bestiality, and obscenity... Every single one of these laws is called into question by today's decision," Scalia wrote.[69]

Scalia was, of course, proven right when the Court, just eleven years later, held that state laws not acknowledging same-sex unions also violated the Fourteenth amendment. The *Obergefell v Hodges* decision was careful to say that its holding did not legalize polygamous unions, but logically there is no way to sanction same-sex, and not also polygamous, relationships.[70]

In fact, a year before *Obergefell*, a federal court held that Utah's law criminalizing polygamy was unconstitutional. "Homosexuals and polygamists do have a common interest: the right to be left alone as consenting adults," the polygamist's lawyer Jonathan Turley wrote before the case was decided. "There is no spectrum of private consensual relations—there is just a right of privacy that protects all people so long as they do not harm others," Turley continued, echoing Mill.[71]

"Our morality laws are falling," Turley later said in celebration after the federal district ruled in his favor, "and we are a better nation for it."

But are we really a better nation now that the government can no longer channel sexual behavior through marriage?

From the first Census that has relevant data—1860 through to 1960—the percentage of American households with a married couple held remarkably steady at around 80 percent. Through a Civil War, Industrialization, two World Wars, and a Great Depression, the American family consensus held firm and the married household thrived. But after Justice Brennan and the Burger Court worked their magic, the American family has never been the same.

By 1980 the percentage of American households with a married couple had fallen to 60 percent; by 2010 it was 50 percent, today it is close to 45 percent.[72] Where before the Burger Court, the married household was the unquestioned foundation of civil society, now married couples are a minority swimming in a sea of alternative lifestyles.

And the most vulnerable among us have been the most affected. Through the 1950s, young black women were actually more likely to be married than young white women.[73] But not after *King v. Smith*. As welfare expanded throughout the 1960s, the percentage of young black women who were married ticked down slightly from 62 percent in 1960 to 56 percent in 1970. By 1980, however, just twelve years after *King*, that number had cratered to just 22 percent.[74] And it has never recovered.

What would Justice Brennan think of his handiwork? Would he even care that marriage was no longer the dominant cultural norm? That probably depends on an application of Mill's harm principle.

Has the dismantling of the state's power to use public policy to channel human sexual behavior through the institution of marriage harmed people or not? As long as the sex is consensual, are other people harmed when unmarried people choose to have sex?

Justice Brennan would most likely answer no. The next chapter will argue yes.

CHAPTER SIX

THE DESTRUCTION OF DEMOCRACY

WHEN PRESIDENT LYNDON JOHNSON GAVE the commencement address at Howard University in June 1965, he acknowledged that "it is not enough just to open the gates of opportunity. All our citizens must have the ability to walk through those gates."[1]

To help blacks achieve equality not just "as a right" but "as a fact," Johnson promised a White House conference titled "To Fulfill These Rights" where an agenda beyond the Voting Rights Act could be developed.

Johnson's speech, and the planned conference, were both inspired by an internal memo written by an assistant secretary of labor named Daniel Patrick Moynihan. That memo, formally titled "The Negro Family: The Case for National Action," warned that even though blacks had recently secured more equal opportunities thanks to the Civil Rights Act, the black community would not see equal results because of a new and growing problem.

Thanks to the recent deterioration of the black family, Moynihan argued, outcomes in the black community would get worse, not better.

Johnson's speech was well received, and planning for a White House conference in the fall went forward, but weeks later portions of Moynihan's memo began leaking to the press. The memo identified a "tangle of pathology" that was afflicting the black community and "at the center of the tangle of pathology is the weakness of the family structure."[2]

"At the heart of the deterioration of the fabric of Negro society is the deterioration of the Negro family," Moynihan wrote. "It is the fundamental source of the weakness of the Negro community at the present time."

These words infuriated some leaders of the civil rights movement. "I'm angry, really angry," Congress of Racial Equality Executive Director James Farmer said in response to the report.

"I intend to spell out this anger in just one more effort to convince somebody, anybody, down in the places of power that the cocktail hour on the 'Negro Question' is over and that we are sick to death of being analyzed, mesmerized, bought, sold, and slobbered over while the same evils that are the ingredients of our oppression go unattended," he concluded.[3]

Psychologist William Ryan denounced Moynihan for "blaming the victim" and Dr. Benjamin Payton of the National Council of Churches organized a conference in New York where one hundred prominent civil rights activists signed a statement calling for "the question of family stability to be stricken entirely from the agenda" of Johnson's upcoming White House Conference on Civil Rights.[4]

The activists won. The White House Conference on Civil Rights was delayed until 1966. The phrase "family stability" was stricken from all conference materials entirely. And by the end of the year Moynihan had been forced out of the Johnson administration.

Which is unfortunate because much, but not all, of Moynihan's analysis was prophetic. "Both white and Negro illegitimacy rates have been increasing, although from dramatically different bases," Moynihan wrote. "The white rate was 2 percent in 1940; it was 3.07 percent in 1963. In that period, the Negro rate went from 16.8 percent to 23.6 percent."[5]

"The evidence, not final, but powerfully persuasive," Moynihan continued, "is that the Negro family in the urban ghettos is crumbling... There are indications that the situation may have been arrested in the past few years, but the general post war trend is unmistakable. So long as this situation persists, the cycle of poverty and disadvantage will continue to repeat itself."[6]

And that is exactly what has happened. The percentage of unmarried births in the black community exploded in the 1970s and has not improved since. According to the most recent numbers available, more than 70 percent of black children are born to an unmarried mother.[7]

What Moynihan did not predict was that the "pathology" of broken families that afflicted the black community would spread to other demographics as well. As noted above, Moynihan was alarmed that the unmarried birth rate among blacks had risen from 16.8 percent in 1940 to 23.6 percent in 1963. But in a similar span of twenty years, the percentage of unmarried births among whites rose from 5.5 percent in 1970 to 20.4 percent in 1990. The Census did not report marriage data on "Hispanics" as a separate racial category until 1970, but that community has also seen unmarried births rise from 23.6 percent in 1980 to 42.7 percent in 2000. Overall, 40 percent of all children born in the United States today are born outside of marriage.[8]

But so what? Who cares if 40 percent of all children and 70 percent of black children are born to unmarried parents? An increasing percentage of Americans sure don't.

In 2006, 49 percent of American adults told Gallup that it was "very important" for a couple that had a child together to get legally married. Just 23 percent said it was not important.[9] By 2013, the gap between those who believe that marriage is important and those who do not had closed to 38 percent pro-marriage, 35 percent blah-marriage.

Today, the blahs have it. A 40 percent plurality of Americans now say that it is not important for a couple that has a child together to get married while just 29 percent hold what was once the pro-marriage consensus position.[10]

This chapter will make the case that the declining number of Americans who believe marriage is important are right. The assault on marriage has been a disaster for the United States. As a direct result of falling marriage rates, America is now more unequal, less socially mobile, more violent, more isolated, more polarized, and less able to project our way of life into the future. The very future of our democracy is at stake.

INEQUALITY

Both income and wealth inequality are rising in the United States, and the decline of marriage is a big reason why.

According to data from the Federal Reserve of St. Louis, while single adults between the ages of twenty-five and thirty-four have a median net worth of $7,341, for cohabitating couples that number rises to $17,372.[11]

This makes sense. Two incomes are better than one, so it isn't surprising that a cohabiting couple would be able to amass about twice the wealth of a single person. Cohabiting couples also by definition have a built-in roommate so they can save on rent. Single people can, and do, often have roommates, but not always.

But something more than combining incomes and sharing rent is going on when a couple gets married. The Fed also found that the median net worth of married couples in that same age group (adults twenty-five through thirty-four) had a median net worth of $68,210. That's a $50,000 marriage premium.

Now, some of that bonus stems from the demographic profile of married people. Married people are, on average, better educated and make more money than single people. But that isn't the whole story.

To be extremely unromantic, think about two business partners that never create a single bank account for their new business, never develop a plan about how their business will grow, and make everyday decisions based on the assumption that their business partner could suddenly abandon the business at any time for any reason.

Compare that venture to two business partners who create a shared bank account, develop a plan for how their business will grow, and sign a contract that binds them to work together permanently. Which of those two businesses would you expect to be more financially successful in ten years? The married couple, of course.

"Married people may be much more likely to have these conversations around what goals they have for their financial future," Cornell University marketing professor Emily Garbinsky says. "There seems to be something very special and unique about deciding to share finances."[12]

Over a lifetime that marriage premium adds up. Penn State sociology professor John Iceland recently took data from every Census since 1960 to identify the most important factors that cause wealth and affluence among families. Iceland found that while race and education both played a big role in the probability that some families become wealthy and others stayed poor, family structure ended up being by far the most important factor.

"Married couples fared better because they experienced larger increases in wages and other important sources of income, such as from investments and retirement," Iceland writes. "The findings suggest that married-couple households benefit from a collective work strategy and economies of scale that increase their likelihood of affluence."[13]

The impact of marriage on inequality only grew over time especially for black families, becoming more salient as fewer and fewer households included a married couple. "The effect of family structure grew in importance and became the most significant factor among blacks," Iceland writes, "not only for poverty, but also for affluence, explaining about a third of the disparity in poverty and affluence in 2015."[14]

Returning to the marriage rates of the American Family Consensus would not completely undo rising inequality, but it would make a significant dent.

MOBILITY

As the gap between the rich and poor has widened in America, the odds of poor Americans becoming rich over their lifetimes has fallen. Americans used to believe that future generations would have a better life than their parents, and now they don't. The American Dream is dying.

According to Opportunity Insights, a research group based at Harvard University that maintains a database of anonymous Internal Revenue Service and Census Bureau records following 20 million Americans from childhood to adulthood, fewer children are growing up to surpass their parents' success than in previous generations. But the decline in social mobility has not been equal.

One important conclusion the researchers found was that there was no racial gap in intergenerational mobility for women. Black and white women who grew up with similar levels of parental income, ended up with similar levels of their own earnings as adults. In fact, black women were about 1 percent higher in income distribution than their white counterparts.[15]

But among black and white men the story was different. Black men who grew up with the same parental income as white men, ended up with much lower earnings compared to their white counterparts as adults. But this result wasn't true for all neighborhoods. There were some neighborhoods that produced far more successful black men than others.

What did those neighborhoods have in common? A high percentage of black fathers living in the home with their black children. More than school quality, more than racial composition, the most predictive factor of upward mobility in a given community for black boys was the presence of black fathers.

There is nothing wrong with black boys in America today that can't be solved by more married black fathers.

To be clear, marriage is not a cure all for disparities in racial outcomes. Marriage does seem to help some demographics more than others, but the help marriage does provide is still substantial.

Also from Harvard, but not associated with the Opportunity Insights project, sociology professor Cristina Cross has compared outcomes of individual children based on how long they spent their childhood in a home with two parents. She then tracked how likely a child is to graduate high school and enroll in college when considering what percentage of their childhood a child spent with a single parent.

Dr. Cross's study found that both white and black children who spent all of their childhood in a single parent home have an almost identical 58 percent chance of graduating from high school on time. As the percentage of time spent in a home with two biological parents increases, the percentage chance that both black and white children graduate from high school also increases, but not at the same rate.

For example, even though both black and white children who spent all of their childhood with a single mother start at the same 58 percent chance of graduating from high school, if black and white children spend half their childhood living with both parents, then their chances of graduating from high school rise to 68 percent and 74 percent respectively. Moving further up the scale to children who spent all their childhoods living with both married parents, the gap widens to 77 percent for black children and 85 percent for white children.[16]

So yes, marriage does seem to benefit white children more than black children. White children who had two parents in their home for their entire childhoods are almost ten percentage points more likely to graduate from high school then black children who also had two parents in the home for their entire childhoods. But the gap between black children raised only by a single parent and those raised by two parents is a much higher twenty percentage points. Not having two parents in the home clearly harms black children.

And for both black and white children, the absence of a father in the home is more detrimental to boys than it is to girls. One 2013 study looking at data collected on over twenty thousand children by the National Center for Education Statistics found that while boys generally misbehaved more often in school than girls, boys from single parent homes were suspended twice as often as boys from homes with married parents. This result held across school quality. Those schools with higher rates of school suspensions had the same gap in single parent boy suspensions that schools with low suspension rates did.[17]

The damage done to boys by not having fathers in the home is bad enough for what it does to one generation, but because of how men and women pair off, having fewer successful men in one generation means even more troubled young boys in the next generation.

Women, understandably, want a marriage partner that is at least as successful, if not more so, than they are economically. Men, throughout history, have cared more about a potential mate's youth and beauty than her economic production potential. But since girls from single mother households are less impacted by not having a father, when marriage declines in a community, that means there are going to be far more successful women than men. We can see this on college campuses today where 60 percent of college students are female as are 66 percent of college graduates.

The fewer marriageable men there are available to women in one generation, the more unmarried families that generation will have, which only leads to an even larger imbalance between men's and women's educations in the generation after that. The result is a never-ending doom loop of more unmarriageable men and more single mothers.

And the more single mothers there are, the fewer fathers in the home, which means more neighborhoods where boys have virtually no chance of becoming productive adults.

CRIME

Neighborhoods dominated by single parent homes are also known to have higher rates of crime, even after controlling for race and income.

Drawing from the same Opportunity Insight data mentioned above, University of Virginia sociology professor Brad Wilcox notes that in 2010, 44 percent of black men who grew up in the low-income Watts neighborhood of Los Angeles were in jail. But for the equally low-income neighborhood of Compton, just two miles south of Watts, just 6 percent of black men were behind bars.

Dr. Wilcox then adds, "There are a number of factors separating these two neighborhoods, but it's fascinating to note that single parenthood was much higher in Watts than it was in Compton when these men were growing up: to be precise, the share of single parents for Watts was 87%, whereas the share of single parents for Compton was 50% in the 1980s, when these men were children."[18]

Harvard University social sciences professor Robert Sampson has done a wider study of 171 cities in the United States looking at the relationship between family structure and crime, specifically homicide and robbery. Sampson found that the more homes without married fathers, the higher the rates of robbery and murder. No other factor, not male employment, population size, or age, was more important than family structure. Lack of married fathers had a particularly large impact on black juvenile homicide offenders. "Family structure is one of the strongest, if not the strongest predictor of variations in urban violence across cities in the United States," Sampson concluded.[19]

Having married fathers in more homes not only decreases crime among young men, but it has a proven ability to help grown men become upstanding citizens as well. One study of Nebraska inmates of all races found that marriage reduces a man's probability of committing another crime by half.[20]

Having a job had only a mixed effect on crime while entering school was almost as beneficial as marriage. This effect did not hold for men who only cohabitated with a new partner. Unmarried men who only moved in with a woman but did not marry her were just as likely to commit crime as single men.

One reason why married men are less likely to commit crime than unmarried men is that other studies have shown that marriage lowers a man's testosterone, the hormone most linked with aggressive behavior.[21]

By both providing role models for young men, and lowering testosterone for grown men, marriage is one of our nation's best proven crime fighters.

ISOLATION

"Loneliness and isolation hurt whole communities," U.S. Surgeon General Vivek H. Murthy recently wrote in the *New York Times*. "Social disconnection is associated with reduced productivity in the workplace, worse performance in school, and diminished civic engagement."[22]

"When we are less invested in one another," Murthy continued, "we are more susceptible to polarization and less able to pull together to face the challenges that we cannot solve alone. As it has built for decades, the epidemic of loneliness and isolation has fueled other problems that are killing us and threaten to rip our country apart."

Murthy is right. Unfortunately, his op-ed failed to identify the biggest cause of America's rising loneliness epidemic: the decline of marriage.

As the percentage of married households has declined, the percentage of Americans living alone has steadily risen. According to the Census, people living alone made up just 8 percent of all households in 1940. By 1970 the number had risen to 18 percent, and it has steadily risen to almost 30 percent today.[23]

Marriage has a long and established track record of reducing loneliness. An authoritative 1998 study found that marriage in particular, not cohabitation or even parenthood, was associated with much lower levels of loneliness in adults. A more recent analysis found that while 20 percent of married Americans reported feeling lonely in 2021, a much larger 40 percent of unmarried adults did. "While marriage is no substitute for sorting out fundamental questions about the meaning and purpose of life," Arizona State University's Christos A. Makridis wrote on his findings, "it does provide a glue that brings people together under common objectives and ultimately makes people happier, on average."[24]

The opioid epidemic has also highlighted the importance of marriage in keeping people tied to humanity. While the never-married and divorced population made up just 32 percent of all adults for the years 1999–2015, that groups accounted for 71 percent of all opioid deaths during that time frame. On the flip side, while 61 percent of the adult population was married for those same years, they accounted for just 28 percent of opioid deaths.[25]

Marriage also has a proven track record of making adults happier and healthier as well. A recent study that followed nurses over a twenty-five-year span found that after controlling for physical health, mental health, and economic variables, women who got married over the twenty-five years of the study were happier than never married women and less likely to suffer from depression. They also were less likely to smoke or suffer from heart disease. These results incorporated the risks of divorce, as women who married but got divorced were included in the got married category.[26]

Studies show that more than any other factor—age, race, gender, education, income, or geography—for both men and women, one's marital status id the greatest predictor of happiness.[27]

Marriage not only binds people into supportive families, but it also is the institution that holds our communities together, although some opponents of marriage will attempt to convince you otherwise.

Sociologists Dr. Naomi Gerstel of the University of Massachusetts and Dr. Natalia Sarkisian of Boston College claim that "marriage is greedy," noting that the 1992 National Survey of Families and Households shows that married people are less likely than single people to have helped their parents or siblings with shopping, running errands, or transportation in the past twelve months. That same survey also showed that married couples were less likely to call or visit their parents or siblings, while a more recent 2004 General Social Survey showed married people were less likely to socialize with friends and neighbors than single people.[28]

Drs. Gerstel and Sarkisian took these survey results and concluded that, "Marriage is greedy for material, emotional, and cultural reasons. Marriages obviously take time and energy—whether for partners to spend time with each other, or to create and maintain the family home. This distracts from investments in other relationships, especially, perhaps, for dual-earner couples already strapped for time by the demands of two jobs."

What Drs. Gerstel and Sarkisian conveniently leave out of their case against marriage, however, is all the other ways that marriage increases people's involvement in their communities.

While it is true the General Social Survey shows that married couples socialize less with neighbors, that very same survey also shows married adults are more likely to talk with their neighbors a few times per month and they are more likely to do regular favors for their neighbors than single people are.[29] Sure, maybe married couples are too busy to come over for drinks at night, but a quick chat in the front yard, or a promise to pick up the mail when a neighbor is on vacation, and married couples are there for you.

Married adults are also much more trusting of strangers than unmarried adults and they are more likely to belong to voluntary associations like the American Red Cross, the Boy Scouts, or a youth sports league. The most typical volunteer for any organization is a married woman between the ages of twenty-five and forty-four.[30]

It is these fundamentally non-political voluntary associations that Alexis de Tocqueville identified as being so fundamental to the strength and wellbeing of American democracy. "Americans of all ages, all conditions, all minds constantly unite," Tocqueville wrote. "Not only do they have commercial and industrial associations in which all take part, but they also have a thousand other kinds: religious, moral, very general and very particular, immense and very small."[31]

"There is nothing that deserves more to attract our regard than the intellectual and moral associations of America," Tocqueville concluded. "We easily perceive the political and industrial associations of the Americans, but the others escape us...One ought however to recognize that they are as necessary as the first to the American people, and perhaps more so."[32]

Americans have never been more lonely or unhappy or less likely to participate in the community organizations that are the backbone of our democracy's civil society, and the decline of marriage is the leading cause why.

POLARIZATION

In addition to finding that single people call their parents more than married people do, Doctors Gerstel and Sarkisian also found that single people were more likely than their married counterparts to be politically active. This includes attending political rallies, signing political petitions, and raising money for political causes. This was especially true for single women.[33]

The decline of marriage since the 1970s, the concurrent rise in the number of single women, and the increased political activism of these single women, is the most underrated political phenomenon of our time.

When Republicans captured the House of Representatives for the first time in forty-two years in 1994, the media were quick to blame "Angry White Males" who, according to President Bill Clinton himself, "don't have great educations."[34]

Google didn't exist in the 90s, but columnist Charles Krauthammer noted that in the ten years before the 1994 election, there were just fifty-nine LexisNexis references to "angry white men," while in just one year after there were 1,400.[35]

For all the press Angry White Males got, however, the shift of white men from the Democratic Party was not that dramatic once compared to similar demographics. Sure, white men with some college moved to Republicans by fifteen points between 1992 and 1994, but white women with some college education also shifted to Republicans by ten points that same year. That's just a five-point difference. Overall, just 60 percent of white men voted for Republicans in 1994.

Moving to 2022, that percentage hasn't really changed. Sixty-three percent of white men voted for Republicans in 2022, including 59 percent of all married men. But there was one group that did stand out. While 56 percent of married women and 52 percent of unmarried men all voted Republican, a whopping 68 percent of single women voted for Democrats.

The greatest untold political story of the last generation is how the Democratic Party has become the party of the Single Woke Female.

In 1960, almost three quarters of adult Americans were married. Now less than half are. In raw numbers there are now more single women in the United States than there are blacks, union members, or college students.[36]

And as their numbers have grown, they have also become more liberal. In 2000, about 30 percent of both men and women between the ages of eighteen and twenty-nine considered themselves liberal. Today, the percentage of young women who consider themselves liberal has soared to 45 percent while the percentage of young men who consider themselves liberal has is still near 30 percent.[37] And as noted above, young women are not only more partisan than they used to be, they are also far more likely to be politically active than young men.

We will explore why single women, particularly white single women, are driven towards political activism in Chapter Seven. For now, all that is needed to know is that it is this block of Single Woke Females that is driving the Democratic Party to the left on some of the most salient issues of our time.

Name any issue over the past twenty years—immigration, the environment, abortion—in every case the Democratic Party has moved far to the left and they have been led left by Single Woke Females.

On immigration, as recently as 2008, the Democratic Party platform read, "We cannot continue to allow people to enter the United States undetected, undocumented, and unchecked," adding that "those who enter our country's borders illegally, and those who employ them, disrespect the rule of the law."[38]

But by 2020, only one candidate for the Democratic Party's nomination opposed the decriminalization of illegal border crossings, and when President Joe Biden was sworn into office, he immediately halted all deportations and began releasing hundreds of thousands of illegal border crossers into the country every month.

We can see the Democrats move left on immigration in polling as well. In 2004, 14 percent of both Republicans and Democrats agreed with the statement that immigrants were "not at all likely" to take jobs from native born Americans. By 2020, an almost identical 16 percent of Republican still believed that same statement while the percentage of Democrats who agreed with it soared to 53 percent.[39] Separately, other polls have conclusively shown that women are far more liberal on immigration than men.[40]

On the environment, as recently as 2015, just 46 percent of Democrats identified climate change as a top priority for Congress. Today that number is 79 percent. Asked if they believed climate change would harm them personally, 69 percent of women said yes, compared to just 48 percent of men, a 21-point gender gap.[41]

And on abortion, as recently as 2000, just 33 percent of Democrats said abortion should be legal under all circumstances. Today, 57 percent of Democrats say abortion should be available on demand for any reason.[42] This move left by Democrats on abortion is driven almost entirely by women. In 1996, 50 percent of men considered themselves pro-choice, a number that has fallen to 45 percent today. Meanwhile, support for abortion has risen from 51 percent among women in 1996 to 63 percent today.[43]

Donald Trump may have turned the partisan rhetoric up from ten to eleven, and there is no doubt he is a culturally polarizing figure, but policy wise, Republican positions on immigration, the environment, and abortion are in the same place they were thirty years ago. Our nation's political polarization is being driven almost entirely from the Left and Single Woke Females are behind the wheel.

DEMOGRAPHIC DECLINE

Just as Justice Brennan was beginning to dismantle the legal underpinnings of the American Family Consensus, Paul Ehrlich's book *The Population Bomb* predicted overpopulation would cause millions to die of starvation within a decade. Ehrlich not only called for the widespread adoption of free contraception and on-demand abortion, but he also floated the possibility of adding sterilants to the water supply in much the same way fluoride is added for better teeth.[44]

Fortunately, despite all the negative messaging from environmentalists, women's stated desire for children has remained remarkably stable since 1950 at around 2.5 children per woman. In fact, according to the latest Gallup survey, 45 percent of Americans say the ideal family size is three or more children. This is a sharp increase from 33 percent in 2003 and is equal to what Americans said way back in 1967.[45]

Unfortunately, women's achieved fertility, the number of children they actually end up having, has declined drastically since the 1950s as the assault on marriage has succeeded. In 1950, by age forty-four the average married woman in America had 3.09 children. The percentage of unmarried women at that time was so small that the average number of children born to unmarried women, just .4, didn't even dent the average number of children for all women aged forty-four which was an identical 3.09.[46]

Fast forward to today, and fertility has fallen significantly. Among all forty-four-year-old women, the average number of children has fallen from 3.09 to 1.99. Single women are having more children now than they did in 1950, rising from .4 to 1.15. But married women are having fewer children, falling from 3.09 to 2.12.

Almost all the decline in fertility in the United States can be accounted for by the decline in marriage. Fewer women are getting married, and unmarried women have only half the children married women do. Additionally, those women that do get married today are waiting longer to do so, limiting the number of children they can have.

Women who get married earlier, start giving birth earlier, and end up with larger families. Half of women who get married in their early twenties end up having at least three children, compared to just 33 percent of women who get married after age thirty. More than 60 percent of women who get married in their thirties have two kids or less.[47]

As women increasingly fail to have the number of children they want, our population is in danger of shrinking. And shrinking populations create several economic and social problems.

On the economic side, the older a population is, the fewer workers there are to support older people that don't work. This means that any growth in productivity achieved by workers gets eaten up by retirees instead of increasing living standards for everyone.

Older populations also require more services (such as health care and food preparation) and fewer goods (such as cars and computers) than younger populations. This means more investments in service industries and fewer investments in infrastructure and manufacturing, sectors that have long provided high stable wages to support married families.

Additionally, most innovations come from younger people, so the older a society is, the less innovative it is and more prone to stagnation and recession. What research there has been done on the economic effect of aging societies, shows that older societies fare far worse economically than young and vibrant ones.[48]

The social damage from declining populations is real too. Fewer children mean fewer siblings who are sources of both support and early interpersonal skill development.

Early in life, kindergartners with siblings are rated by their teachers as having better communication skills and higher self-control than kindergarteners without siblings. These advantages appear to accumulate through to the fifth grade.[49]

Later in life, many Americans point to their siblings as both their closest friends and a person they know they can call in an emergency.[50]

Further down the road, fewer children means less material and emotional support for the elderly. One study found that the percentage of seventy-five-year-old adults with children has already declined from 85 percent in 2008, to 76 percent in 2002, and if present trends continue, will continue to fall below 60 percent by 2060. Elderly adults with adult children are known to have better mental and physical health outcomes than those that do not.[51]

But demographic decline is more than just a social or economic issue. It is also, literally, an existential issue. To put it simply, the future belongs to those who show up. If your culture is not projecting itself into the future, it is dying.

Replacement level fertility is 2.1 births per woman. Currently the United States is almost a half-birth below that at 1.64 births per woman. That's not good. But it is better than Japan's 1.34 and much better than South Korea's .78. Unless South Korea finds a way to turn their birth rate around, their population of 50 million will shrink in half to 25 million in just two decades.[52]

Unless our marriage rates improve, we will share South Korea's fate.

WHAT GOES ON BEHIND CLOSED DOORS

At the end of the last chapter, we quoted law professor Jonathan Turley who, in arguing for the legalization of polygamy said, "There is no spectrum of private consensual relations—there is just a right of privacy that protects all people so long as they do not harm others."

This is a popular sentiment shared by most Americans: What two consenting adults do by themselves in private isn't anyone's concern as long as they are not harming others.

But what goes on behind closed doors doesn't always stay there.

As established above, the decline of marriage has led to higher levels of income inequality. Separately, research has found that economic inequality produces unequal democratic participation and representation, with wealthier families both more likely to participate in democracy and see their preferred candidates win election.[53] Income inequality has also been shown to decrease the trust poor citizens have in the government, which in extreme cases can lead to political violence.[54]

There is also evidence that decreased economic mobility caused by the decline of marriage weakens democracy. Individuals that experience upward social mobility have been shown to be more supportive of democracy, while those that have not are less supportive. Upward social mobility has also been shown to increase trust in strangers and institutions, another predicate for strong democracy.[55]

Turning to crime, scholars have long recognized that public security is one of the most basic conditions needed for democracy to function.[56] Studies show that victims of crime have lower levels of support for democratic political institutions, less interpersonal trust, and a tendency to prefer radical change.[57] High levels of crime have been shown to cause citizens to leave their home less, participate in community activities less, and generally disengage from their neighbors.[58] How is democracy supposed to function if people don't feel safe leaving their homes?

The evidence that increased polarization undermines democracy is so old even the authors of the Constitution recognized its danger. They may have called it "violence of faction" but James Madison warned in Federalist 10 that political polarization led to the "public good" being "disregarded" in favor of "the conflicts of rival parties."[59]

More recently, researchers have found that political polarization "weakens respect for democratic norms, corrodes basic legislative processes, undermines the nonpartisan stature of the judiciary, fuels public disaffection with political parties, exacerbates intolerance and discrimination, diminishes societal trust, and increases violence throughout the society."[60]

What consenting adults do in private may not directly harm other people, but when government policy does not encourage sex to be channeled through marriage, or worse, when government policy actively punishes marriage as government policies do today, everyone suffers, particularly those most vulnerable among us.

CHAPTER SEVEN

MARRIED TO THE STATE

DURING PRESIDENT BARACK OBAMA'S REELECTION campaign in 2012, a cartoon character named "Julia" was created to illustrate the life of an average American. Clocking in at just fourteen panels, the "Life of Julia" followed a faceless white woman from the ages of three to sixty-seven. We see her go to preschool, graduate from college, dye her hair orange, get a job as a web designer, go back to her natural dark hair, have a child, start her own business, and then retire.

At every step of the way the campaign was at pains to show how government programs made Julia's life possible. At age three she enrolls in Head Start, at eighteen she qualifies for a Pell Grant, at thirty-one she receives free prenatal care, at forty-two she qualifies for a Small Business Administration loan, and at sixty-seven she comfortably retires—because the evil Mitt Romney was prevented from cutting her Social Security benefits by 40 percent. (*PolitiFact* labeled this last panel false.)

What we never see in the Life of Julia is a man, let alone marriage to one. Thanks to government programs created by Democrats, and expanded by Obama, Julia has no need for a husband. That's because Julia is married to the state.

Nine years later, Joe Biden introduced a similar single woman named Linda intended to promote his "Build Back Better" agenda. Linda hails from Peoria, Illinois. When we first meet her, she is already pregnant. Again, no man in sight. As we watch her raise her son Leo, the proposed Biden agenda provides first discounted childcare and then free prekindergarten. By the time Linda retires, the state is there for her again, this time footing the bill for subsidized elder care.

Whatever problems the Lindas and Leos of the world may face, according to the Biden White House, the solution is not a husband for Linda or a father for Leo; it is government funded care for them both. Linda, too, is married to the state.

GENDER LINKED FATE

Both Julia and Linda were created for the same reason: Democratic operatives know that single women are not only already one of the largest voting blocks in the party (outnumbering both blacks and Latinos) but also the fastest growing. Inculcating single women's group identity is a huge priority for Democratic campaigns…and it is working.

In 2012, among all women, Obama won by eleven points, 55 percent–44 percent. But he lost among married women 46 percent–53 percent. He lost among married men as well. But where he cleaned up was among single women who he won by an overwhelming 67 percent to 32 percent margin.

If Obama would have faced a 1960 electorate, where single women made up just 5 percent of voters, married women would have carried the day for Romney. The only reason Obama was able to win in 2012, was because the single woman electorate had grown to 25 percent of all voters.

Importantly, the gap in voting between married and unmarried women was not driven by race. Among all white women, Romney won 56 percent to 42 percent. But among unmarried white women, Obama won, 49 percent to 39 percent.

Biden continued Democratic dominance among single women in 2020. While Trump won married men and women 55 percent to 44 percent and 51 percent to 47 percent respectively, Biden won single women 63 percent to 36 percent. And, as noted in the last chapter, the Democrats expanded that lead in 2022, winning single women by a 68 percent to 31 percent margin.

As the gap in voting patterns between married and single women has grown, researchers have begun to theorize and study why. One recent paper that looked at a survey of more than 2,000 women, found that single women, especially single white women, are more likely to identify with other women generally. Unmarried women feel that if women in general are doing well, then they too are doing well themselves. The authors called this mindset a "gender linked fate."[1]

Married women, on the other hand, are more likely to identify with the needs of their husbands and children. They are more likely to share income and resources with their husbands and are therefore more concerned with their husband's wellbeing than the wellbeing of women they don't know.

Another study following women's political preferences through the Youth Parent Socialization survey from 1964 through 1996 found that women who once considered themselves liberal and voted for Democrats, were more likely to vote for Republicans after they got married. Conversely, married women who had been Republicans and then got divorced were more likely to become Democrats.[2]

Other studies show that having children makes both men and women more conservative. Since, as we discussed in the last chapter, married women are far more likely to have children than unmarried women, the more unmarried women there are, the more potential childless Democratic women voters there will be.

That marriage and children moderates women politically makes sense. Marriage binds men and women together into a long-term project of cooperative care for both each other and their children. Married women see their husband's interests, and their children's interests, as their own. Single women do not have these personally created family bonds to other men. Sure, they may have been born into a family with a father and maybe even a brother, but these are not men that single women chose to make the central focus of their lives. A married woman has chosen to make her husband and her children a part of her identity. Single women, by contrast, feel a stronger amorphous "gender linked fate" with millions of other single women they do not even know.

The triumph of "intersectionality" on college campuses has also greatly contributed to the rejection of marriage by white women in particular. When law professor Kimberle Crenshaw first coined the term intersectionality in 1989, she was specifically addressing the failures of both "feminist theory" and "antiracist policy discourse" to "accurately reflect the interaction of race and gender."[3]

"These problems of exclusion cannot be solved simply by including black women within an already established analytical structure," Crenshaw wrote. "Because the intersectional experience is greater than the sum of racism and sexism, any analysis that does not take intersectionality into account cannot sufficiently address the particular manner in which Black women are subordinated."[4]

This was relevant to the study of law, Crenshaw explained, because only using the existing gender and race lenses often left black women unprotected. For example, an employer may show they did not discriminate because they hired plenty of black men and white women, but such a defense left black women no recourse. Viewed through the intersectionality lens, in a hierarchy of victimhood, black women were at the top, above black men and white women, with white men at the bottom.

Intersectionality has since moved on from race and gender to include religion, disability, physical appearance, and most importantly for our purposes, sexuality. A black straight woman faces compounded oppression due to her gender and race, but a black queer woman is oppressed due to her gender, race, and sexuality.

By adding sexuality to the hierarchy of intersectional oppression, white women are afforded new avenue to distance themselves from the top of the privilege ladder. As a straight white woman, an individual is just one step away from being the pinnacle of oppression, a straight white man. But by claiming to be queer, white women can now put two rungs between themselves and the source of all evil.

And that is what we see happening. Gallup has been tracking self-reported gender identity for years and there has been a marked rise in Americans identifying as LGBTQ. But drilling down into the data, it quickly becomes obvious that the movement away from identifying as heterosexual is concentrated not only in the youngest generation, but among young women in particular.

According to Gallup, the percentage of Americans self-identifying as LGBTQ has grown from 3.5 percent in 2012 to 7.6 percent in 2024. But while the LGBTQ identity of Generation X and above still hovers around 3.5 percent, it is the LGBTQ identification of Generation Z that has exploded.[5]

Over a fifth of Gen Z youth now identify as LGBTQ, a fad driven entirely by young women claiming to be bisexual. Almost 30 percent of Gen Z women now claim LGBTQ identity, including 20 percent of Gen Z women who claim to be bisexual. By contrast, among Gen X women, less than 5 percent claim to be LGBTQ and just 2.8 percent say they are bisexual. LGBTQ self-identification is also much weaker among Gen Z men as just 10.6 percent identify as LGBTQ at all, and just 6.9 percent say they are bisexual.[6]

The celebration and consecration of LGBTQ identification by the progressive movement provides many lost young women searching for connection a new tribe to call home. This new identity, however, is deeply hostile to heterosexual marriage and encourages women to become clients of the Democratic Party's expansive welfare state, a system which we will now show is designed to push single women as far away from potential husbands as possible.

ONE TRILLION DOLLARS

As we noted in Chapter Five, thanks to the Supreme Court's decision in *King v. Smith*, the current welfare state is an oddly jealous husband. Under current program design, single women are allowed to sleep with as many men as they want, however often they want, and the state doesn't care. The state doesn't even mind if a single woman cohabitates with another man. But God forbid a woman might want to make a long-term promise of sexual fidelity to a single man in the form of marriage. That is when the state gets crazy jealous and cuts her off.

Liberal academics often attack the claim that the growth of the welfare state is a cause of the decline of marriage by noting that the real value of cash payments to single mothers has shrunk significantly since peaking in 1975. And they are right, inflation has eaten away at the money delivered through the program most associated with the word welfare, the Aid to Families with Dependent Children program, since renamed Temporary Assistance for Needy Families (TANF) in 1996. TANF payments and participation in the program has also shrunk significantly since the program was reformed and renamed.

But what these same academics ignore is the explosion of other means tested programs that also discriminate against marriage. In addition to AFDC/TANF, Congress has since passed:

- the Food Stamp Act of 1964 which created what is now known as the Supplemental Nutrition Assistance Program (SNAP);
- the Economic Opportunity Act of 1964 which created Head Start;
- the Social Security Amendments of 1965 which created Medicaid;
- the Child Nutrition Act Amendments of 1972 which created the Women, Infants, and Children (WIC) program;
- the Social Security Amendments of 1972 which created the Supplemental Security Income (SSI) program;
- the Housing and Community Development Act of 1974 which created Section 8 housing subsidies;
- the Tax Reduction Act of 1975 which created the Earned Income Tax Credit (EITC);
- the Balanced Budget Act of 1997 which created the Children's Health Insurance Program (CHIP);
- and the Affordable Care Act of 2010 which expanded Medicaid and created health insurance premium subsidies.

Together these programs send over $1 trillion worth of means tested benefits to eligible families every year.[7] Every single one of these programs discriminates against married families in a similar way that AFDC/TANF does. No empirical study has ever measured the combined impact of all these marriage penalties. But evidence from recent safety net expansions show they do play a role.

A 2021 paper, for example, compared marriage rates in states that were early adopters of the Affordable Care Act's Medicaid expansion with marriage rates in states that did not expand Medicaid. The study found that for adults over age twenty-six without a college education, the likelihood of being newly married decreased by 6.9 percent in states that expanded

Medicaid.[8] This is exactly the demographic we would expect to see marriage penalties affect behavior.

Another study looked at a hypothetical couple with two children where one partner earned $24,000 and the other earned $20,000. Looking at just the benefits from the Earned Income Tax Credit, the Child Tax Credit, the Supplemental Nutrition Assistance Program, Section 8 housing assistance, Medicaid, and the Affordable Care Act, the paper found that this couple earning just $44,000 a year, would face a yearly $10,500 penalty if they got married.[9]

$10,500 a year is a lot of money to go missing for a couple making $100,000 a year, let alone a couple making just $44,000.

SEPARATE AND UNEQUAL MARRIAGE POLICIES

Many Americans may be surprised to learn that our federal tax and safety net programs punish instead of promote marriage. A common feminist lament is that the government unfairly subsidizes marriage while punishing single people, and for some married couples there are small benefits to marriage, but not nearly as large as most people think.

Lisa Arnold and Christina Campbell, co-founders of Onely.org (a website dedicated to "questioning heteronormative bias"), recently claimed in the *Atlantic* that government discrimination costs single people $1 million over a lifetime. But on closer inspection, their calculation is comically bad, with over $750,000 of the supposed single penalty coming from the fact that married people live together and share a mortgage while single people don't have a partner to help pay the rent.[10]

Some high-earning married couples do pay less in taxes, as Arnold and Campbell correctly note, but this is not true in all cases. Generally, those couples where one spouse makes more than the other get a marriage bonus, while couples with more equal incomes pay a marriage penalty.

For Arnold and Campbell's calculation, they used a woman making $80,000 and a husband making $103,000. They found the married woman paid $3,875 less in taxes than her single counterpart in a single year, netting out to a lifetime $155,000 single "penalty." But these numbers could easily have been different if the couple earned equal incomes.

The Social Security program also provides a substantial marriage bonus, but only for couples with unequal earnings and even then, the benefit isn't realized until someone retires. This is a nice bonus for older, wealthy married couples, but it does nothing to help young couples buy a house, get married, and start a family.

In fact, the entire Social Security system is a huge transfer of wealth from poor working families who have the payroll tax subtracted from their meager paychecks every month, to wealthier non-working older couples. If anything, Social Security is just another big government program that makes it harder for young couples to get and stay married.

Our government basically has two separate and unequal marriage policies. For wealthy families, the government hands out marriage bonuses through the tax code and Social Security system. A CEO making millions of dollars who has a wife at home working part time gets a huge marriage bonus every year through our current tax laws. Then when that same CEO retires, his wife can claim a Social Security payment every month up to half the size of his. It is good to be wealthy and married in America.

For the working poor, however, the story is completely different. For the forty percent of Americans who use at least one means tested welfare program, getting married can trigger the loss of thousands of dollars in benefits a year. Is it any surprise then that marriage is weakest among this group?

"KIND OF...YEAH"

That our government punishes marriage for working class people isn't widely known among college educated Americans, but it is better understood among the working poor.

A 2016 poll by the *Los Angeles Times* asked men and women in poverty, "How often do you think unmarried adults choose not to get married to avoid losing welfare benefits?" Almost a quarter of respondents (24 percent) answered "almost always" while another 23 percent said "often."[11] Among all adults, the 2015 American Family Survey found that 31 percent of Americans knew someone who chose not to get married "for fear of losing welfare benefits, Medicaid, food stamps, or other government benefits."[12]

Anecdotal evidence isn't hard to find either. When the Institute for Family Studies recently conducted focus groups of working-class parents in Ohio, Atlanta, and San Antonio, one working mother told the discussion leaders, "Yes, I chose not to marry," she explained. "I get a lot of assistance for my children for myself, so if I did marry or put any other type of income in, I would not qualify for anything."[13]

Another working mother in Georgia said it was unfair for her to have "to choose between marrying a man she loves or losing the benefits that she has." She is absolutely right. It is unfair.

Even the proudly single women in Rebecca Traister's book *All the Single Ladies* acknowledge that marriage penalties play a role in their romantic decision making. Emmalee, an employed mother of a toddler who lives with, but is not married to, the father of her child, told Traister she participated in the food stamp, Medicaid, and WIC programs.

"I'm able to survive. I get a little help from the government without being married," Emmalee told Traister. "If I was married I probably wouldn't get that extra help from them." Asked if the possibility of losing government benefits was "wholly" behind her decision not to marry, Emmalee responded, "Not my end result, but kind of yeah."[14]

Traister, of course, immediately discounted Emmalee's response by noting that cash welfare benefits have declined since the 1970s, which as we noted above is true. But Emmalee doesn't receive cash welfare benefits. She gets food stamps, Medicaid, and WIC. These are all huge government programs that have only expanded in size and value since the 1970s. But for the welfare state's jealous marriage penalties, maybe Emmalee would be married to the father of her child, and not the state.

FOR EVERY DOLLAR INVESTED

After decades of continued poverty concentrated among single parent households, even feminists like Traister have been forced to admit that single parent households are falling behind. But instead of husbands, Traister says there is another thing that could help single parent households: "Money."

Well, money and government programs to provide care for the children of single mothers so they can work. Going back to the Fact Sheet accompanying the Linda and Leo slide show, the White House explains, "The high cost of childcare continues to make it hard for parents—especially women—to work outside the home and provide for their families. These costs are especially significant for mothers and people of color, exacerbating inequality and harming the economic security of their families."[15]

To prevent children from single parent homes from falling behind, the Biden White House calls for "high-quality early care and education" that can "lay a strong foundation" for "education and training opportunities later in life."

"This is especially important for children from low-income families," the Biden White House explained, "who too often start school without access to high-quality educational opportunities."

"The President's plan, and especially its investments in the care economy, would increase labor force participation by almost a full percentage point, with even greater gains for women" another White House fact sheet explains, "and boost the economy's real GDP growth by 10 to 15 basis points."

It all sounds like such a win-win. Under these feminist family policies, women would get just enough parental leave so that they can bond with their newborn children, but not too much that it would hurt their professional careers. Their children would then be swept into day care where highly trained professionals would give them the best supervision based on the latest scientific research. As these children became toddlers, they would be transferred into state-of-the-art prekindergarten programs that would prepare them for school.

If only our society could muster the political will to invest in this "care economy" then single parent households could close the gap with married households and the damage from the decline of marriage would be undone.

If only it were all true.

Much of the liberal faith in the ability of government programs to replace marriage can be traced back to the work of one man: the University of Chicago's Nobel prize winning economist James Heckman.

Dr. Heckman has made a career out of publicizing the results of two early childhood programs: the Perry Preschool Project out of Ypsilanti, Michigan in the 1960s and the Carolina Abecedarian Project out of

Durham, North Carolina in the 1970s. Both programs were quite small, with the Perry Preschool Project studying just 123 children and Carolina Abecedarian Project looking at 111. Both programs studied only low-income black families.

The Perry Preschool Project included two and a half hours of preschool a day for participating three- and four-year-olds. Each child also received a one-and-a-half-hour home visit every week from a teacher, where their mothers were instructed on how best to support their child's development.[16]

The Carolina Abecedarian Project was even more invasive, enrolling infants at just eight weeks of age and providing eight hours of intensive care five days a week all the way through age five. Children also received home visits every other week to provide parents with activities to complement what was being taught at school.[17]

Both studies found that children selected for the intensive instruction and home visit programs were more likely to graduate high school, more likely to go to college, less likely to have a criminal record, and were healthier as adults.

Anytime you hear an advocate use a statistic like "for every dollar invested in high-quality early childhood programs for low-income children" the government gets back "$7.30 in benefits," they are most likely referencing one of these two programs.[18]

According to Dr. Heckman, the results of these studies show that "the highest rate of return in early childhood development comes from investing as early as possible, from birth through age five, in disadvantaged families."[19] There are two big problems, however, with transferring the results of Ypsilanti and Durham to thousands of communities nationwide.

First, the intensive services provided by the programs bear no resemblance to even the most generous early childhood development programs introduced in Congress. Mandated staff to child ratios vary by state and by age, with some states not including numerical limits at all. For infants, the Abecedarian Project had one caregiver for every three children. California, the most progressive state in the union, only requires one for every four.

By age five, the Abecedarian Project averages one teacher for every six students, which is the same ratio The Perry Preschool Project had for their three- and four-year-olds. California only requires one teacher for every twelve children aged three and up. Childcare and preschool are already insanely expensive in California and doubling the staffing requirements for these institutions would only send the price tag much higher.

And that's not even considering that the Perry program also included a teacher going to literally every child's home every week in addition to their classroom duties. The Abecedarian program had similar visits every other week. No state mandates that, nor does any legislation in Congress. Not only would it be insanely expensive, but all these visitations could be considered highly intrusive for many single parents.

More importantly, the two studies were exceedingly small. Fifty children enrolled in one program in one city compared to fifty children in a control group from the same city doesn't really tell us anything about a nation of 300 million. There have also been significant questions raised about how families were selected for the treatment and control groups for each study as well as how families in each group were tracked through the years.

Most importantly, however, when early education programs have scaled up, they have consistently failed to produce anything close to the results achieved by the tiny Durham and Ypsilanti experiments.

WE WANT A MAGIC BULLET

The largest study examining the effectiveness of early childhood education was the Department of Health and Human Services Head Start Impact Study. First created as part of the Economic Opportunity Act of 1964, Head Start provides education, nutrition, and health services to over a million low-income families nationwide. As popular as the program was politically from the start, the government had never conducted its own study of how effective the services were.

In 2002, HHS commissioned a study of five thousand children who applied to participate in the Head Start program. Children were randomly assigned to intervention and control groups, with control group families free to pursue other day care or early education opportunities outside of Head Start.

In 2010, HHS finally published their first results. While the children who received Head Start services did show some initial gains in their health and cognitive skills compared to the control group, those gains disappeared by the first grade.[20] Two years later in the third grade, HHS checked in on study participants again. Still nothing.[21]

So much for seven dollars in benefits for every one dollar invested.

More recently, Vanderbilt University decided to take advantage of Tennessee's free preschool program to do their own randomized study. The Tennessee Voluntary Prekindergarten program serves 18,000 children from low-income families statewide every year, and the program is always oversubscribed. Since Tennessee picks students randomly to allocate the limited number of spots, a perfect research opportunity was waiting to be explored.

Under the leadership of Dr. Dale Farran, researchers followed almost 3,000 children, some of whom were admitted to the program, and others that were not. Like the Head Start study, at first results were positive. Children who participated in the program entered kindergarten with better skills than the control group.[22]

But when Vanderbilt followed up with those same children in the third grade, they were disappointed with what they found. Children who had participated in Tennessee's preschool program had worse math and science scores than the children in the control group. Things only got worse by the sixth grade when the preschool group produced lower scores than the control group in math, science, and reading. Not only did they fall short academically, the preschool beneficiaries were also more likely to be in special education, were more likely to have been in trouble in school, and were more likely to have been suspended.

"It really has required a lot of soul-searching, a lot of reading of the literature to try to think of what were plausible reasons that might account for this," Dr. Farran told NPR after publication of the sixth-grade results. But, she added, "this is still the only randomized controlled trial of a statewide pre-K program and I know that people get upset about this and don't want it to be true."[23]

But it is true.

Many tried to dismiss these results by attacking the quality of the Tennessee preschool program. But as Dr. Farran notes, the teachers in the

Tennessee Voluntary Prekindergarten were highly trained and credentialed. She thinks that high training may even be part of the problem. "There have been three very large studies, the latest one in 2018, which are not showing any relationship between quality and licensure," Dr. Farran noted. The program's one teacher for every ten students ratio isn't as intensive as Perry Preschool's six-to-one ratio, but it is better than California's twelve-to-one ratio and most other state's ratios.

"We tend to want a magic bullet," Dr. Farran continued. "Whoever thought that you could provide a four-year-old from an impoverished family with five and a half hours a day, nine months a year of preschool, and close the achievement gap, and send them to college at a higher rate?" she asked. "I mean, why? Why do we put so much pressure on our pre-K programs?"[24]

People put so much pressure on pre-K programs because their world view depends on those programs making up for the negative impact of missing fathers. If government funded preschool can't close the gap between married families and single parent homes, then the entire feminist project is in doubt.

But what about universal childcare? Maybe the problem with Head Start and other government funded preschool programs is that they target low-income families. Maybe if the government provided a highly regulated high quality universal day care benefit designed for everyone, that could help improve child development outcomes.

The Canadian province of Quebec started doing exactly that in 1997, offering subsidized childcare, five dollars a day for all families, in highly regulated non-profit centers with strict qualifications and high mandated wages for all caregivers. Economists then studied the impacts to both parents and children from the subsidized universal day care in the long term.

For employers, the subsidized day care was great. Quebec experienced rapid growth in the maternal labor force after the program was introduced. The results for children, however, especially in the long term, were not as encouraging.

On the bright side, economists found no negative impacts from universal childcare on the cognitive skills of children by the time they became adults. But non-cognitive outcomes did not turn out as well. Researchers found that increased day care use led to worse health outcomes, worse life satisfaction, increased aggression, and higher rates of criminal activity, especially among boys.[25] If the goal of universal day care is to alleviate the disadvantage boys face without fathers in the home, then universal day care appears to make the problem worse.

FATHERHOOD WITHOUT MARRIAGE

After decades of bad results, some liberals have finally begun to recognize that government programs are failing boys from single parent households. In his book, *Of Boys and Men*, Brookings Institution fellow Richard Reeves documents the declining state of boys and men in America, noting that already more than 45 percent of all adult women in the United States have a college degree compared to just 35 percent of men.[26]

As their education has fallen behind, so has men's earning power. Adjusting for inflation, most American men earn less today than their counterparts did in 1979, and for those that did not graduate high school they are earning 14 percent less. In light of these declining wages, it is not terribly surprising that more than 10 percent of working age men (ages twenty-five to fifty-four) are not working or looking for work. That is the highest percentage ever in American history.[27]

Considering these bleak statistics, it is understandable that men account for 67 percent of all drug overdose deaths and 77 percent of all suicides.

Reeves even acknowledges the role that missing fathers have played in the decline of men, writing, "Engaged fatherhood has been linked to a whole range of outcomes from mental health, high school graduation, social skills, and literacy to lower risks of teen pregnancy, delinquency, and drug use."[28]

"A study in the state of Georgia found that infant mortality rates were twice as high among children whose fathers were not listed on their birth certificate (a proxy for paternal involvement) after taking account of differences in health conditions and socioeconomic background," Reeves adds.[29]

But instead of embracing the one institution that has a multi-millennium long track record of successfully tying fathers to mothers, Reeves, as noted in the introduction, celebrates the decline of marriage. "Marriage and motherhood are no longer virtually synonymous," Reeves writes. "About 40% of births in the U.S. now take place outside marriage, up from just 11% in 1970... From a feminist perspective, which to be clear is my perspective, these are marvelous developments."[30]

"Marvelous development." That's what Reeves thinks of the decline of marriage.

So, what does Reeves call for to replace marriage? His last chapter is titled "NEW DADS: Fatherhood as an Independent Social Institution." In other words, he wants to create a new role for fathers completely divorced from marriage.

"These policies are intended to support the development of a new model of fatherhood," Reeves writes, "suited to a world where mothers don't need men, but children still need their dads."

"There is no residency requirement for good fatherhood," Reeves asserts. "The relationship is what matters. Fatherhood matters just as much as ever in a world of women's economic independence, but necessarily in a reinvented form."[31]

In his quest to "reinvent" fatherhood, Reeves calls for paid paternal leave so new fathers can provide equal care for their children in the first months after their birth, $1 billion in scholarships for men to get degrees in health care and education, and child support reform that would allow men to substitute care given to their children in place of cash given to mothers.

Underlying all of Reeves' preferred policies is the belief that government can socially engineer into men the same desire and capacity for caregiving that already exists in women. "The way we get divided into our false notions of masculine and feminine is what we see as children," Reeves quotes Gloria Steinem.[32]

But Steinem is just plain wrong. Our notions of what is masculine and feminine are not socially constructed. They come from our genes which were shaped by thousands of years of evolution. Having mothers be the primary caregivers for children is not something men invented in 1950, or 1776, or even 10,000 BC.

In every human society across time, mothers have always been the primary caregivers. Yes, fathers do help with childcare. In some hunter-gatherer tribes men provide more care than men in America do today (and in many they provide far less.) But even in the most egalitarian, care-giving tribe, mothers still provide most of the care for their children.[33]

For hundreds of thousands of years, mothers in hunter-gatherer bands stayed with their infants twenty-four hours a day for the first two years of their life.[34] They slept with their babies, carried them while they collected food, and breastfed them when they were hungry. Humans are mammals. We are literally defined by the mother's unique ability to provide milk through her mammary glands. No parental leave policy or health care scholarship fund is going to change this biological fact.

Just as importantly, there are common male archetypes across cultures and time as well. Humans are unique in our capacity to fight and compete as a group. For hundreds of thousands of years, it was the men who most successfully banded together to fight and defeat other less well-organized groups of men, and it was the most successful fighting bands of men that survived and passed their genes onto the next generation. Even today boys across cultures will spontaneously form groups that compete against other groups of boys. This is a genealogical artifact of our hunting and gathering days.[35]

It is through these competitive group interactions that boys learn to become men. Unorganized groups will lose to cohesive groups. So, boys learn to follow rules and respect authority. In any competition, nothing ever goes perfectly according to plan. Group competition teaches boys to control their emotions and stay cool when things go wrong. And of course, physical strength and toughness are valuable in pretty much any physical competitive activity.

Strength. Toughness. Composure. Respect for rules and authority. These are the attributes that are associated with masculinity across cultures. Also, in every culture, men are expected to protect the women in their lives, particularly those they live with.

Reeves seems to forget this when he claims, "there is no residency requirement for good fatherhood." Biologically, he's just plain wrong. Just as the hormone oxytocin floods a mother's nervous system to help her bond with her child, new fathers often experience a similar decrease in testosterone and increase in prolactin. The decrease in testosterone helps curb men's desire to impregnate other women, and the increased prolactin helps stimulate parental care.

But these changes in fathers' hormone levels only occur if they are living with the mother of their child.[36] Fathers out shacking up with other women simply do not experience the same hormonal changes that resident fathers do. Other studies have shown that wage gains associated with fatherhood do not accrue to non-residential fathers. Only those fathers that live with the mother of their children put in the effort and discipline to see their wages rise.[37]

Reeves—a good liberal—may celebrate the ability of women to raise children without fathers, but he never really grapples with what these fathers are supposed to do if the mother of their child doesn't want them around. Clearly Reeves expects them to be dutiful parents, putting in just as much effort into providing care as mothers do. But what if Reeves' new "fatherhood as an independent social institution" isn't as fulfilling as Reeves hopes it is? What if these fathers meet new women, women that actually want to live with them? Are they supposed to be celibate for the rest of their lives?

This is a real problem that Reeves completely ignores. Without marriage to bind one man and one woman into a long-term project of cooperative care, what is to stop both men and women from having multiple children with multiple partners?

In fact, as marriage has declined, that is exactly what is happening. Of men who father a child outside of marriage, 50 percent of them go on to have a child with another woman. Overall, about 15 percent of men and about 20 percent of women in the United States today have children with more than one partner.[38] The United States is the world leader in this multipartner fertility statistic. No nation has more mothers with children from more than one father than us.[39] And as marriage continues to decline, which again Reeves claims to think is "marvelous," these numbers will only go up.

The chances that a mother will have children with more than one father, however, is not equally distributed demographically. Mothers without a college degree are three times more likely to experience multipartner fertility than mothers that graduated college. Among men with just a high school education, 43 percent of men with at least two children, have those children with multiple partners. Among men with a college degree, just 5 percent of fathers with multiple children have them with multiple mothers.

Multipartner fertility is tough on both parents and children. Studies show that both mothers and fathers who have children with more than one partner report significantly higher rates of depression and less satisfaction with parenting. Children who have half-siblings are significantly more likely to use drugs and more likely to get in trouble at school compared to children with only one set of parents.[40]

It's not difficult to imagine why multipartner fertility is so stressful for both parents and children. When a father has biological children in two homes it is impossible for him to split his time and resources evenly. Inevitably there is going to be conflict between the mother of his oldest children and the mother of the children he is currently sleeping with.

Reeves may wish it were not so, but men will always devote more care and resources to the biological children of the mother he is currently living with. Research shows that when fathers who don't live with the mother of their children go on to live with another woman and father her children, they devote less time and less resources to the children from the old relationship.[41] Reeves's new "Fatherhood as an Independent Social Institution" theory has nothing to offer these abandoned children.

Reeves also ignores the danger that children are exposed to when unmarried men are brought into the home. According to a 2005 University of Chicago study, young children who live in households with an unrelated man are nearly fifty times more likely to die from an inflicted injury (such as being shaken or struck), as compared to children living in a home with both biological parents.[42]

Unmarried young women are also less safe from men than their married counterparts. According to a 2018 University of Pennsylvania study, 80 percent of all domestic violence comes from unmarried couples, not married couples.[43] Unless single mothers plan to stay celibate for the rest of their lives, they and their children are much safer in a married relationship than in a single parent household.

WE NEED EACH OTHER

Like anything in life that is worth doing, parenting is hard. While both mothers and fathers have an instinctual desire to care for children, unfortunately the how is not hard wired into our bodies. Keeping a child fed and dry and warm is highly context specific. The knowledge and skills necessary to provide for a child on the Mongolian steppe in 1200 AD is vastly different from what is needed in suburban northern Virginia in 2020. Even something as biologically rooted as breastfeeding is not innate. New parents have to learn how to provide that care.

Then there is the constant worrying about whether your child is developing normally. Are they eating too much? Too little? Are they crying too much? Is their speech developing normally? Do they have enough friends at school?

These are difficult questions for anyone to navigate. Is it really that radical an idea to suggest that parenting is easier for two parents who love each other, who support each other through these challenges, than it is for one person, regardless of their sex?

And that is just the emotional side of parenting. There are also the logistics. Cooking, cleaning, shopping, changing diapers, taking out the trash. Aren't all these services easier to carry out with two people working as a team than by one person on their own?

Gloria Steinem did not come up with the feminist rallying cry "a woman needs a man like a fish needs a bicycle"—but she did popularize it. Reeves mostly embraces the sentiment, agreeing that we live in "a world where mothers don't need men," but he at least allows that "children still need their dads." Steinem didn't even allow that concession.

It is good to see thinkers on the left admit that it is difficult for mothers to raise children all by themselves, even with government help. It is becoming increasingly clear that children, especially boys, need fathers. The question is how to ensure fathers play a significant role in their children's lives. Reeves thinks this can be accomplished without marriage. Thousands of years of human history say otherwise.

But more importantly, Reeves and Steinem are wrong about women too. Women do need men just as much as men need women. Both men and women have innate biological needs for physical and emotional intimacy. And for the 98 percent of the population that is straight, those needs can only be met by a member of the opposite sex. Regardless of which sex we are, we need each other, not the state.

Pew recently came out with a study that made headlines showing that 50 percent of single people aren't interested in dating. But that same poll found that 70 percent of Americans were already in a romantic relationship. And when you drilled down into the percentage of single people who were not interested in dating, it was overwhelmingly made up of widowed and divorced women over the age of sixty-five. Meanwhile, 67 percent of single men under forty were looking for a romantic partner, and for single women under forty it was 61 percent.[44]

So yes, a widowed sixty-five-year-old woman probably does need a man like a fish needs a bicycle. But the rest of us still crave emotional and physical connection with a partner of the opposite sex, and the state cannot provide that.

CHAPTER EIGHT

WHY MARRIAGE WORKS

IN HER RECENT BOOK *THE Two Parent Privilege*, University of Maryland economics professor Melissa Kearney makes a specific effort to avoid any discussion about "why" marriage works. "It's simply not my expertise on marriage, coming to it as I do as an economist," Kearney writes. "I am focused on marriage as an institution that is defined by two people combining and sharing resources in a long-term contract. If you are looking for a book about marriage and love," Kearney continues, "this is not that book."[1]

Kearney's choice is understandable. She is writing for a liberal audience that has fully imbibed the cultural relativism at the heart of the sexual revolution. Many of them are not ready to hear explanations for why some cultural norms are better than others, about why human desires for physical and emotional intimacy are best channeled through monogamous marriage.

But *this* book is ready to have that discussion, and *this* is that chapter.

THE POWER OF LOVE

To take a step back, why do we love? I don't mean romantic love, although we will get there soon. Why are mothers drawn to cuddle and feed their babies? Why are husbands driven to protect their wives? Why do brothers and sisters stick up for each other in school?

These behaviors are not unique to humans. Almost all male birds help their mates build and protect a nest for at least one season, and in some bird species, for life. In chimpanzee communities, when a mother dies, her youngest children are often adopted and cared for by their older siblings.

There is something deep within most animals that draws us into meaningful relationships with each other. In fact, it can be argued (and was argued in Chapter One) that the reason humans are as successful as we are, is because we have developed the capacity and desire to form and maintain the world's deepest and most complex relationships.

When we think of evolution in animals, we usually think of small mutations within a species that can create advantages in certain environments for certain mutations. For example, on an island where insects are a plentiful source of food, a bird species may slowly evolve long thin beaks and sharp claws that are better at harvesting insects compared to their original short-beaked, nut-eating ancestors.

But for single-celled organisms evolution is often different. Two separate species of single-cell organisms can combine to form a more complicated organism that has advantages over other simpler single-cell entities. Just such a merger happened between the ancestors of your mitochondria and your nucleated cells over 1 billion years ago.

After the merger, the mitochondrion specialized in processing energy while the larger cell handled the rest of the organism's other functions. By working together, thus allowing each to specialize in certain functions, the overall union became more effective at surviving and reproducing. With the mitochondrion able to process fifteen times more energy than other cells without energy-processing specializers, this new symbiotic team became the basis for all animal life on earth.

Cooperation and specialization have since become the dominant strategy for all complex life. Of course, single and multicell organisms don't think about strategy or cooperation like we do. Instead, billions and billions of random mutations became experiments the results of which favored those changes that included more cooperation and specialization.

The advantages of cooperation and specialization are not limited to single organisms. As animals have become more complex, they have also gained the capacity to cooperate with each other, and those animals that have evolved a capacity to cooperate often succeed over those that don't in most environments. This cooperation can be seen in behaviors as complex as wolves hunting in a pack, or as simple as one cat grooming another.

Of course, not all animals have the same capacity for bonding and cooperation. When dogs are separated from their owners, for example, they exhibit the same kind of stress behaviors that infants exhibit when they are separated from their mothers. Cats, however, seem not to care when their owners are gone and often ignore them when they are present.

Dogs may even have a greater capacity for bonding then humans, particularly interspecies love. In addition to forming deep bonds with their human masters, as long as a dog is raised with another animal, any animal, the dog will bond with that animal.

Raise a dog with humans and it will bond with humans. Raise a dog with sheep and it will bond with sheep. You can even raise a dog with a cheetah, and it will bond with cheetahs.

The same is not true with the dog's closest relative the wolf. Wolves have not spent the last fifteen thousand years being rewarded by humans for being as friendly as possible. As a result, wolves do not form the same relationships with other species that dogs do and require far more interaction when young to become friendly with humans at all.

Scientists have even identified the genes in dogs that, in humans, are associated with Williams-Beuren syndrome, a symptom of which is indiscriminate friendliness. People who have these genes are extremely outgoing and treat almost everybody they meet as a friend, just like dogs.[2]

While indiscriminate friendliness poses its own unique problems for humans, it has worked out great for dogs. For every one surviving wolf on the planet, there are at least three thousand dogs. From a Darwinian standpoint at least, friendliness has made dogs a big winner compared to their wolf relatives.

"The animal world tells us again and again and again that love is really important," Patrick Abbot, an associate professor of Biological Sciences at Vanderbilt University explains. "There doesn't seem to be any obvious advantage to the one that is grooming. It is work. You give up something for yourself for another. Whether animals know they are loving or not, it is clearly advantageous to them to do it."[3]

Entire books have been written trying to define love, but I think Abbot has hit upon the essential elements necessary for our purposes. Love is work. It is an act you take that helps cement a relationship that ultimately ends up helping you too.

DRIVEN BY EMOTIONS

The tricky part about love is that we don't always know what relationships will ultimately be advantageous to us. That is where our emotions, and the chemicals in our bodies that drive those emotions, come in. Informed by millennia of evolutionary wisdom, our body produces certain hormones in certain situations which tend to guide us towards behaviors that in general are ultimately beneficial for us, even if that benefit is not immediately obvious.

For example, when a mother hears a baby cry, her body releases a hormone called oxytocin which triggers nurturing desires in the mother's brain. This same hormone is delivered into women's bodies when they feel stressed, causing a desire for physical contact with a loved one.

Men are far from immune. Physical contact, including cuddling but especially sexual contact, causes a rush of oxytocin in both men and women. With this hormone surging through our systems, both sexes are more likely to form emotional bonds with their partner.[4] As discussed in Chapter One, a similar hormone, vasopressin, is released in male prairie voles during sex, triggering pair-bonding and parenting behaviors in the tiny rodents. This hormone is also active in humans. Men with genes that are especially friendly to vasopressin transmission have been shown to have happier marriages.[5]

As much as we might wish to be purely intellectual creatures, the unavoidable fact is that our human bodies crave affectionate physical contact. The need for touch is not as immediate as our need for oxygen, water, and food, but it is real, and when it is not met our bodies and minds suffer.

In orphanages where children's strict material needs were met (food, clothing, education), but they were denied affectionate physical contact growing up, the children were found to be both developmentally behind those raised with their parents and more prone to physical illness.[6] Studies have also found that all of us, but especially men, are less healthy and less happy when we are deprived of physical affection.[7]

The emotions that drive us to seek love from others, also protect us from others taking advantage of us. We feel anger when someone does not reciprocate the generosity we show them. We feel jealousy when a romantic partner strays. For both men and women there are real evolutionary disadvantages to investing in a relationship where the other person does not reciprocate.

Men in a romantic relationship could lose their investment in affections for a woman entirely. If a man devotes himself to a woman, but that woman is impregnated by another man, the first man has lost any chance his genes will survive into the next generation. That is why, evolutionarily speaking, jealousy pays off. Men who care if their romantic partners are faithful have a far better chance of seeing their genes passed into the next generation.

Women too have much to gain from a faithful man. If a woman did not care if her romantic partner had sex with other women, that woman could expect less resources from that man for each additional woman he became involved with. If a man is romantically involved with three women, then the resources he can produce will be divided three ways. But if a woman jealously protects her man's attentions, then she gets all his resources and help.

There is also a natural division of labor between the sexes, especially since we are mammals. As mentioned in the last chapter, as mammals we are literally defined by a mother's unique ability to provide milk through her mammary glands. This biological fact has positioned mothers to be the primary caregiver for children for millennia. Fathers can and do help care for children, but for the hundreds of thousands of years we existed as hunter-gatherer bands, mothers cared for their infants twenty-four hours a day for the first two years of their life.

This does not mean that mothers were ever wholly dependent on men or that they didn't produce many, if not most, of the calories eaten by a family. Mothers have been pulling double duty as economic providers and caregivers since the dawn of humanity. But as we discussed in Chapter One, as amazing as mothers are, they need help raising children. They can't do it alone.

And monogamous marriage has proven to be the best way to get mothers the help they need to raise children.

As discussed in Chapter Two, almost all societies throughout written history were polygamous, not monogamous. But as discussed in Chapter Three, since the spread of Christianity and the subsequent rise of democracy, the world has recently become majority monogamous again. Monogamy has simply proven itself more conducive to human flourishing. Let's review why.

PROBLEMATIC POLYGAMY

In Chapter Two we explained why polygamous societies have a math problem. In even a moderately polygamous society where most marriages are monogamous, the polygamous marriages monopolize so many women that it is not uncommon for 40 percent of all men to be left without a wife. It is these unmarried men, cut off from the physical contact they need to be happy, that pose the biggest problem for polygamist cultures.

Data has conclusively shown that the greater the percentage of unmarried men there are in a nation's population, the greater the rates of rape, murder, assault, theft, and fraud. Inequality, unemployment, and urbanization also lead to more crime, but the presence of large numbers of unmarried men is an even bigger predictor of crime.

More competition between males over mates also drives men to seek greater control over their own daughters and sisters. As a result, polygamous countries have the lowest age of marriage for women and the highest age gap between husbands and wives. This spousal age gap has proven to be the most accurate predictors of spousal homicide.[8]

Polygamous households are also more divisive than monogamous households. Monogamous households have lower rates of abuse, neglect, and homicide than their polygamous counterparts. On the national level, monogamous countries have less domestic violence, less maternal mortality, and less sex trafficking, even after controlling for wealth. Infant and child mortality are also higher in high polygamy countries roughly double the rate of similar monogamous countries.[9]

Considering how poor a foundation for human development the polygamous home is, it is not surprising that the most comprehensive study of 156 countries shows that monogamous societies are more populous, less authoritarian, less corrupt, and wealthier than polygamous ones.[10]

The evidence above might not be enough to convince the Jonathan Turleys of the world that monogamy is superior to polygamy, but it should be enough to push most cultural relativists to admit that the Supreme Court was right to affirm Congressional action against the practice of polygamy almost two hundred years ago.

NOT SO CONSENSUAL NON-MONOGAMY

But what if the problem with polygamy is just that it is a little too patriarchal, that it allows men to monopolize women sexually, but not the other way around? What if we could all just be a little freer and tolerate the sexual dalliances of our partners? What if we could embrace the polyamorous relationships that are more common in the gay community?

"Gay male couples are the least likely to divorce," America's most popular sex advice columnist Dan Savage correctly notes. "Straight couples are more likely [to divorce], lesbian couples most likely. Lesbian couples and straight couples are most likely to be monogamous; gay couples are least likely to be monogamous. Correlation ain't causation, but it would seem that gay male couples are doing something right by defusing the bomb that explodes so many straight and lesbian relationships."[11]

Savage then makes the case that the only problem with the sexual revolution is that it hasn't gone far enough. "More straight people have at least entertained the thought of there being possibilities, which ironically is the stated fear from the 70s and 80s...that gay people led these hedonic lifestyles and straight people were going to be tempted to adopt gay, hedonic lifestyles. And we've kind of seen that come to pass."[12]

Plainly, Savage is right. Acceptance of polyamorous lifestyles has risen right along with acceptance of gay marriage. New York City now offers legal recognition of polyamorous relationships as do the Massachusetts cities of Somerville, Cambridge, and Arlington.

To help his readers navigate this new world of sexual promiscuity, Savage recommends *The Ethical Slut* by Janet Hardy and Dossie Easton, which he describes as the "Code of Hammurabi where ethical non-monogamy is concerned."[13]

Published in 1997, as this largely San Francisco–Bay Area phenomenon began to go mainstream, *The Ethical Slut* does indeed lay out some hard rules for those interested in practicing polyamory. In the book, Hardy and Easton claim that "controlling sexual behavior didn't seem to be that important outside the propertied classes until the Industrial Revolution," which as we covered in Chapter Two, would be a big surprise to anyone who read the actual Code of Hammurabi.

Hardy and Easton go on to argue that "the nuclear family…is a relic of the twentieth century middle-class."

"Marriage," they claim, "is no longer essential for survival." "Human nature will win out," they confidently claim. "We are horny creatures and the more sexually repressive a culture becomes, the more outrageous its covert sexual thoughts and behaviors will become."[14]

Not that Hardy and Easton endorse a completely promiscuous lifestyle where people can have sex with whoever they want, whenever they want. "It is very important to us to treat people well and do our best not to hurt anyone," Hardy and Easton write. To make sure people are not harmed, Hardy and Easton place consent at the center of their moral universe. "First and foremost, ethical sluts value consent," they write.[15]

This consent system requires polyamorists to be honest with themselves and others. Polyamorists must be excellent and patient communicators, able to both express their deepest desires and listen to what others are truly saying.

While polyamorists must be "respectful" of other people's feelings, Hardy and Easton say polyamorists are under no obligation to change their behavior to accommodate other people's needs. "What you are not responsible for is your lovers' emotions," Hardy and Easton write. "You can choose to be supportive—we're great believers in the healing power of listening—but it is not your job to fix anything."

If a partner feels jealous, Hardy and Easton argue that is their problem, not yours. For Hardy and Easton, jealousy is just a social construct invented when humans transitioned from nomadic hunter gathering to sedentary agriculture. Since jealousy is learned, Hardy and Easton believe, it can also be unlearned. And they devote a whole chapter to describing exercises designed to help people evolve past it.

Hardy and Easton stress that there is no "villain" when someone feels jealous. It is wrong for polyamorists to blame others when they feel this. "You cannot deal constructively with jealousy by making other people wrong," they write. "Like it or not, the only person who can make that jealousy hurt less or go away is you."

Hardy and Easton even suggest that learning to master your jealousy can lead to spiritual enlightenment. "Working to change your emotions requires that you open up, be willing to feel, flinching when necessary, becoming more conscious. Isn't that what spirituality is, an opened and expanded consciousness?"

Aside from achieving a higher state of being by overcoming our petty possessive impulses and our need to control others' behavior, Hardy and Easton note that the real driving force behind polyamory is, of course, the pleasure of being able to have guilt-free sex with multiple partners.

"Releasing physical tensions, relieving menstrual cramps, maintaining mental health, preventing prostate problems, making babies, cementing relationships, and so on are all admirable goals, and wonderful side benefits of sex," they write. "But they are not what sex is for. People have sex because it feels very good, and they feel good about themselves. Pleasure is a complete and worthwhile goal in and of itself."[16]

But is sexual pleasure such a worthwhile goal when it inflicts so much emotional pain on your romantic partners?

Easton recounts a story about a lover she took who had trouble adjusting to Easton's polyamorous desires. "My lover is late coming home. I hope she is alright—this morning she left in tears," Easton writes. "And it's my fault, my choice, my responsibility. I am asking my lover to go through the fire for reasons most of the rest of the world consider frivolous if not downright reprehensible. I cannot, will not, be monogamous."

The punch line of the story is that after immense emotional pain, Easton and her lover break up. Easton, of course, counts herself blameless. She has every right to maximize her sexual pleasure, and it is not her fault her lover failed to unlearn the jealous feelings impressed upon her by an oppressive patriarchal society.

But the polyamorists are just factually wrong. Jealousy was not invented alongside agriculture as a mechanism to control female desire and female bodies. It is an emotion ingrained into both sexes over millions of years of evolution. The vasopressin raging through our bodies when we have sex with another person, helps us form tight emotional bonds that can only be broken through immense psychological pain.

Jealousy gets a bad rap, and understandably so. One common way, but not the only way, jealousy can be channeled is through violence. Most domestic abuse does come from men violently punishing their female partners for making them feel jealous. This behavior is unequivocally bad.

But violence is not the only way to channel jealous emotions. In fact, it is not even the most common way. Men do not have a monopoly on jealousy. Women are just as likely to be jealously protective of their partners and the intensity of their jealousy is just as strong as a man's.

We feel jealous when we sense our partner is thinking of leaving us. This has always been a very real possibility. All societies throughout time have had divorce of some kind. But violence and vigilance are not the only ways to keep your partner.

University of Texas psychology professor David Buss has researched behaviors couples use to retain their current partner, and then he checked in on newlyweds five years after they got married to see how often these tactics were used and how successful they were.[17]

In addition to the more classic behaviors we associate with jealousy (snooping through others' belongings, calling at odd hours to make sure a partner is not with a member of the opposite sex, flirting with other people to make our partner angry) Dr. Buss found that couples also sought to retain their mates by trying to better meet their needs.

Such behaviors included buying a spouse flowers, telling their spouse they love them, helping their spouse when they need assistance, improving one's physical appearance, and meeting the other partner's sexual desires (i.e. having sex with each other, not letting a spouse have sex with someone else).

Turns out that the most effective strategy for mate retention for both husbands and wives is regular displays of love and kindness. Husbands who failed to perform acts of love and commitment were far more likely to have a wife that was thinking of getting a divorce and vice versa.

The motivation for doing things that will please your romantic partner can come from a lot of places. It can come from naked sexual desire, pure altruistic impulse to help a loved one, and it can even come from the nauseating fear of potential loss that is jealousy. These emotions drive us to please our partners because maintaining long-term relationships has proven to be an effective way to project one's genes into the future. Suppressing these emotions is painful because it is a denial of our humanity.

Once jealousy is acknowledged as a valid emotional response to extra-partner pairings, the entire ethical construct of non-monogamy falls apart.

"The problem is that with many of these couples one partner wants it and the other says yes because she's afraid that he will leave her," Dr. Janis Abrahms Spring told the *New York Times*.[18] If the consent for extra-partner sex is only being secured through emotional blackmail, if "ethical" non-monogamy is built on completely disregarding the entirely justified jealous feelings of others, then it really isn't properly given consent at all.

And what data we do have on polyamorous relationships, backs Dr. Spring up. A recent study from the Wheatley Institution and the School of Family Life found that heterosexual men were four times as likely than heterosexual women to desire a non-monogamous relationship.[19] Other studies have found heterosexual polyamorous couples are more likely to get divorced than people in traditional monogamous relationships.[20]

Non-monogamy may work for Savage and other gay male couples, but for most heterosexual couples, polyamory is a recipe for emotional abuse and misery.

COHABITATION COMPLICATIONS

Another rising substitute for marriage is cohabitation. Cohabitation has become so common, in fact, that it has in some ways replaced marriage. The proportion of women that have ever cohabitated has nearly doubled over the past twenty-five years, rising to the point that the number of adults who have ever cohabitated is now higher than the number who have ever been married.[21]

As cohabitation's popularity has grown, however, its stability has not. Cohabitation used to be a common stepping stone to marriage. In the 1980s about 40 percent of cohabitations had transitioned into marriages within five years, by the 2010s, however, that percentage had dropped to 20 percent.[22]

Those cohabitations that don't transition to marriage are highly likely to dissolve. One study found only 44 percent of first cohabitations remained intact two years later.[23]

What was once a stepping stone to marriage has now evolved into a merry-go-round of serial shacking up. Not only are more women today likely to experience multiple cohabitations, but the time between cohabitations is falling. In the 1980s, of the few women that did have multiple cohabitations, the average length between cohabitations was about four years. Now, far more women are living through multiple cohabitations and the length between the cohabitations has fallen to just two years.[24]

Similar data comparing past generations of men is not available, but looking at today, those men that have cohabitated are more likely than women to have cohabited with multiple partners. What appears to be happening in communities where marriage has broken down, is that a minority of men is enjoying serial cohabitations with multiple women.

It is not so much a concurrent neo-polygamy, but an asynchronous neo-polygamy.

Despite the instability of cohabiting unions, it has become increasingly common for cohabitating partners to start a family. Most of the increase in unwed childbearing since the 1970s is due to the rise of births to cohabiting couples. Today, almost 75 percent of women agree that it is acceptable to have and raise children in cohabiting unions, and almost 60 percent of unwed births are to cohabiting mothers.[25]

Unfortunately, these cohabiting unions, even with children added, are not as stable as marriages. Half of children born to cohabiting parents see their parents' relationship end by their third birthday, compared to just 10 percent of married parents. Fast forward to age twelve and two-thirds of cohabiting parents have separated compared to just 25 percent of married parents.[26] Additionally, studies have found that children whose fathers have children with multiple women often live in neighborhoods with greater physical disorder than their peers from married families.[27]

Not only are children in cohabiting households much more likely to become children in single parent households, but compared to children in married families, children raised in cohabiting families are more than twice as likely to be suspended or expelled from high school.[28] Studies also show that among black families in particular, children do better when their mother marries a stepfather, but do worse when she only cohabitates with a new man.[29]

The problem with cohabitation is that it often involves a mismatch in expectations between partners. In other words, couples often start cohabitating for different reasons and with different goals in mind.

Researchers at the University of Michigan and Bowling Green State recently conducted focus groups with working class and middle-class cohabiting couples from southeast Michigan and Toledo, Ohio, to discover why they chose to live together, but not marry. They discovered a big difference in motivation for cohabitation between men and women.[30]

While both men and women viewed cohabitation as just a temporary stage to gauge whether or not they were truly compatible with their partner, women were much more likely to worry that cohabitation decreased their bargaining power in the relationship, thus delaying marriage. Women said moving in together was a deterrent to marriage because it allowed men to enjoy the benefits of a relationship (sex) without making the commitment. The ultimate goal of cohabitation for most women is marriage, while most men didn't see the link.

The men interviewed for the study were four times more likely to name sex as their primary motivation for cohabitation, and the notion that cohabitation is more sexually satisfying than dating was emphasized more by men. "I think one of the reasons that people do want to move in together is because they have, you know, sex, and I think that is the driving force behind a lot of this," one male participant eloquently explained.[31]

Part of the reason marriage works is that it involves a public acknowledgment that something is fundamentally changing in the relationship.

There is a clear meeting of the minds between two parties. A deep and new commitment is being made, one which the rest of the community through cultural norms can be deputized into supporting. Cohabitation simply doesn't elicit the same kind of honest discussions about a couple's intentions that marriage does, nor does it bring in the surrounding community to help the couple keep their promises to each other.

HOOK UP HANG UPS

Of course, men and women don't have to be married, or live together, or be in any type of relationship at all, in order to have sex. They could just hook up. And to be fair, men and women have been hooking up outside of marriage for as long as marriage has existed.

But before the latest assault on marriage, there was always an expectation that physically intimate relationships would become marriages eventually. There was never an established cultural norm that relationship-free sex was acceptable or even encouraged. But there is now.

In order to ensure successful professional careers, feminists like Hanna Rosin, author of *The End of Men: And the Rise of Women*, are encouraging women to embrace hookup culture. Women have made "unbelievable gains" in recent decades, Rosin notes, and "those gains depend on sexual liberation."[32]

"[Women] are more likely to have a college degree and, in aggregate, they make more money," than men, Rosin explains. "What makes this remarkable development possible is not just the pill or legal abortion but the whole new landscape of sexual freedom—the ability to delay marriage and have temporary relationships that don't derail education or career."

"To put it crudely," Rosin continues, "feminist progress right now largely depends on the existence of hookup culture. And to a surprising degree, it is women—not men—who are perpetuating the culture." And research shows Rosin is right: women who identify as feminist are much more likely to endorse hookup culture than women that don't.[33]

Rosin may be right that it is mostly women, not men, perpetuating hook up culture. But unless all these women are hooking up with each other, it does require at least some male participation. And while most men may not like the new hook up scene, a few do come out as big winners.

The first key to understanding hook up culture where long-term relationships are verboten, is to recognize the differences between the short- and long-term mating strategies of men and women.

When looking for a long-term mate, both men and women have the same top priority: finding a partner that loves them. As we discussed earlier, love can be defined as acts that are consistent with developing a long-term beneficial relationship with another person. When looking for a long-term mate, both men and women look for behaviors that indicate a prospective partner is committed to building a life together. These behaviors include giving up romantic relationships with other prospective partners, converting to a partner's religion, or investing in communal resources (like a house or a car).

For long-term mates, women also prize kindness, dependability and emotional stability. Physical perfection is not a deal breaker for women when looking for long-term mates, and instead of focusing on the current wealth or earning power of potential partners, women look for signs of future productive potential like intelligence and hard work.

When looking for short-term mates, however, women suddenly become very picky about the physical attractiveness of their partners. For casual sex, women only want the strongest, best looking, most masculine men. Wealthy men that are willing to shower women with gifts are also successful at obtaining casual sex.

Smart, kind, hardworking, average looking guys of modest means need not apply for hook ups. Most women simply are not interested.

For men, youth and beauty are always priorities when looking for mates, both in the short- and long-term context. But where women are much pickier when it comes to casual sex, men are the opposite: They are much more willing to lower their standards for one-night stands.[34]

These universal differences in short- and long-term preferences create highly unequal outcomes in casual short-term hookup dating markets. The most attractive and wealthy men get all the women they want. Poor, average looking guys are out of luck.

We can see this playout on dating apps. On Tinder, for example, the top 10 percent of men get 58 percent of all likes while the bottom 50 percent of men get just 4 percent.[35] OkCupid has published data from their app showing similar results. Women rate 80 percent of men as unattractive, meaning the top 20 percent of men get almost all the messages from women.[36] Data from Hinge tells a parallel story with the top 10 percent of guys receiving 60 percent of likes from women.[37]

These results show that while millions of average looking men are receiving virtually no interest from women online, women are dealing with attractive men who have the leverage to make them choose between short-term sexual relationships or no relationship at all.

A similar scene has developed on college campuses where, according to author Susan Walsh, the most popular men have formed "soft harems" of willing women.

High status college men, according to Walsh, usually maintain one official girlfriend and then have a waiting roster of "neo-concubines" ready for easy hookups. "There used to be more assortative mating," Walsh told the *Atlantic*, "where a five would date a five. But now every woman who is a six and above wants the hottest guy on campus, and she can have him… for one night."[38]

This hookup culture may be essential to the professional success of women, but is it making them happy? It doesn't seem so.

For starters, women in long-term relationships have more and better sex than women who just have casual sex. Women are far more likely to achieve orgasm with a long-term partner than with a casual hook up, and they are far more likely to say they are satisfied with their love lives.[39]

Research has also found that women who practice casual sex are more likely to suffer from anxiety and reduced life satisfaction and their chances of suffering from depression goes up with each additional hookup partner they add to their history.[40]

If the negative effects of hookup culture on women were only temporary, if they were able to rebuild their romantic lives after they started their careers and went on to achieve healthy marriages, then maybe hookup culture wouldn't be so bad. But that doesn't seem to be the case.

Research shows that the more men a woman has sex with before she gets married, the more likely her eventual first marriage will end in divorce. It turns out the optimal number of sexual partners to have before marriage is actually not zero. Virgins have a higher rate of divorce than women who only sleep with their husbands before their wedding day. Women who have slept with just their husband, and one other man, also have lower odds of divorce than virgins. But after two partners, for every additional partner a woman adds to her history before she gets married, the likelihood that her first marriage will end in divorce goes up.[41]

WHERE THERE IS MARRIAGE, THERE HAS ALWAYS BEEN DIVORCE

Fortunately for women, marriage is no longer the economic necessity that it once was. Women can and do provide for themselves economically today, and they are, in fact, becoming better at providing for themselves than men.

But life is about more than economic success. Most women are either married or want to be married. According to Gallup, just 5 percent of American women have never been married and say they want to stay that way.[42] And as we touched on in Chapter Six, married women are, on average, more happy and less likely to suffer from depression than single women.

Now marriage is no guarantor of happiness. No human institution is. There are unhappy marriages and many of them end in divorce. In every society where marriage is found, so is divorce. The Code of Hammurabi had no less than three laws governing divorce. The Roman empire had no fault divorce laws that would be the envy of California. All a man or woman had to do was say, "I divorce you" and the couple was split. This practice left many older women, whose husbands wanted new—often younger—wives scrambling to support themselves.

It is in this context that Jesus said in the Sermon on the Mount:

> It was also said, 'Whoever divorces his wife, let him give her a certificate of divorce.' But I say to you that anyone who divorces his wife, except on the ground of unchastity, causes her to commit adultery; and whoever marries a divorced woman commits adultery.[43]

Jesus does alter the teaching on divorce from the law of Moses here, but he still identifies at least one acceptable ground for divorce: unchastity. Questioned by the Pharisees after the Sermon on the Mount about the change, Jesus explains, "It was because you were so hard-hearted that Moses allowed you to divorce your wives, but from the beginning it was not so." This may sound like an outright ban on divorce, but then Jesus continues, "And I say to you, whoever divorces his wife, except for unchastity, and marries another commits adultery."[44]

So even in Christianity, there has always been divorce and annulment, which is functionally a divorce. What specifically was required to qualify for annulment has changed throughout Church history, and is still highly contested today, but again, the Church has never been beyond declaring certain marriages invalid.

For our more secular concerns, every state in the nation has always allowed divorce, although it has become much easier to secure a separation since the no-fault divorce revolution of the 1970s. But is the increase in the ease of divorce a positive development?

For marriages that are emotionally or physically abusive the answer is an unequivocal yes. High-conflict marriages are bad for both the adults involved and any children present in the household. But surprisingly few divorces stem from high-conflict situations. As many as two-thirds stem from low-conflict marriages where at least one partner was completely surprised there was a problem in the relationship at all.[45]

And it is these low-conflict marriages ending in divorce that appear to be most damaging to children. When a child experiences divorce because one parent has simply become unhappy with the current state of the relationship, that child is more likely to have their faith in love and commitment irreparably harmed. It turns out that children from high-conflict divorces are less likely to get divorced themselves than those who lived through low-conflict divorces.[46]

Additionally, almost half of divorced adults wished they had worked harder to save their marriage and 30 percent of divorced adults say they would have been interested in reconciliation services if they were available.[47] Worse, there is strong evidence that the existence of no-fault divorce laws make it less likely people will get married in the first place. Thanks to the uneven spread of no-fault divorce laws across the country, economists can look at how the implementation of no-fault divorce affected mating behaviors.

University College London economics professor Imran Rasul used Centers for Disease Control data along with Census numbers to show that those states that adopted no-fault divorce laws first, saw a significant decline in marriage rates. States that adopted equitable division of property rules for divorce proceedings also showed significant reductions in new marriages.[48]

Economists have theorized that men, especially those without college degrees, are a lot less willing to put in the effort to get good jobs and make themselves marriage material when it is easy for women to divorce them at any time for any reason. With fewer marriageable men available, fewer women are able to find suitable mates, and the number of marriages declines. So, what marriage offers couples in terms of added long-term stability, no fault divorce regimes appear to undermine.

MARRIAGE IS THE WORST, EXCEPT FOR EVERYTHING ELSE

To review, as much as we may want to believe we are all rational creatures coldly calculating the costs and benefits of each of our choices, the reality is that we are mostly driven by our emotions to meet our biological needs, needs that have been shaped by millions of years of evolution. If we feel hungry, we seek out food. If we feel tired, we seek a safe place to sleep. If we feel lonely, we seek to form intimate relationships with others.

This need for intimacy is not as pressing as the needs for food and rest, but we still suffer if we do not get it. When we do seek to meet our intimacy needs, we are hardwired to emotionally bond with those we are physically intimate with, especially when that intimacy involves sex. But sex is never just physical for humans; there is always an ingrained emotional component as well.

The relationships we form by meeting our intimacy needs become the basis of how we cooperate with others to perform tasks we could never accomplish on our own. Cultural norms then help shape the rules and expectations surrounding these relationships and some of these cultural norms have proven to be more conducive to human development than others.

As much as cultural relativists may protest, the simple fact is that cultures built around monogamous marriage are just better at delivering human flourishing than other cultures. Polygamous cultures leave too many men without any way to meet their physical and emotional intimacy needs. This makes cooperation between men difficult and leads to higher rates of crime and violence.

Polyamory doesn't work because, as much as some may wish it were not so, even in today's enlightened world, humans are still jealous creatures. We don't want another person stealing the time and affection and resources of the mates we have built relationships with.

Cohabitation fails to provide the same stability as marriage because there is no widely accepted understanding of what cohabitors owe each other. Instead of this lack of expectations leading to more honest conversations between cohabitors, it often leads to less, leaving a big mismatch between what most men and women are hoping to get out of the relationship.

Finally, hookup culture fails to meet most men's and women's needs because of the discrepancy in dating preferences for short-term relationships between the genders. The result is a highly unequal neo-polygamist dating environment where the most desirable men sleep with as many women as they want, and the women that sleep with them are left unfulfilled by the sex they do get and the emotional commitment they don't.

Marriage does not guarantee anyone's happiness. The exchange of promises between a man and a woman is just the beginning of a lifetime of work spent listening to another person, comprehending their needs, and then meeting them. This work is hard. A lot of people fail to do it. Many marriages fall apart. But no institution better channels our primal emotions of loneliness, lust, anger, jealousy, and joy into the productive behavior of loving another person, then monogamous marriage.

For too long, we have prioritized individual exploration and sexual gratification over the formation of stable long-term family bonds. Where once the entirety of American family law was built on the confident belief that the monogamous married family was the best environment for the development of human flourishing, now individual wants and desires reign supreme. The American family, and the nation itself, has suffered as a result.

CHAPTER NINE

MAKE MARRIAGE GREAT AGAIN

NOT EVERY UNIVERSITY HAS A luxury sports facility specifically built just for its women's volleyball team, but the University of Southern Mississippi does. Officially called "the Wellness Center," the $8 million structure includes multiple indoor volleyball courts, seating for roughly one thousand spectators, a weight room, locker rooms, classrooms, administrative offices, and additional meeting space. And all it took to secure the funding was a scandal involving the governor's office, the state's director of the Department of Human Services, a Hall of Fame quarterback, and a retired professional wrestler.

The story of Southern Mississippi's infamous volleyball stadium begins back in 1996 in Washington, D.C.

When Congress reformed what was the Aid to Families with Dependent Children (AFDC) program into the Temporary Assistance for Needy Families (TANF) program, it significantly increased the discretion states had over the federal welfare funds sent to them by the Department of Health and Human Services (HHS).

As long as states used the funds to accomplish four broad purposes, states could spend the money pretty much however they wanted. Those four purposes included: 1) providing assistance to needy families so that children may be cared for in their own homes; 2) ending the dependence of needy parents on government benefits by promoting job preparation, work, and marriage; 3) preventing and reduce the incidence of out-of-wedlock pregnancies; and 4) encouraging the formation and maintenance of two-parent families.

Under these guidelines, Mississippi was supposed to be either giving their TANF dollars directly to needy families or using it on programs to promote work and marriage and reduce out of wedlock births. Instead, state officials turned the TANF program into a slush fund for their own pet projects. One of those projects ended up being a volleyball stadium sought by a former Green Bay Packer who just happened to have once played quarterback for the University of Southern Mississippi Golden Eagles.

On July 24, 2017, Brett Favre, WWE professional wrestler Ted DiBiase, Mississippi Department of Human Services Director John Davis, Mississippi Community Education Center president Nancy New, and her son Zach all met at The Rock, the Golden Eagles football stadium, to discuss the financing of a new women's volleyball stadium. Favre's daughter was set to play on the team as a freshman that coming fall.

Both federal and state regulations prevent TANF funds from being spent on "brick and mortar" projects, but Nancy and her son Zach came up with a clever work around. They would characterize the money given to the University as a "lease" for educational facilities funneled through the New's Mississippi Community Education Center. Favre would also get paid an additional $1.1 million for radio public service announcements promoting "family stability" by another nonprofit, the Family Resource Center. Favre would then donate that money to the university to help complete funding of the volleyball stadium.

"If you were to pay me, is there any way the media can find out where it came from and how much?" Favre texted Nancy after the plan was hatched.[1]

"No, we never have had that information publicized," New responded.

Five years later those very texts, and a whole bunch more, were publicized after they were included in court documents filed by the state of Mississippi seeking that $1.1 million, plus interest, back from Favre.

Favre quickly paid up, as did Ted "The Million Dollar Man" DiBiase who had been paid $722,299 to help underprivileged teens through his Heart of David Ministry.

The News, however, were not able to return the $4 million they allegedly embezzled from the nonprofits they ran, and Department of Human Services Director John Davis eventually pleaded guilty to state and federal fraud and conspiracy charges for the misuse of over $77 million in TANF funds.

HOW WELFARE REFORM FAILED

This is not what Congress intended when they passed welfare reform in 1996.

The old AFDC program had been a target of Republican ire for decades. In his famous 1964 speech endorsing Barry Goldwater for president, Ronald Reagan, who wouldn't become governor of California until three years later, recounted a story a state judge had recently shared with him.

"Not too long ago, a judge called me here in Los Angeles," Reagan said. "He told me of a young woman who'd come before him for a divorce. She had six children, was pregnant with her seventh. Under his questioning, she revealed her husband was a laborer earning 250 dollars a month. She wanted a divorce to get an 80 dollar raise. She's eligible for 330 dollars a month in the Aid to Dependent Children Program. She got the idea from two women in her neighborhood who'd already done that very thing."[2]

Welfare as an enemy of marriage would be a Republican theme for decades to come.

After Republicans won the House of Representatives for the first time in over forty years in 1994, President Bill Clinton saw an opportunity to tack towards the center just in time for his reelection campaign. Announcing "the end of welfare as we know it," Clinton signed the Personal Responsibility and Work Opportunity Reconciliation Act of 1996 and went on to cruise to reelection that same year.[3]

The 1996 welfare reform legislation had three basic goals: 1) replace welfare with work; 2) decrease the number of children born out of wedlock; and 3) promote marriage. By instituting a five-year time limit for receiving benefits and requiring recipients to meet weekly work, job training, or job searching goals, the 1996 welfare reform was a huge success on the first goal. Welfare caseloads were cut in half in just five years while child poverty fell too.

But the 1996 welfare reform bill completely failed on its other two goals. In fact, it has arguably made them worse. The number of children born out of wedlock has only risen since 1996, and the percentage of households headed by married couples continues to fall.

The failure of the 1996 welfare reform bill to raise marriage rates isn't that surprising when you take a closer look past what the legislation said it was trying to accomplish and examine what it actually did. While the findings of the bill pay lip service to marriage as "the foundation of a successful society," the policy in the legislation doesn't really do anything to help secure that foundation.

The bill did allow states to extend TANF eligibility to married couples, but it did not require them to do so, nor did it help them pay for such a reform. It also included a rule that for a married family to qualify for TANF, both parents had to meet the program's work requirements. This means that working families who wanted to have a traditional household where one parent worked and one did not, were prevented from doing so by law. In congressional testimony, Wisconsin Department of Children and Families Secretary Eloise Anderson testified that this rule created a "disincentive to marry or be in a stable family." She was right.[4]

University of Wisconsin researchers found that while the 1996 welfare reform law worked wonders at increasing single mother labor force participation, the wages of men with equal levels of education fell over the same time. As more single mothers with low education worked, and more men with low education saw their wages fall, more low education men became undesirable marriage partners.[5] Looking at Center for Disease Control and Prevention data on marriages and divorces between 1989 and 2000, the RAND Corporation confirmed that this "independence effect" led to the formation of fewer marriages after welfare reform became law.[6]

By prioritizing work over marriage, the 1996 welfare reform got a lot more single mothers into the workforce, but it also made it harder for them to get married.

Not all news out of the 1996 welfare reform's marriage promotion efforts has been bad. While less than one percent of all TANF spending has gone to programs supporting "two-parent family formation and maintenance," some states have used that small amount of money to establish real marriage education programs that didn't involve volleyball courts or professional wrestlers.

In 2006, HHS's Administration for Children and Families (ACF) contracted with the research firm Mathematica to evaluate a number of marriage education programs nationwide, including one in Oklahoma that was partially funded by TANF dollars.

The Oklahoma program taught relationship skills to low-income married and unmarried couples who were either expecting or recently had a baby. Couples could choose from a six-week program with weekly five-hour sessions, or a ten-week program with weekly three-hour sessions. Once enrolled in the program, participants were given weekly cash incentives to show up, participate, and finish the curriculum.

After fifteen months, Mathematica checked in with both program participants, and other couples that had been randomly assigned to a control group. Researchers found that program participants were more likely to still be in a romantic relationship than control group couples and reported higher levels of relationship happiness and fidelity than control group couples did.[7]

Program participants also reported greater levels of father involvement in the lives of their children. But while program participants reported more positive opinions of marriage, they were no more likely to be married than control group couples.

Mathematica visited program participants and control group couples again after thirty-six months and found whatever differences there had been between the two groups, had since disappeared. Like Head Start's early benefits, marriage education benefits also seem to fade. On the bright side, however, the children of program participants were slightly more likely to still be living with both parents than were the children of couples from the control group. But again, there was no difference in marriage rates.[8]

A later 2012 study of a different TANF funded marriage education program also showed some small initially positive results. This program served low-income married couples who either had children or were expecting. In addition to a yearlong curriculum on relationship skills, the program also offered support services to address program participation barriers and connect participating families with other government services they were eligible for.

Researchers found that a year after the program began, "the program group showed higher levels of marital happiness, lower levels of marital distress, greater warmth and support, more positive communication, and fewer negative behaviors and emotions in their interactions with their spouses."[9]

Two years after the program was over, researchers returned to the participating couples and control groups and found that those who participated in the program "had higher levels of marital happiness; lower levels of marital distress and infidelity; greater warmth, support, and positive communication; and fewer antagonistic and hostile behaviors with their spouses."[10]

At no point, however, did the researchers find that program participants were more likely to stay married than the control group.

Summarizing the available evidence, what little research we do have on marriage education is slightly positive. The programs do seem to improve the quality of some relationships and they can encourage fathers to stay with the mothers of their children. But they do not seem to increase the chances that a couple will get or stay married. This result is discouraging for those hoping that the decline in marriage can be solved through classroom instruction.

Is marriage dead then? Have we reached a point of no return for what was once the foundational building block of American society? Not if we look at what other countries have accomplished.

A NEW HOPE

When the Berlin Wall fell in 1989, Hungary had a high marriage rate compared to most other former communist countries. But as Hungary absorbed American culture, American sexual norms began to take root. Most importantly, cohabitation began to replace marriage. In just one decade the marriage rate in Hungary was cut in half, and fertility fell right along with it.

Hungary stayed at the bottom of European rankings for marriage and fertility until Viktor Orban's Fidesz party won control of parliament in 2010. That next year, Hungary adopted a new constitution that committed the government to "protect the institution of marriage" and established "the family as the basis of the nation's survival."[11]

Fidesz then began rolling out a number of pro-marriage policies including subsidized home loans for married couples with at least three children, student loan forgiveness for married couples, and subsidies for minivans.

Then in 2019, Fidesz added a new loan program available only for young newlyweds. Married couples could get a $35,000 loan with extremely low monthly payments. Then as the married couple had children, tranches of the loan balance would be erased for each child born. If the couple had three children and was still married after ten years, the entire loan would be forgiven.

Not only would $35,000 help a ton of working-class families achieve the financial stability they need to get and stay married here in the United States, but $35,000 goes a lot farther in Hungary than it does in the United States. An equivalent amount in this country, considering the average wages in each, would be about $130,000.

On marriage, these programs have been an immense success. The marriage rate in Hungary has soared 92 percent since 2010 and the nation went from ranking twenty-eighth among European nations in new marriages to number one today. As marriage has risen, births outside marriage have fallen from 48 percent in 2010 to 30 percent today. Divorce has also fallen by almost 40 percent.[12]

As marriage has recovered, fertility has begun to recover too, though not as dramatically. From a low of 1.25 children per woman in 2010, Hungary has upped that number to 1.6 today. If the next generation keeps pace with the progress of the current generation, Hungary can reach its goal of 2.1 births for every woman by 2030. Only two other European countries (Austria and Germany) have managed to raise their birthrates over the past decade.

There are also success stories closer to home.

Before the end of the draft in 1973, marriage was virtually unknown among enlisted soldiers. "If the Army wanted you to have a wife it would have issued you one," the saying went. But with an all-volunteer force, the military had to work to both attract young men and women to sign up and keep them in service. The Pentagon made a bet that making it easier for young soldiers to get and stay married would both attract people into the military and provide a stable foundation for service once there.

In addition to providing stable employment for high school graduates right as factory jobs were fading, the military not only provides housing subsidies to married couples (single soldiers have to sleep in the barracks), but they also give outright cash bonuses for marriages.

So, just as the Supreme Court was dismantling the American Family Consensus in the 1970s, the military was making itself family friendly. And it worked.

Where the percentage of enlisted men that were married was just 30 percent in the 1950s, today 60 percent of enlisted men are married, and the marriage rate for officers is an even higher 90 percent. United States service members aged eighteen to twenty-four are now twice as likely to be married as their civilian counterparts. After studying the military's success in "reinstitutionalizing" marriage, sociology professor Jennifer Lundquist noted that, "It is therefore striking to find a context like the U.S. military, in which marriage rates bear an anachronistic resemblance to those of the 1950s."[13]

Both Hungary and the U.S. military show that the right policies can change a culture that has abandoned marriage into a culture that embraces marriage. But it will not be easy.

First, we need to change the way we think about family issues. Too often marriage, if it is thought of at all, is considered just one issue among many. A legislator will have a position on crime, taxes, immigration, climate change, and sometimes marriage. Instead of being just one policy among many, marriage needs to become the guiding priority for all issues. Instead of asking what tax policy will cause the most economic growth, or which immigration policy will create the most jobs, we need to be asking, "Does our tax system make it harder or easier for Americans to get or stay married? What immigration policy is best for American families?" Currently, no legislator does this.

There are some office holders who are moving in the right direction though.

Senator Josh Hawley of Missouri proposed a parent tax credit that would offer working families (those with earned income higher than $7,540 a year) a $6,000 fully refundable tax credit for single parents and $12,000 credit for married parents. That is an explicit $6,000 bonus for married households. And since it is fully refundable, many lower-income parents with no net tax liabilities would receive a check from the government every month.

On the campaign trail, Senator J.D. Vance of Ohio proposed giving government loans to married couples that would be completely forgiven if the couple stayed together and had children, like Hungary. As President Donald Trump's Vice Presidential pick, Vance has since suggested raising the Child Tax Credit to $5,000. This would be available to all families, regardless of income, thus avoiding a marriage penalty.

Once we reorientate our priorities to what truly matters, building a stable environment for families to grow and thrive, marriage will bounce back.

TURNING MARRIAGE PENALTIES INTO MARRIAGE BONUSES

The biggest obstacle to family formation today is the $1 trillion that our federal and state governments spend every year punishing marriage. Every means tested safety net program today penalizes working class people who try to get married. This includes not only welfare (TANF), but also food stamps (known as the Supplemental Nutrition Assistance Program or SNAP), Head Start, the Women, Infants, and Children (WIC) program, Supplemental Security Income (SSI) program, Section 8 housing subsidies, the Earned Income Tax Credit (EITC), Medicaid, the Children's Health Insurance Program (CHIP), and the Affordable Care Act.

It is not a coincidence that the same working-class families that rely on these programs that punish marriage, are the same working-class families that are the least likely to get and stay married.

Reforming these programs so they no longer punish marriage will be difficult. Senator Mitt Romney of Utah introduced legislation in 2021 that, among other things, eliminated both TANF and the EITC in favor of a monthly cash benefit for every child, regardless of their parent's income. Parents would have received $4,200 a year for every child under six and $3,000 a year for every child between the ages of six and eighteen. No new money would have been spent under the plan, the new child benefit would have been paid for by what had been spent on TANF, the EITC, and the Child Tax Credit.

While the plan was greeted warmly by some Democrats, champions of the 1996 welfare reform law attacked the plan for eliminating the work requirements in the TANF program. They worried that without those work requirements, single mothers would be more likely to exit the labor force and stay home with their children.

But as the Niskanen Center's Samuel Hammond pointed out, when a similar child benefit was introduced in Canada, single mothers and married college educated women increased the number of hours worked every year. Married women without a college degree, however, were more likely to stay home. So yes, the end result of a child benefit would probably be less work outside the home, but the lost hours working would come almost entirely from married women who still have a working husband in the home.[14]

Is it really that bad if married non-college educated women with working husbands exit the labor force to personally care for their children if they are given a cash benefit for each child? Might that even be a good thing? As the Institute for Family Studies' Lyman Stone notes, "The reality is that if a person has to choose between driving an Uber or taking care of their four-year-old, society and that child is probably better off with a little more parent-child time and a little less time at work."[15]

For many working-class parents, a child benefit might even be cheaper than childcare subsidies. One working class mother told an Ohio focus group, "I did the math, and for my kids to go to the daycare they go to, if I didn't get help for four children to go every week, it's almost five grand a month to go... If I stay home and they don't have to help pay for childcare, then that would help the government itself."[16]

Is it really so crazy to suggest that the government should compensate parents for the care they provide their own children? Bringing a new child into the world and providing the care they need to become a self-sufficient adult is an extremely valuable benefit to society. But how valuable is it?

When the federal government performs a cost-benefit analysis for any new regulation (say for example forcing power plants to install new equipment that lowers the amount of air pollution they produce), it places a $10 million value on every life saved. So, if a new regulation would cost power plants $1 billion to implement, but would also save one thousand lives, the government would say that the cost is worthwhile.

Now paying every parent $10 million for every child they produce is a fiscal impossibility, but if we are going to reform how we spend the $1 trillion we spend on means tested programs every year, maybe we could find at least some room for paying parents for the very real work they do in raising the next generation.

As promising as Romney's plan was, however, it simply was not ambitious enough. "You get rid of TANF and you implement a child allowance, you still have the panoply of other safety net benefits each with their own marginal tax rates," the American Enterprise Institute's Scott Winship noted. "That doesn't change with a child allowance." Winship is right.[17]

We can't just eliminate marriage penalties in one or two programs and expect the culture around marriage to change for the families that are eligible for other benefits. We need to be sure to uproot the marriage penalties in all safety net programs too. That's a big lift. But it should be viewed as an opportunity, not a problem.

No one person purposefully designed our current social safety net. It is more like a many layered patchwork of programs, each with its own complicated set of eligibility requirements and delivery systems. But there is also a ton of money flowing through these programs. We could simplify them and streamline them into one or two benefit programs that not only don't penalize marriage, but instead incentivize it.

Maybe the end result of such a reform could look like Hungary's loan program, where couples are given the equivalent of a $130,000 loan at marriage and then that balance is forgiven for each child they have until it is completely eliminated after a third child. Or it may end up looking more like Romney's monthly cash benefit only larger and paid for by eliminating other means tested programs.

There are many possible solutions. And the details of those solutions absolutely do matter. But instead of making the elimination of child poverty the goal, or getting more mothers into the workforce, the goal should be to make it easier for more young people to get and stay married. That should be the guiding principle for all safety net programs as they are reformed.

MAKING MEN MARRIAGEABLE

Another safety net program that is undermining marriage, although not by creating marriage penalties, is the Social Security Disability Insurance program. First created in 1956, SSDI was originally only available to workers between the ages of fifty and sixty-five, but within the first ten years of the program that age was lowered to thirty.

To qualify for benefits, an SSDI applicant must have worked at least three months every year after turning twenty-one, and they need an assessment from a doctor that they are "unable to do [their] past relevant work or any other substantial gainful work that exists in the national economy." Benefits levels are tied to how much an applicant earned before they were injured, with a maximum payment of $3,600 and an average payment of about $1,400.

SSDI was a relatively unknown program until a flood of people applied for and received benefits from the program during the recession of 1974. Congress responded by requiring the Social Security Administration to review more eligibility decisions, lowering benefit levels, and requiring beneficiaries to reapply every three years.

The reforms succeeded in lowering the SSDI rolls for about a decade, but after a series of sensational news stories about sympathetic people denied benefits, Congress undid those reforms in 1984. Since then the number of beneficiaries has skyrocketed, including some rural counties where one in four adults are on SSDI. Overall, 5 percent of working age adults, mostly men, are on the program.

SSDI is not the only reason nearly 9 million working age men are not in the labor force today, but it is a big part of the problem. Program beneficiaries are limited in the number of hours they can work in a week, functionally trapping them in idle poverty.[18]

It is far past time for Congress to revisit SSDI reform. They were able to lower SSDI roles before and they can do it again. Doctors should not be allowed to make a living giving the green light to SSDI patients and the SSA needs the mandate and resources to review more cases. Beneficiaries with ailments that have a chance of improving should also have to reapply for benefits every three years. Many of these men would be working if the government wasn't paying them not to.

Increasing male employment in particular is important for reviving the institution of marriage. One seemingly odd confirmation of this comes from studies of lottery winners. There is no better way to study what a sudden increase in wealth means for one's marriage prospects than a lottery. And what researchers have found, both in the United States and in Europe, is that when men win the lottery they are more likely to get married and have children, but when women win the lottery they are no more likely to get married and, in fact, they are more likely to get divorced.[19]

This result is not due to the fact that men love family and women don't. Both men and women value family highly. It does have to do with the different qualities men and women are looking for in a potential mate. Men want a woman who is loving and kind and physically attractive. They generally do not care how wealthy she is or how much money she makes. Accordingly, when a woman wins the lottery her relative mate value doesn't change. But women generally do value how many resources a man can command. The higher a man's income is, the more likely he is to be married. So, when a man wins the lottery, he does suddenly become a lot more desirable to many women.

As for the increase of divorce when women win the lottery, those divorces are mostly concentrated among low-income women and women married to older men. Researchers speculate that those women most likely chose their pre-lottery husbands for economic reasons, and once their financial situation changed, they thought they could find a new man with other desirable traits.

If our goal is to increase marriage, then we should be looking for opportunities to raise male wages. And there are many things the federal government can do that would raise men's wages without harming the wages of women. One easy way to raise male wages is to make America a country that builds things again.

In 1900, it took the city of New York just four and a half years to build a twenty-eight-station subway system. Fast forward to the year 2000 and the three-station Second Avenue subway expansion took seventeen years to build.

In California between 1950 and 1970, the state managed to build enough dams and levees to store twenty million acres feet of water. In the fifty years since, despite multiple droughts and a doubling of the population, the state has only added another seven million acres feet of storage. Left in its natural state, without any aqueducts bringing water from other rivers lakes, the Los Angeles River watershed only supported around five hundred thousand people. Today, thanks to dams and aqueducts, it supports ten million. California's continued growth depends on water, but they just stopped building new water storage.

And across the country, between 1956 and 1992, the federal government built almost fifty thousand miles of new roads for the interstate highway system. But where once highway construction was affordable and easy to build, now spending per mile of construction has increased threefold since the 1960s.[20]

If we could just build more things, subways, dams, roads, power plants, transmission lines, and so forth, we could create hundreds of thousands of good high paying construction jobs, jobs that would go mostly to men because of their physically demanding nature.

Why did our nation stop building things? What happened around 1970 that suddenly made construction so difficult?

NEPA is what happened.

The same year Earth Day was created, 1970, the National Environmental Policy Act became law. On its face NEPA sounds like a reasonable policy: Any action by the federal government that could have a significant environmental impact should first undergo an environmental assessment. That assessment must identify all environmental harms caused by the project and discuss reasonable alternatives that would have a smaller impact on the environment.

Making federal agencies assess the environmental harm caused by their actions and consider reasonable alternatives, sounds nice, but Congress put some real teeth into how NEPA was enforced. NEPA included a citizen suit provision that empowered any American to sue in federal court and block a government project.

No one really knew just how powerful NEPA was until 1973 when a University of Tennessee biology professor successfully used the law to block construction of the Tellico Dam which was funded by the Tennessee Valley Authority. Turns out the Little Tennessee River was home to something called a "snail darter" and the TVA never analyzed how the dam would impact the habitat of that particular species of fish.

The case went all the way to the Supreme Court before the snail darter finally won…temporarily.[21] It took a special act of Congress to exempt the Tellico Dam from NEPA to get the project finished.

Now, Congress can't take the time to exempt every infrastructure project from NEPA—and the costs of compliance are steep. The average NEPA environmental impact statement takes four and a half years to complete and runs 575 pages.[22] If an environmental group finds even one thing wrong with the statement, it can send the entire project back to the drawing board.

Fortunately, NEPA isn't written in stone. Instead of ignoring the law for specific projects, Congress should just reform the law itself. We could narrow who is allowed to sue under the law, forcing plaintiffs to show that they personally would be harmed if a construction project went forward. We could shorten the time plaintiffs are allowed to sue. And we could require federal agencies to complete all environmental assessments in a matter of months, not years.

Federal agencies would still be required to study the environmental impacts of their actions, but they would have to do it quickly and environmental activists would be limited in their power to drag the process out.

Projects would be completed faster. The cost of projects would go down. More projects would get funded. More construction jobs would be created. More families would get started. It's a win win.

In addition to making it harder to build things here in the United States, leaders in both parties have made it easier for wealthy Americans to invest overseas. The result has been a disastrous hollowing out of our nation's manufacturing jobs and expertise.

Before the United States approved of China's admittance to the World Trade Organization, we were the largest trading partner of 152 countries in the world. Now more than twenty years later, we are the largest trading partner of just fifty-seven nations, while China enjoys that honor with 128 countries.

In just the first ten years after China joined the WTO, we lost one million manufacturing jobs, about a third of the entire sector. MIT economist David Autor estimates that these manufacturing job losses led to the loss of an additional one million jobs in other sectors, bringing the total job loss from China's ascent into the WTO to 2.4 million.[23] Other studies have found that in domestic labor-intensive industries, trade with developing nations has depressed non-college educated worker wages by as much as 5.5 percent.[24]

Entire communities were decimated by China's entrance into the WTO, especially in the Midwest, South Atlantic, and Deep South, the very regions that have seen a steep rise in the SSDI claims mentioned previously.

This is not what was supposed to happen. "China will compete for some low-wage jobs with Americans," Nobel laureate Robert Solow said during the debate over whether to approve China's entrance into the WTO. "And their market will provide jobs for higher wage, more skilled people. And that's a bargain for us."[25]

But those higher wage jobs never materialized. At least not in large enough numbers to offset what was lost in the manufacturing sector. Business investment ended up falling to the lowest share of GDP on record.[26] Productivity declined. Our economy lost the industrial base capacity to make products, like computer chips and airplanes, in industries we once dominated. The economy has created more jobs that require a college degree, but only at half the pace that our higher education system pumped out new graduates.[27]

The problem is not that capitalism suddenly stopped working in the year 2000. The problem is that globalization undermines the fundamental assumptions that make capitalism work.

In theory, if a factory is not competitive an investor will move their capital from that project to another project where workers are being more productive. This works great when investors can only move their money within their own country. A factory in Toledo might fail but a more productive factory in Akron will soak up investment and more productive jobs will be created here in the United States. Affected workers can even move from Toledo to Akron.[28]

But what if instead of an investor taking their money out of Toledo and putting it into Akron, they put it into Beijing? Then how does that help American workers? In theory, as long as the capitalists in Beijing use that investment to make their workers more productive, then their workers will then have more buying power to spend on goods that American workers still produce here.

But what if a country takes actions to depress their workers' wages, as China has done since 2000? What if a country chooses to debase its currency so that its exports are more attractive to Americans, but American imports are more expensive for Chinese workers?

Suddenly this is not a good deal for American workers. Sure, the wealthy investor class becomes richer as their investments in China pay off, but American workers get nothing. No one is investing in their capacity to become more productive and compete with Chinese firms. The result is fewer jobs and lower wages for American workers, especially for men in the manufacturing sector, which leads to fewer marriages and more failed communities.

It doesn't have to be this way. We don't have to make it so easy for wealthy Americans to invest overseas, especially in China. We spend so much leverage in trade negotiations protecting American investors overseas when we shouldn't be protecting them at all. If a foreign government or actor takes an unfair chunk of an overseas investment, too bad, you should have invested that money here at home.

The United States does not have a bilateral investment treaty with China, and it should stay that way. But more should be done to disentangle ourselves from what has been a one-sided relationship with China's authoritarian regime. Congress should prohibit both People's Republic of China ownership of American assets (like farmland and factories) and American investment in PRC-controlled firms. We should also revoke China's most-favored-nation trading status and impose tariffs to break up Chinese supply chains into the American market.

Really, we should rethink giving automatic trade preferences to any developing nation with weaker labor and environmental protections than our own. American workers shouldn't have to compete on an unlevel playing field that favors workers from other countries with lower regulatory burdens than ours.

Free market ideologues may cry "protectionism," but the end result of tariffs (higher costs for consumers, but more profits for domestic manufactures) are no different than any of the other tactics other nations use to boost their exports (such as suppressing wages or deflating currency). We simply have to decide what is more important to us: that global corporations and the overwhelmingly wealthy class that owns their stock get higher returns on their investments, or that American workers get higher wages so it is easier for them to start and maintain families?

Trade isn't the only aspect of globalization that is lowering wages for American workers. As University of Minnesota history professor Steven Ruggles notes in his history of the American family, the "golden age of wage labor" for young men just happened to coincide with the lowest percentage of foreign-born workers in the American economy.[29] With fewer foreign laborers in the labor pool, employers were forced to raise wages.

That all changed with the Immigration and Nationality Act of 1965, which made it much easier for low-skilled immigrants to legally enter the country. As a direct result, our nation now has a higher percentage of foreign-born workers in the nation today than ever before. And the American worker has suffered accordingly.

Free market ideologues have a just-too-perfect story on immigration just as they do on trade. In theory, low-skilled immigrants make it easier for high-skill natives to be more productive and earn more money. For example, a dual-earning college graduate couple may have more time to invest in their careers as doctors and lawyers if they can pay immigrants lower wages to clean their house and mow their lawn. New jobs have been created, our most skilled workers can now work more hours, our gross domestic product has gone up, everyone is supposedly better off.

Well not everyone. The wages of native workers' go down if their skill sets are similar to those of immigrants'. According to Harvard University economist George Borjas, a 10 percent increase in the number of workers with a particular set of skills lowers the wages of native workers with those same skills by about 3 percent.[30]

This means that for someone who did not graduate from high school and earns about $25,000 a year, their annual income has dropped by about $1,500 a year as the size of the low-skilled workforce has grown by roughly 25 percent over the last two decades.

You can see the impact of low skill immigration on native worker wages in real time. Often when a factory is raided by immigration officials, it can lose up to 75 percent of its workforce in a single day. And then those factories (often food processing plants) are forced to replace their employees with native workers—and every time those companies are forced to court native workers by offering them higher wages.

In 2006, for example, thirteen hundred illegal immigrants were arrested at six meat processing plants across the Midwest and plains states (including Colorado, Iowa, Minnesota, Nebraska, Texas, and Utah). All six facilities resumed production on the same day of the raids and full production was resumed within five months. Except, in order to fill all those jobs so quickly, the company had to raise wages for all workers by almost 10 percent.[31]

Having a ready supply of cheap foreign labor is, of course, a boon to big business. Borjas estimates that on aggregate employers enjoy $50 billion in higher profits every year thanks to the lower wages they are able to pay thanks to high levels of immigration.[32]

Higher levels of immigration also make it harder for displaced native workers to find new jobs. Immigrants often settle in areas with high demand for labor, which decreases the rewards native workers would reap from moving to that city from a community that may not be thriving. Research shows that much of the decreased mobility among American workers over the last twenty years is due to the decreased benefits of moving from one struggling city to a growing one, thanks to higher levels of immigration.[33]

Just like with trade, we have the ability to control immigration levels in this country. If we could muster the political will, we could regain control of our borders and only let in a set number of high-skill immigrants every year. By decreasing the numbers of low-skilled immigrants we can increase the wages of working-class Americans and make it easier for them to start and maintain successful families.

Our country also must do a much better job of developing the skills of those born here. Combined, federal, state, and local governments spend about $200 billion a year subsidizing higher education with most of that money going towards helping adults earn college degrees. As a result of this spending, more Americans now have a college degree than at any point in American history.

The problem is that the economy is not creating jobs that require a college degree as fast as colleges are producing graduates. Since 2000, over 22 million workers with a college degree entered the labor force but only 10 million jobs requiring a college degree were created.[34]

Those that do graduate are often forced to do so with mounting levels of debt. Between 1992 and 2018 the average sticker price at four-year public schools more than doubled. Some of these increased costs stem from the explosion in new administrative positions like Diversity Equity and Inclusion officers. Since 2008, colleges have employed more administrators than actual in-classroom faculty. Some institutions like Yale and Stanford have more administrators than students.

Another cause of rising tuition appears to be the increasing generosity of federal loans. Many studies have been done looking at the relationship between the rise in student loan benefits and rising tuition, with some papers finding that colleges, particularly the most selective colleges, are able to raise tuition by sixty cents for every one dollar increase in student loan aid.

Whatever the cause of rising college prices, the resulting increase in the number of Americans with college debt and the size of that debt is undeniable. In 2005, just 30 percent of twenty-two-year-olds had student loan debt and the average balance was $13,000. By 2014, the percentage of twenty-two-year-olds with student loan deb had risen 45 percent while the average balance rose to $16,000.[35]

Considering that student loan debt burdens are the highest at the same time that adults are looking to start families, it is not surprising that rising student debt levels have been shown to decrease the likelihood adults will get married. One recent study found that for each additional $5,000 in student debt, a debtor is 8 percent less likely to be married.[36]

Instead of pumping more money into an already bloated higher education system that is turning out more college graduates than our economy needs, we need to shift that money to other options, like high-quality vocational training.

Governors and mayors should be working harder at connecting high schools with regional employers that could provide workplace training to students who have no intention of going to college. Governors should be given the power to accredit these programs, so they are eligible for the higher education aid we already spend today.

Existing four-year college institutions should also be forced to take some accountability for the students they are charging so much tuition to educate. In addition to students being on the hook for student loans, colleges should be on the hook too; not for a full amount of a student's payments, but maybe like 10 percent. This would incentivize colleges to do a better job keeping a lid on rising tuition while making sure their graduates are gainfully employed so they can repay their loans.

What we should absolutely not do is what President Joe Biden has done which is to give tens of thousands of borrowers blanket loan forgiveness. This policy only encourages bloated schools to raise tuition even higher without creating any new incentives to lower costs or make sure they are properly preparing graduates for the job market.

It also largely benefits the wealthiest students who took out the largest loans for advanced degrees in law and medicine. Doctors and lawyers are doing just fine in this economy, they do not need an additional taxpayer handout, especially when we are doing so little to help non-college graduates the training they need to improve their skills.

We also need to do more to stop young men from making bad choices. As discussed in Chapter Five, the ubiquity of online pornography has led some men to substitute the immensely rewarding but difficult job of building a relationship with a real woman, with the ease of instant online gratification. Other men that still have the drive to seek the company of real women, have also been polluted by porn into thinking that their partners want to, or expect to be choked. The result is a generation of young women who are rightly afraid of physical intimacy with the porn addled brains of today's young men.

We could start to address the problem by requiring age verification for all pornographic sites as many Republican states have already done. But while that would be a good first step, it is not nearly enough. The Department of Justice needs to make a renewed commitment to bringing obscenity cases against pornographers, particularly the most hardcore pornographers that depict violence against women like choking and slapping. Today's Supreme Court is far more conservative than the Burger Court, and the damages from pornography, which has become far more ubiquitous, are harder to deny. It may be time for the Court to revisit its holding in *Miller*.

On the other hand, it may be too soon to ask the Supreme Court to revisit its 2018 *Murphy v. National Collegiate Athletic Association*, which allowed states to legalize online sports betting, but the early evidence is that the expansion of online betting his been an epic disaster economically, especially for young men. One study found that in those states that have legalized online betting, bankruptcies are up 30 percent and households are now more likely to be delinquent on auto loans and credit cards. The study also found that it was young men in low-income counties that were hardest hit.[37]

If we want to maximize the number of marriageable men available to women, something is going to have to be done about online gambling. It may be difficult to ban it in states that have already legalized it, but Congress can at least ban advertising for the product as they have done for cigarettes and other tobacco products.

AFFORDABLE FAMILY FORMATION

Even if we do manage to raise wages by reforming NEPA, rebalancing trade, restricting low-skilled immigration, and improving people's skills, that won't help much if we don't make it easier for young couples to afford a home and start a family in. Since 2000, home prices have more than doubled nationally, with those cities with the highest job growth also featuring the fastest growth in home prices.

Multiple studies show that higher housing costs in a city correspond with lower marriage rates.[38] This is completely understandable. Young couples need a private space they can make their own to start a life together.

You can see this in the average age of first marriage throughout U.S. history. Whenever it has been easier for young couples to afford their own home, the average age of marriage has fallen. When it is difficult to afford a home, the average age of first marriage rises.[39]

Existing policies designed to make housing affordable simply don't work. The home mortgage deduction mostly benefits older wealthier couples who use their subsidies to add on to their existing homes. It does nothing to help a young couple afford their first home.

What we need to do is make it easier for developers to build more new homes and in the case of home construction, environmental regulations like NEPA aren't always the main problem. Local zoning rules are often to blame, rules that restrict where housing can be placed and what types of housing can be built. These rules are often so strict that most cities couldn't be built today if they had to meet the current zoning requirements when they were first constructed. It is estimated that 40 percent of the buildings in New York City today would not be approved today if they were proposed as currently built.[40]

In most localities the main zoning requirement driving home prices higher is the minimum lot size. Does a town want one lot to fit five families into five row homes or one family living in one big house? A lot of times local governments will try to raise home values and keep lower-income people out of their communities by setting minimum lot sizes so high that only wealthy families could afford to build there.

Localities will often purposefully limit how many square feet apartments are allowed to have with the express purpose of limiting the number of families with children that live there. Some cities will zone entire buildings or neighborhoods as restricted to "the elderly" thus making it impossible for a young family with children to buy a house there at all. Minimum parking requirements and regulations forbidding day care centers are also ways localities purposely try to price out young families.

The federal government shouldn't dictate what types of housing should be built where, but it still does have plenty of leverage over state governments through the billions it sends them every year through the Community Development Block Grant and HOME Block Grant programs. Some cities like Houston, Texas, have done a remarkable job making it easy for developers to build housing, with thousands of new units coming on the market every year. Other cities like San Jose, California, haven't added any new net housing in fifty years.

The federal government doesn't have to micromanage every locality's zoning regime, it could just allocate federal dollars to those states that add the most units. If Texas is responsible for building 20 percent of all new housing in a given year, they should get 20 percent of all federal housing dollars. If California built no new net housing last year, they should get nothing. Studies show it doesn't matter what type of housing gets built, as long as new units are being added, whether they are luxury units or "affordable" units, as long as new units are added, the price of housing will go down. We just need to get developers building.

Another cost that has risen sharply for families in recent decades is childcare, which has tripled in price since 1990. Again, the blame largely falls on increased regulation.

The main driver of rising childcare costs (in addition to regulations on fire safety, CPR requirements, and square footage) is child-to-staff ratios. These vary by state, and by age, with younger children requiring a lower staff ratio and those states that have the lowest child-to-staff ratios also having the highest childcare prices.

One study found that raising those child-to-staff ratios by just one child across all age groups would lower childcare costs by up to 20 percent.[41]

Another factor driving up childcare costs is education requirements for day care providers. The more education a state requires, the higher the price of childcare in that state. Requiring lead teachers to have at least a high school diploma raises childcare costs between twenty-five and 50 percent.[42]

Instead of reducing regulations and bringing the cost of childcare down, some want to go in the other direction. The District of Columbia, which already has the nation's highest childcare prices, recently passed a new regulation that requires all childcare providers to have at least a two year's associate's degree. And the Biden administration wants to require that day care providers nationwide get paid as much as kindergarten teachers do. That would nearly double the average pay of the country's day care providers. Such a new regulation would almost certainly double the price of day care nationwide too.

Parents need more flexibility when finding day care solutions for their family not less. They don't need the state or the federal government snooping into their homes and regulating their caregiving solutions. In addition to state governments deregulating their childcare sectors, the federal government should exempt all money paid for childcare services from the federal unemployment tax. If a family wants to pay a neighborhood high school or college kid to look after the children for a couple of hours every afternoon, or one or two days a week, they shouldn't have to involve the Internal Revenue Service in the transaction. If one mother in the neighborhood wants to take in three or four others' children each day, let her do that—and let the other mothers pay her. Let's not make a federal case out of it.

In addition to making housing and childcare more affordable, we also need to make work itself more family friendly. One of the main ways firms in the retail, food, and hospitality industries have increased productivity over the last two decades is through just-in-time scheduling. By only calling in employees when they are absolutely needed, firms can lower labor costs by not having employees standing around waiting while business is slow. In the leisure and hospitality industries, most workers receive their work schedules with just a week's notice.[43]

This makes planning for family events like weddings, vacations, and graduations impossible. In one focus group of working-class parents in Ohio, legislation requiring employers to give their employees their work schedules at least two weeks in advance was the most widely accepted policy in the group. One particularly conservative factory worker in the group, someone who would have been against paid parental leave and childcare subsidies because of the higher taxes they would require, thought the two-week schedule requirement was a no-brainer.

"I think there's no debate on this one," he said. "I don't think there's a problem with it." Another participant added, "I think in the end it makes bigger companies show courtesy to their employees."[44]

Mothers looking to achieve work-life balance through part-time work would particularly benefit from such a policy change. The Bureau of Labor and Statistics has found that mothers in part-time jobs predominately work in industries less likely to have advanced schedule notice.[45] Requiring all businesses to provide their workers this courtesy, a courtesy that was common just a generation ago, would make it easier for married mothers to reenter and stay attached to the work force.

Big business should be forced to show their employees a little more courtesy. Especially if it means they can better care for their families.

RECHANNELING SEX THROUGH MARRIAGE

Undoing the welfare penalties in our social safety net would go a long way to undoing the damage done by Justice Brennan and the Burger Court in dismantling the state's power to channel sex through marriage. Adding a marriage bonus would help even more.

Some might want to go even further, reversing some of the legal pillars of the assault on monogamy like *Eisenstadt v. Baird* and *King v. Smith.* These are unnecessarily fraught tasks.

The political constituency for limiting birth control to married couples is extremely small. Few people want to deny illegitimate children the same rights and benefits as legitimate children. Fifty years ago, couples overwhelmingly waited until marriage before moving in together. That is no longer the case today. Most (70 percent) married couples cohabitated before they tied the knot.

Not only is cohabitation the most commonly observed behavior among married couples today, but it is also the preferred sequence for the vast majority of women. Asked to put a series of relationship milestones in their preferred order, this is how most women envision their romantic life playing out: 1) partner meets family; 2) couple has sex; 3) couple moves in together; 4) couple gets married; 5) couple buys a house; and then finally 6) couple has a child.[46]

A full two-thirds of women say they want to cohabitate before they get married, and 60 percent say they want sex before marriage. Nothing against those who do wait till their wedding day, but that custom really does seem to be a relic of the past.

That most women want sex before marriage does not mean they are out looking for casual hookups. The median number of lovers of a woman's lifetime is still just three (compared to five for men). And when we look at which women are most likely to still be married by age forty, an ideal number of lovers before marriage does emerge, and that number is not zero. Also, as we covered earlier, once a woman goes past one extra partner besides her husband, the odds of her first marriage ending in divorce go up with each new man she sleeps with before marriage.[47]

The best path to a stable marriage appears to include premarital sex, but only with someone who you think could be a good marriage partner. It also appears to help couples when purposefully choose cohabitation as a conscious step towards marriage, instead of something they slide into because it's convenient.

One study of over one thousand unmarried Americans between the ages of eighteen and thirty-four circled back five years later and found 418 of those individuals were married. Researchers then asked respondents a series of questions about their relationship, including whether or not they "slid" into cohabitation, or made a deliberate decision to do so to advance the relationship. The more strongly respondents categorized the move to cohabitation as a decision rather than a slide, based on a five-point scale, the more likely they were to report a happy marriage.[48]

With 70 percent of married couples cohabiting before marriage, this too is a bridge we can't uncross. We can encourage couples, however, to be more deliberate in their relationship choices and to communicate to their partners where they hope cohabitation is going.

What we should not do is try and legitimize cohabitation into a quasi-marriage status. Part of the reason marriage works is that it involves a public acknowledgment that something is fundamentally changing in the relationship. There is a clear meeting of the minds between two parties. A deep and new commitment is being made, one the rest of the community can be deputized into supporting—through social norms. If we were to extend marriage rights and protections to cohabitations, marriage would lose its power as a shared public signal of enduring commitment.

There is also much we can do to keep existing marriages intact. As it is today, our divorce system incentivizes only one outcome: messy, drawn-out divorces that end in huge payouts for divorce lawyers. Divorce law, as it is established today, is designed to benefit only one class of people: divorce lawyers. Families that might benefit from staying together don't have anything, or anyone, pushing them in that direction.

States that wanted to help keep more families together could combine a one-year waiting period for parents seeking a divorce with mandatory education on the negative impacts divorce has on children. Most states already require divorcing parents to take a brief course on how to manage being a divorced parent, these pro-marriage education courses could easily be added on the existing systems.

These waiting periods would, of course, not apply to cases where physical abuse was alleged. States could also allow judges to consider which party is suing for divorce when making final custody, child support, alimony, and property division decisions. If the party being sued for divorce has not engaged in any grievous behavior, like abandonment or verbal abuse, then that should factor against the party suing for divorce. Such an incentive structure would encourage those seeking an easy way out of a low-conflict marriage to reconcile with their spouse.

Not only would the end of no-fault divorce for low-conflict marriages save a lot of salvageable relationships, but as we covered earlier, when single men know that the divorce bond cannot be so easily cast off, they invest more in making themselves marriage material, which would also mean more marriages overall.

THE CABBAGE FIELD TEST

Inveighing against the revolutionaries of his time who, like Marx and Engels, were questioning the need for family, the British Catholic reactionary G.K. Chesterton wrote, "An honest man falls in love with an honest woman; he wishes, therefore, to marry her, to be the father of her children, to secure her and himself. All systems of government should be tested by whether he can do this."

"If any system, feudal, servile, or barbaric, does, in fact, give him so large a cabbage-field that he can do it, there is the essence of liberty and justice," Chesterton continued. "If any system, Republican, mercantile, or Eugenist, does, in fact, give him so small a salary that he can't do it, there is the essence of eternal tyranny and shame."

The United States is failing the cabbage field test. Too many honest men are no longer able to secure a salary large enough to attract a woman, marry her, and start a family. Over half of all households in this country have no married couple in them. Men and women are marrying later, if at all, and when they do, they are not having enough children to make sure their values survive into the next generation.

As a nation, we have lost sight of what should be most important in life: family. But hope is not lost. Politics can change a culture. We can reorientate our policies so that they are once again centered on family. We can make marriage great again.

CONCLUSION

REFLECTIONS ON THE REVOLUTION IN FAMILY FORMATION

IN 1789, SOON AFTER THE Storming of the Bastille, a French aristocrat sent a letter to an Irish-born member of the United Kingdom's House of Commons, asking for his opinion on the French Revolution.

Edmund Burke, who had already earned a reputation as both a supporter of independence in the American colonies, and as an opponent of slavery, wrote back a scathing letter which not only predicted the coming Reign of Terror which would see the murder of tens of thousands, but also the rise of a "popular general" who would become "master of your assembly, the master of your whole republic."[1]

Burke was not able to identify Napoleon by name, but he described the tyranny that would be needed to bring order to France after the manner in which the *Ancien Regime* had been dispatched. "Rage and phrenzy will pull down more in half an hour, than prudence, deliberation, and foresight can build up in a hundred years," Burke wrote.

Not that Burke was an apologist for the French crown. He was well aware of France's problems before the revolution, as well as of the inequities of his own nation's rule. "A state without the means of some change, is without the means of its own conservation," Burke wrote.

The question is then how to change a state of affairs, without destroying all that is good within it. "It is with infinite caution that any man ought to venture upon pulling down an edifice which has answered in any tolerable degree for ages the common purposes of society, or on building it up again," Burke said.

The laws and customs of marriage that served our common purposes for hundreds of years have been torn down without any caution. But that does not mean we should rebuild the old structure just as it was before. In 1776, wives could own no property, keep no wages, and had no recourse for physical or sexual abuse from their husbands. No good will come from going back to that regime.

Women have made tremendous gains in the workplace, and to the extent they truly want to spend time working for wages, that is a good thing. Women are proving to be remarkably successful in our increasingly information and service-based economy and it would be a huge loss if their talents were restricted.

But not all women seek fulfillment in the workplace, and even those that do, don't necessarily want work outside the home to be a full-time job.

Surveys show that only 23 percent of married mothers with a child under the age of eighteen say they want to work full-time. The vast majority of married mothers, 76 percent, would prefer to either work part-time (53 percent) or not at all (23 percent). Even among unmarried mothers with children most (51 percent), would prefer to work either part-time (36 percent) or not at all (15 percent), compared to 49 percent that want full-time work.[2] And it is not just mothers with low skill careers who choose not to work full-time. The proportion of women who do not work outside the home is U-shaped as you move up the income scale.

For families where a husband earns less than $25,000 a year, 35 percent of mothers don't work outside the home. But for husband's making $70,000, just 25 percent of mothers don't work outside the home. But when you move further up the scale to husband's making more than $250,000 a year, the percentage of mothers who don't work outside the home bounces back up to 45 percent. And the women choosing to stay home, especially at the higher income levels, are highly educated. Among husbands who make $70,000 a year, 20 percent of their wives with college degrees don't work outside the home. But for husbands who make more than $250,000, even among women with a college degree, 52 percent of mothers choose not to work outside the home.[3]

If anything, our current public policies are forcing mothers to work when they don't want to. While just 32 percent of all mothers say they want to work full-time, 57 percent do. And while most married mothers say their ideal would be to work part-time (53 percent), just 15 percent of married mothers manage to meet that goal.[4]

If our objective is to help mothers achieve the work-life balance they want, then we should be making it easier for women to work part-time instead of advocating for policies like government run day care and pre-K that push them into the workplace full-time.

Making sure women have the opportunity to succeed professionally has been a positive change over the last seventy years. We should conserve it. But pushing them into the workplace when they would rather devote time to their families, all in the name of gender equity, is not helpful. Especially when it comes at the cost of stable family formation.

It was clear to the founders of our nation, as well as foreign observers like Alexis de Tocqueville, that the married, monogamous, nuclear family was the foundational unit of American society. It was the secret to our success.

To quote the second President of the United States, John Adams, again, "The foundations of national morality must be laid in private families. In vain are schools, academies, and universities instituted if loose principles and licentious habits are impressed upon children in their earliest years."

This does not mean single mothers are morally inferior in any way. Fathers die. Husbands can be abusive. Every society, including ours at the founding, has divorce. Single motherhood happens. And we should do all we can to help them.

But one of the best ways we can help single mothers raise their children, is to make sure they are surrounded by married households. Children need to see the nuclear family at work. Boys especially need positive male role models that play productive, cooperative, gentle, and loving roles in the lives of wives and children.

By ignoring the positive role married fathers play in children's lives, by creating a social safety net that actively punishes mothers who want to have a married father in the home, we have created whole communities where married fathers are virtually extinct.

By tearing down the legal framework that channeled human sexual desire through the institution of marriage, and by telling people they were free to find sexual fulfillment however they desired, we have unleashed a "rage and phrenzy" that is empowering the worst demagogues among us, just as it did in revolutionary France.

Without the stability and cooperation of married families, too many single parent and cohabitating families are falling behind financially while their married counterparts pull ahead.

Without positive role models in the home, too many young boys are growing up directionless, uninspired, and often violent. This is not only contributing to higher crime in some neighborhoods, but it is also creating an intergenerational feedback loop of unmarriageable men that has made upward social mobility unattainable for many communities.

Without husbands and sons to sympathize with, many women are turning away from family and towards politics as their primary source of identity and fulfillment. This is leading to an increasingly polarized political environment where compromise is impossible, and the worst actors are encouraged to prioritize their own fame over finding real policy solutions.

And as more men and women fail to find mates that share their worldview, fewer children are born, fueling a demographic decline that only increases isolation, makes our society older and less dynamic, and hinders economic growth.

The path towards a further decline in monogamous marriage is a dark one. More polarization, more inequality, and more violence. If you thought the January 6 and the Black Lives Matter riots were bad, an America with less marriage will only have worse unrest.

As astonishingly diverse as the global human population is today, we all share one thing in common: We all come from an unbroken chain of ancestors who successfully passed their genes from one generation to the next.

Human nature has been argued about for centuries, but at the end of the day our thoughts, feelings, emotions, and actions all emanate from just one source: the innate drive of the genes within us to continue that unbroken chain.

Marriage is a cultural norm, a norm that as this book has shown has shifted throughout time. At first, we were mostly monogamous, then mostly polygamous, then monogamous again, and now we may be slipping out of monogamy once more.

At all times however, whatever marriage norms existed, they all had one thing in common: marriage is always and everywhere about managing who is allowed to have sex with whom. Or to put it another way, who is allowed to pass their genes into the next generation.

When we combine these conclusions, when we realize that human behavior is driven by the innate drive of our genes to pass themselves into the next generation, and that marriage is the governing cultural norm about who gets to pass their genes into the next generation, what institution could possibly be more important to the future of humanity than marriage?

How can we call ourselves a democracy when we are not giving all our citizens an equal shot at forming a family and contributing to the future of humanity? As the assault on marriage continues, it is the least fortunate among us that are being prevented from enjoying a stable family life.

The question we have to ask ourselves is whether we want this growing inequality to continue, or whether we want to do everything we can to restore monogamous marriage norms, strong families, and stable communities, for everyone.

"What is liberty without wisdom and without virtue?" Burke asked before France tore itself apart in murderous rage. "It is the greatest of all possible evils; for it is folly, vice, and madness, without tuition or restraint."

Sexual desire is such a powerful force, it was folly to ever believe we could tear down the old rules for channeling its energy without building anything new to replace them. Marriage and family don't have to be luxury goods for the wealthy. An America where more people are married is an America where more people have children and feel connected to our nation's past and future. The path to a more perfect national union goes through more monogamous unions for its citizens.

ENDNOTES

Introduction

1 Tucker Carlson, "The Andrew Tate interview," X: Ep. 9, July 11, 2023 https://twitter.com/TuckerCarlson/status/1678873144201818115
2 "Andrew Tate x Nelk Boys," July 28, 2022, Ep. 52, *Full Send*, Podcast https://open.spotify.com/episode/7zTZba9JE0wTuucxizRzI2.
3 Marlene Dixon, "*Why Women's Liberation?*" (Chicago: Chicago Women's Liberation Union, 1963).
4 Betty Friedan, *It Changed My Life: Writings on the Women's Movement* (Cambridge: Harvard University Press, 1963).
5 Antoinette Radford, "Who Is Andrew Tate?," BBC News (2023).
6 Tate x Nelk Boys, *Full Send*, podcast, July 28,2022.
7 Dan Savage, "Why Monogamy Is Ridiculous," *Big Think*, podcast, June 20, 2011.
8 "Monogamy, explained," *Netflix: Explained* (2018). Available at https://www.youtube.com/watch?v=DCGyLjBjuGI.
9 Stephanie Coontz, *Marriage, A History: How Love Conquered Marriage* (Cambridge: Penguin Books. 2006).
10 YouGov, poll of 1000 U.S. Citizens. Interview dates September 23-25, 2016. https://d3nkl3psvxxpe9.cloudfront.net/documents/tabs_OP_Relationships_20160925_Sd5Ie9n.pdf
11 "Understanding the Increase in Moral Acceptability of Polygamy," Frank Newport, Gallup.com https://news.gallup.com/opinion/polling-matters/313112/understanding-increase-moral-acceptability-polygamy.aspx 2020.
12 Richard Fry and Kim Parker, "Rising Share of U.S. Adults Living Without a Spouse or Partner," Pew Research Center, October 5, 2021.
13 Peter Ueda, "Trends in Frequency of Sexual Activity and Number of Sexual Partners Among Adults Aged 18 to 44 Years in the US, 2000-2018," *JAMA Network Open* (2020).

14 Daniel Cox, "The State of American Friendship: Change, Challenges, and Loss," American Enterprise Institute Library, 2021.

15 Joint Economic Committee, *An Overview of Social Capital in America*, 115th Congress, 1st session, 2017.

16 United States Census Bureau, "Home Alone: More Than A Quarter of All Households Have One Person," 2023, https://www.census.gov/library/stories/2023/06/more-than-a-quarter-all-households-have-one-person.html; Pew Research Center, "Trust and Distrust in America," 2019, https://www.pewresearch.org/politics/2019/07/22/trust-and-distrust-in-america/.

17 Menelaos Apostolou, "Sexual Selection Under Parental Choice: The Role of Parents in the Evolution of Human Mating," *Evolution and Human Behavio*r (2007).

18 Joseph Henrich, et al., "The Church, intensive kinship, and global psychological variation," *Science* (2019).

19 Kyle Harper, "The First Sexual Revolution," *First Things* (2018).

20 "The landscape of marriage and cohabitation in the U.S.," Pew Research Center, Washington, D.C. (November 6, 2019) https://www.pewresearch.org/social-trends/2019/11/06/the-landscape-of-marriage-and-cohabitation-in-the-u-s/

21 Wendy Wang and Brad Wilcox, "The Married-Mom Advantage," the *Atlantic* (December 2022).

22 Richard Reeves, *Of Boys and Men* (Washington, DC: Brookings Institution Press, 2022).

23 Richard Reeves, "Dads matter, period," *Of Boys and Men*, Substack (October 1, 2022) https://ofboysandmen.substack.com/p/dads-matter-period.

24 Louise Perry, *The Case Against the Sexual Revolution* (Oxford: Polity, 2022).

25 Melissa Kearney, *The Two-Parent Privilege: How Americans Stopped Getting Married and Started Falling Behind* (Chicago: University of Chicago Press, 2023).

26 Joe Klein, "Daniel Patrick Moynihan Was Often Right," *New York Times*, (May 15, 2021).

Chapter 1

1 Plato, *The Republic*, translated by Desmond Lee (New York: Penguin Classics, 2007).

2 Karl Marx and Friedrich Engels, *The Communist Manifesto* (New York: Penguin Classics, 2015).

3 Friedrich Engels, *The Origin of the Family, Private Property and the State* (New York: Penguin Classics, 2010).

4 Heidi Hartmann, "The unhappy marriage of Marxism and feminism: towards a more progressive union," edited by Linda Nicholson, *The Second Wave: a Reader in Feminist Theory* (New York: Routledge Press, 1997).

5 Martha Fineman, "Why Marriage?" *Virginia Journal of Social Policy & the Law*, Vol 9, No. 1, (2001).

6 Henry Lewis Morgan, *Ancient Society* (Tucson: University of Arizona Press, 1985).

7 Engels, *The Origin of the Family.*

8 Jane Goodall, "Learning from the Chimpanzees: A Message Humans Can Understand," *Science*, (December 18, 1998).

9 Jane Goodall and Guy Kawasaki, TedX, September 2018, https://www.ted.com/talks/dr_jane_goodall_guy_kawasaki_dr_jane_goodall_dbe_with_guy_kawasaki.

10 Anne Pusey and Kara Schroepfer-Walker, "Female Competition in Chimpanzees," *Philosophical Transactions of the Royal Society of London* (2011).

11 Joseph Henrich, *The Secret of Our Success*, (Princeton: Princeton University Press, 2016).

12 Henrich, *The Secret of Our Success.*

13 Karen Kramer and Amanda Veile, "Infant Allocare in Traditional Societies," *Physiology & Behavior*, (2018).

14 L.J. Young, et al., "Neuroendocrine Bases of Monogamy," *Trends in Neuroscience* (1998).

15 A. Ophir et al., "Variation in the neural V1aR predicts sexual fidelity and space use among prairie voles," *Proceedings of the National Academy of Sciences* (2008). https://pubmed.ncbi.nlm.nih.gov/18212120/

16 Randolph Nesse, *Good Reasons for Bad Feelings: Insights from the Frontier of Evolutionary Psychiatry* (New York: Dutton, 2019).
17 H. Walum, et al., "Genetic variation in the vasopressin receptor 1a gene associates with pair-bonding behavior in humans," *Proceedings of the National Academy of Sciences* (2008).
18 Christopher Boehm, *Hierarchy in the Forest: The Evolution of Egalitarian Behavior*. (Cambridge: Harvard University Press,1999).
19 Henrich, *The Secret of Our Success.*
20 Ryan Schacht and Karen Kramer, "Are We Monogamous? A Review of the Evolution of Pair-Bonding in Humans and Its Contemporary Variation Cross-Culturally," *Frontiers in Ecology and Evolution* (2019).
21 Steven J.C. Gaulin, "Paternal confidence and paternal investment: A cross cultural test of a sociobiological hypothesis," *Ethology and Sociobiology* (1980).
22 Lawrence Keeley, *War Before Civilization: The Myth of the Peaceful Savage* (Oxford: Oxford University Press, 1996).
23 Lawrence Keeley, *War Before Civilization: The Myth of the Peaceful Savage* (Oxford: Oxford University Press, 1996).
24 Bernard Chapais, *Primeval Kinship: How Pair-Bonding Gave Birth to Human Society* (Cambridge: Harvard University Press, 2008).
25 Schacht and Kramer, "Are We Monogamous?"
26 Menelaos Apostolou, "Sexual Selection Under Parental Choice: The Role of Parents in the Evolution of Human Mating," *Evolution and Human Behavior* (2007).
27 Christopher Ryan and Cacilda Jetha, *Sex at Dawn: How We Mate, Why We Stray, and What It Means for Modern Relationships* (New York: Harper Perennial, 2011).
28 Lynn Saxon, *Sex at Dusk: Lifting the Shiny Wrapping from Sex at Dawn* (CreateSpace Independent Publishing Platform, 2012).
29 Ryan and Jetha, *Sex at Dawn.*
30 Saxon, *Sex at Dusk.*
31 Ryan and Jetha, *Sex at Dawn.*
32 Saxon, *Sex at Dusk.*
33 Boehm, *Hierarchy in the Forest.*

Chapter 2

1 Kurt Alt, et al., "A massacre of early Neolithic farmers in the high Pyrenees at Els Trocs, Spain," *Scientific Reports* (2020).
2 Laura Betzig, "Means, variances, and ranges in reproductive success: comparative evidence," *Evolution and Human Behavior* 33 (2012) 309–317.
3 Mark Dyble, et al., "Engagement in agricultural work is associated with reduced leisure time among Agta hunter-gatherers," *Nature Human Behaviour*, no. 3 (2019): 792–796.
4 James C. Scott, *Against the Grain: A Deep History of the Earliest States* (New Haven: Yale University Press, 2017).
5 Ian Kujit, "Evidence for food storage and pre domestication granaries 11,000 years ago in the Jordan Valley," *Proceedings of the National Academy of Sciences of the United States of America* (2009).
6 Kirk Endicott, "Property, power and conflict among the Batek of Malaysia," *Hunters and Gatherers: History, Evolution and Social Change*, edited by Tim Ingold (New York: Routledge, 1998).
7 Timothy Kohler, "A deep divide between rich and poor dates back millennia," *Nature* (2017).
8 Scott, *Against the Grain.*
9 Laura Betzig, "Eusociality in History," *Human Nature* (2014).
10 Monika Karmin, et al., "A recent bottleneck of Y chromosome diversity coincides with a global change in culture," *Genome Research* (2015).
11 Exodus 21:7-11. New Revised Standard Version.
12 Upinder Singh, *A History of Ancient and Early Medieval India: From the Stone Age to the 12th Century* (London: Pearson Publishing, 2009).
13 John Strong, "Aśoka's Wives and the Ambiguities of Buddhist Kingship," *Cahiers d'Extrême-Asie*, (2002).
14 Paul Gooldin, "Polygyny and Its Discontents: A Key to Understanding Traditional Chinese Society," *Sexuality in China: Histories of Power and Pleasure*, edited by Howard Chiang (Seattle: University of Washington Press, 2018).
15 Ben Raffield, "The Slave Markets of the Viking World," *Slavery and Abolition* (2019).

16 Ibn Fadlan, *Ibn Fadlan and the Land of Darkness: Arab Travelers in the Far North,* translated by Caroline Stone (London: Penguin Classics, 2012).
17 Ben Raffield, "Male-biased operational sex ratios and the Viking phenomenon: An evolutionary anthropological perspective on Late Iron Age Scandinavian raiding," *Evolution and Human Behavior* (2017).
18 Sunna Ebenesersdóttir, "Ancient genomes from Iceland reveal the making of a human population," *Science* (2018).
19 This example is tweaked from Joseph Henrich's "The puzzle of monogamous marriage," *Philosophical Transactions of the Royal Society of London* (2012).
20 Chris Tyler-Smith, "The Genetic Legacy of the Mongols," *American Journal of Human Genetics* (2003).
21 Nehemia Levtzion, *Corpus of Early Arabic Sources for West African History* (Princeton: Markus Wiener Publishers, 2011).
22 Ibn Battuta, *Travels in Asia and Africa-1325-1354* (Adelaide: Hassell Street Press, 2021).
23 Mark Tran, "Mali conflict puts freedom of slave descendants in peril," the *Guardian*, October 23, 2012.
24 Camilla Townsend, *Fifth Sun: A New History of the Aztecs*, (Oxford: Oxford University Press, 2019).
25 Townsend, *Fifth Sun.*

Chapter 3

1 Susan Lape, "Solon and the Institution of the Democratic Family Form," *The Classical Journal* (2002).
2 Lape, "Solon and the Institution of the Democratic Family Form."
3 Victor Davis Hanson, *The Other Greeks: The Family Farm and the Agrarian Roots of Western Civilization*, (Berkeley: University of California Press, 1999).
4 Plato. The Republic. Book VIII.
5 George Mousourakis, *A Legal History of Rome* (New York: Routledge, 2007).
6 Aldo Schiavone, *The End of the Past: Ancient Rome and the Modern West* (Cambridge: Harvard University Press, 2000).

7 Mary Beard, *SPQR: A History of Ancient Rome* (New York: Norton, 2015).

8 Kyle Harper, *From Shame to Sin: The Christian Transformation of Sexual Morality in Late Antiquity* (Cambridge: Harvard University Press, 2013).

9 Harper, *From Shame to Sin.*

10 Matthew 19:4-6. New Revised Standard Version.

11 1 Corinthians 6:16-19. New Revised Standard Version.

12 1 Corinthians 7:2-4. New Revised Standard Version.

13 Romans 16:1-2.

14 1 Timothy 3:11.

15 Rodney Stark, *The Rise of Christianity,* (San Francisco: HarperOne, 1996).

16 Stark, *The Rise of Christianity.*

17 Joseph Henrich, et al., "The Church, intensive kinship, and global psychological variation," *Science* (2019).

18 Tom Holland, *Dominion: How the Christian Revolution Remade the World (*New York: Basic Books, 2021).

19 David Herlihy, *Medieval Households* (Cambridge: Harvard University Press, 1985).

20 Jack Goody, *The Development of the Family and Marriage in Europe* (Cambridge: Cambridge University Press 1983).

21 Nicholas Vincent, *Magna Carta: A Very Short Introduction (*Oxford: Oxford University Press, 2012).

22 Alexis de Tocqueville, *Democracy in America,* translated by James Schliefer (Liberty Fund website, 2010) https://oll.libertyfund.org/

23 Tocqueville, *Democracy in America.*

24 James Wilson. "Lectures on Law," *Collected Works of James Wilson,* edited by Kermit Hall (Carmel: Liberty Fund, 2007.

25 Wilson, James. Lectures on Law.

26 Joseph Story, "Natural Law," *Encyclopedia Americana,* edited by Francis Lieber (Philadelphia: Carey and Lea, 1832).

27 Nancy Cott, *Public Vows: A History of Marriage and the Nation* (Cambridge: Harvard University Press, 2000).

28 Cott, *Public Vows.*

29 Cott, *Public Vows.*
30 Cott, *Public Vows.*
31 Peter Gray, "Marriage, parenting, and testosterone variation among Kenyan Swahili men," *American Journal of Biological Anthropology* (2003).
32 David Herlihy, *Medieval Households* (Cambridge: Harvard University Press, 1985).

Chapter 4

1 Jacob 2:27. The Book of Mormon
2 Cott, *Public Vows.*
3 *Reynolds v. United States.* 98 U.S. 145. 1878.
4 *Murphy v. Ramsey.* 114 U.S. 15. 1885
5 *Late Corporation of the Church of Jesus Christ of Latter-Day Saints v. United States.* 136 U.S. 1. 1890.
6 "Mormons more likely to marry, have more children than other U.S. religious groups," Pew Research Center, Washington, D.C. (May 22, 2015) https://www.pewresearch.org/short-reads/2015/05/22/mormons-more-likely-to-marry-have-more-children-than-other-u-s-religious-groups/
7 Spencer Klaw, *Without Sin: The Life and Death of the Oneida Community* (New York: Penguin Books, 1994).
8 Elizabeth Cady Stanton, *Elizabeth Cady Stanton: As Revealed In Her Letters, Diary And Reminiscences* (Whitefish: Kessinger Publishing, 2007).
9 Stanton, *As Revealed In Her Letters, Diary And Reminiscences*
10 Elizabeth Cady Stanton, Declaration of Sentiments. 1848.
11 Elizabeth Cady Stanton, Declaration of Sentiments. 1848.
12 Cott, *Public Vows.*
13 Elizabeth Cady Stanton, "Mrs. Elizabeth Cady Stanton's Address at the Decade Meeting on Marriage and Divorce," in *A History of the National Woman's Rights Movement for Twenty Years*, edited by Paulina Wright Davis (Journeymen Printers Cooperative Association, 1871).
14 Edmund Morris, *The Rise of Theodore Roosevelt* (New York: Random House, 2001).

15 Allan Carlson, *The American Way* (Moscow: Canon Press, 2003).
16 Carlson, *The American Way.*
17 Theodore Roosevelt, *The Foes of Our Own Household* (New York: George H. Doran, 1917).
18 Carlson, *The American Way.*
19 Theodore Roosevelt, "Address to the New York State Agricultural Association," *The American Presidency Project*, https://www.presidency.ucsb.edu/node/270557
20 Carlson, *The American Way.*
21 Theodore Roosevelt, "Remarks Before the Mothers' Congress," *The American Presidency Project,* https://www.presidency.ucsb.edu/node/343746
22 Theodore Roosevelt, "Sixth Annual Message," *The American Presidency Project,* https://www.presidency.ucsb.edu/node/206216
23 Theodore Roosevelt, "Remarks in Osawatomie, Kansas," *The American Presidency Project* https://www.presidency.ucsb.edu/node/358608
24 Roosevelt, *The Foes of Our Own Household.*
25 Gwendolyn Mink, *The Wages of Motherhood: Inequality in the Welfare State 1917-142* (Ithaca: Cornell University Press, 1995).
26 Susan Ware, *Holding Their Own: American Women in the 1930s* (Woodbridge: Twayne Publishers, 1984).
27 Carlson, *The American Way.*
28 Steven Ruggles, "Patriarchy, Power, and Pay: The Transformation of American Families 1800–2015," *Demography* (2015).
29 Stephanie Coontz, *The Way We Never Were: American Families and the Nostalgia Trap* (New York: Basic Books, 2016).
30 Ruggles, "Patriarchy, Power, and Pay."
31 Ruggles, "Patriarchy, Power, and Pay."
32 David Brooks, "The Nuclear Family Was a Mistake," the *Atlantic*, 2020.
33 Steven Ruggles, *Prolonged Connections: The Rise of the Extended Family in Nineteenth-Century England and America* (Madison: University of Wisconsin Press, 1987).
34 John Witte, *The Western Case for Monogamy Over Polygamy* (Cambridge: Cambridge University Press, 2015)

Chapter 5

1 "Going All the Way: Public Opinion and Premarital Sex," Roper Center for Public Opinion Research, Ithaca, New York (July 7, 2017) https://ropercenter.cornell.edu/sites/default/files/wp-content/uploads/2018/03/output_1520352458.htm
2 "Majority Considers Sex Before Marriage Morally Okay," Gallup (May 24, 2001) https://news.gallup.com/poll/3163/Majority-Considers-Sex-Before-Marriage-Morally-Okay.aspx
3 United States Congress, Joint Economic Committee. (December 11, 2017). *Love, Marriage, and the Baby Carriage: The Rise in Unwed Childbearing,* https://www.jec.senate.gov/public/index.cfm/republicans/analysis?ID=E0C3BA6E-840A-4B5E-A5BF-B43FC0BB5331
4 Jean-Jacques Rousseau, *Emile* (New York: Penguin Classics. 2007).
5 Jean-Jacques Rousseau, *Discourse on the Origin and Basis of Inequality Among Men* (Cambridge: Hackett Publishing, 1992).
6 Rousseau, *Discourse on the Origin and Basis of Inequality Among Men.*
7 Rousseau, *Discourse on the Origin.*
8 Rousseau, *Discourse on the Origin.*
9 Rousseau, *Discourse on the Origin.*
10 Rousseau, *Emile*
11 John Stuart Mill, *On Liberty* (Cambridge: Hackett Publishing Company,1978).
12 Mill, *On Liberty.*
13 Mill, *On Liberty.*
14 Mill, *On Liberty.*
15 Mill, *On Liberty.*
16 Cleveland v. United States, 329 U.S. 14. 1946.
17 Margaret Mead, *Coming of Age in Samoa: A Psychological Study of Primitive Youth for Western Civilisation* (New York: Harper Perennial, 1971).
18 Mead, *Coming of Age in Samoa.*
19 Mead, *Coming of Age.*
20 Mead, *Coming of Age.*
21 Derek Freeman, *Margaret Mead and Samoa: The Making and Unmaking of an Anthropological Myth* (New York: Penguin Books,1986).

22 Paul Shankman, *The Trashing of Margaret Mead: Anatomy of an Anthropological Controversy* (Madison: University of Wisconsin Press, 2009).
23 Paul Shankman, "The History of Samoan Sexual Conduct and the Mead-Freeman Controversy," *American Anthropologist* (1996).
24 Alfred Kinsey, *Sexual Behavior in the Human Male* (Bloomington: Indiana University Press,1948).
25 Judith Reisman, *Kinsey, Sex and Fraud: The Indoctrination of a People* (Lafayette: Vital Issues Press, 1990).
26 Frequently Asked Questions About the Kinsey Institute, Kinsey Institute, 2024, https://kinseyinstitute.org/about/kinsey-institute-faq.php
27 Frequently Asked Questions About the Kinsey Institute.
28 James Jones, *Alfred Kinsey: A Life* (New York: W. W. Norton, 1997).
29 Chandra, Anjani and Mosher, William. Sexual behavior, sexual attraction, and sexual identity in the United States: Data from the 2006–2008 National Survey of Family Growth. National health statistics reports. 2011.
30 Michael Wiederman, "Extramarital Sex: Prevalence and Correlates in a National Survey," *Journal of Sex Research* (1997).
31 Wilhelm Reich, *The Sexual Revolution: Toward a Self-Regulating Character Structure* (New York: Farrar Straus and Giroux, 1936).
32 Sigmund Freud, *Civilization and its Discontents* (New York: W.W. Norton, 2010).
33 Freud, *Civilization and its Discontents.*
34 Freud, *Civilization.*
35 Reich, *The Sexual Revolution.*
36 Wilhelm Reich, *The Invasion of Compulsory Sex-Morality* (New York: Farrar Straus and Giroux, 1931).
37 Ervin Drake, "Morals: The Second Sexual Revolution," *Time*, January 24,1964.
38 Daniel Horowitz, *Betty Friedan and the Making of the Feminine Mystique* (Amherst: University of Massachusetts Press, 1998).
39 Horowitz, *Betty Friedan and the Making of the Feminine Mystique.*
40 Simone de Beauvoir, *The Second Sex* (New York: Vintage, 2011).

41 De Beauvoir, *The Second Sex.*

42 Carole Seymour-Jones, *A Dangerous Liaison: A Revelatory New Biography of Simone DeBeauvoir and Jean-Paul Sartre* (New York: Abrams Press. 2009).

43 Betty Friedan, *The Feminine Mystique* (New York: W.W. Norton, 2013).

44 *Griswold v. Connecticut* 381 U.S. 479. 1965.

45 *Griswold v. Connecticut* 381 U.S. 479. 1965.

46 *Eisenstadt v. Baird* 405 U.S. 438. 1972.

47 *Eisenstadt v. Baird* 405 U.S. 438. 1972.

48 *Eisenstadt v. Baird* 405 U.S. 438. 1972.

49 *King v. Smith* 392 U.S. 309. 1968.

50 *King v. Smith* 392 U.S. 309. 1968.

51 *King v. Smith* 392 U.S. 309. 1968.

52 *Roth v. United States* 354 U.S. 476. 1957.

53 *United States v. Miller* 425 U.S. 435. 1976.

54 Roger Ebert, "Review: The Devil in Miss Jones," the *Chicago Sun Times*, June 13,1973.

55 Richard Corliss, "When Porno Was Chic," *Time*, March 29, 2005.

56 Tim Alberta, "How the GOP Gave Up on Porn," *Politico*, December 2018.

57 *Pope v. Illinois* 481 U.S. 497. 1987

58 Tim Alberta, "How the GOP Gave Up on Porn," *Politico*, December 2018.

59 Robert Richards, "Obscenity Prosecutions and the Bush Administration: The Inside Obscenity Prosecutions and the Bush Administration: The Inside Perspective of the Adult Entertainment Industry," *Jeffrey Moorad Sports Law Journal* (2007)

60 Christina Camilleri, Justin T. Perry, Stephen Sammut, "Compulsive Internet Pornography Use and Mental Health: A Cross-Sectional Study in a Sample of University Students in the United States," *Frontiers in Psychology* (2020).

61 Daniel Cox, "How Prevalent is Pornography," *Institute for Family Studies*, May 3, 2022.

62 Chyng Sun, "Pornography and the Male Sexual Script: An Analysis of Consumption and Sexual Relations," *Archives of Sexual Behavior* (2014).

63 Michael Malcolm, "Are Pornography and Marriage Substitutes for Young Men?" *Eastern Economic Journal* (2015).
64 Peggy Orenstein, "The Troubling Trend in Teenage Sex," *New York Times*, April 12, 2024.
65 Debby Herbenick, "Diverse Sexual Behaviors in Undergraduate Students: Findings From a Campus Probability Survey," *The Journal of Sexual Medicine* (2021).
66 Debby Herbenick, "Feeling Scared During Sex: Findings From a U.S. Probability Sample of Women and Men Ages 14 to 60," *Journal of Sex and Marital Therapy* (2019).
67 Paul Wright, "Pornography Consumption and Sexual Choking: An Evaluation of Theoretical Mechanisms," *Health Communication* (2021).
68 *Lawrence v. Texas* 539 U.S. 558 .2003.
69 *Lawrence v. Texas* 539 U.S. 558. 2003.
70 *Obergefell v. Hodges*, 576 U.S. 644. 2015.
71 Jonathan Turley, "One Big, Happy Polygamous Family," *New York Times*, July 20, 2011.
72 Household and Family Characteristics: March 1980. Current Population Reports. United States Census Bureau. Households and Families: 2020. 2020 Census Briefs. United States Census Bureau.
73 Erol Ricketts, "The origin of black female-headed families," *University of Wisconsin-Madison Institute for Research on Poverty* (1989).
74 Belinda Tucker and Claudia Mitchell-Kernan, "Trends in African American Family Formation: A Theoretical and Statistical Overview," from *The decline in marriage among African Americans: Causes, consequences and policy implications* (New York: Russell Sage Foundation, 1995).

Chapter 6

1 Lyndon Johnson, "Commencement Address at Howard University," *The American Presidency Project,* https://www.presidency.ucsb.edu/people/president/lyndon-b-johnson
2 United States Department of Labor, Office of Policy Planning and Research, Daniel Patrick Moynihan, "The Negro Family: The Case for National Action," 1965.

3 David Carter, *The Music Has Gone Out of the Movement: Civil Rights and the Johnson Administration, 1965-1968* (Chapel Hill: The University of North Carolina Press, 2009).

4 Thomas Meehan, "Moynihan of the Moynihan Report," *New York Times*. July 31, 1966.

5 United States Department of Labor, Office of Policy Planning and Research, Daniel Moynihan, "The Negro Family: The Case for National Action," (1965).

6 Moynihan, "The Negro Family."

7 Centers for Disease Control and Prevention, National Vital Statistics Reports, "Births: Final Data for 2021," (2023).

8 Data from National Vital Statistics Reports.

9 Lydia Saad, "Americans Have Complex Relationship With Marriage," *Gallup News Service,* May 30, 2006, https://news.gallup.com/poll/23041/Americans-Complex-Relationship-Marriage.aspx

10 Marriage. Gallup Historical Trends. Online.

11 Fenaba Addo and Lowell Ricketts, "As Fewer Young Adults Wed, Married Couples' Wealth Surpasses Others," *In the Balance*, Federal Reserve Bank of St. Louis (January 1, 2019), https://www.stlouisfed.org/publications/in-the-balance/2018/as-fewer-young-adults-wed 2019.

12 Julia Carpenter, "Moving in Together Doesn't Match the Financial Benefits of Marriage, but Why?" *Wall Street Journal*, November 7, 2022.

13 John Iceland, "US disparities in affluence by household structure, 1959 to 2017," *Demographic Research* (2020).

14 Iceland, US disparities in affluence by household structure.

15 Raj Chetty, et al., "Race and Economic Opportunity in the United States: An Intergenerational Perspective," *Quarterly Journal of Economics* (2020).

16 Christina Cross, "Racial Ethnic Differences in the Association Between Family Structure and Children's Education," *Journal of Marriage and Family* (2019).

17 Marianne Bertand and Jessica Pan, "The Trouble with Boys: Social Influences and the Gender Gap in Disruptive Behavior," *American Economic Journal: Applied Economics* (2013).

18 Bradford Wilcox, "The Family Geography of the American Dream: New Neighborhood Data on Single Parenthood, Prisons, and Poverty," *Institute for Family Studies* (2018).

19 Robert Sampson, "Unemployment and Imbalanced Sex Ratios: Race-Specific Consequences for Family Structure and Crime," *The decline in marriage among African Americans: Causes, consequences and policy implications* (New York: Russell Sage Foundation, 1995).

20 Jule Horney, et al., "Criminal Careers in the Short-Term: Intra-Individual Variability in Crime and Its Relation to Local Life Circumstances," *American Sociological Review* (1995).

21 Lee Gettler, et al., "Longitudinal evidence that fatherhood decreases testosterone in human males," *Proceedings of the National Academy of Sciences* (2011).

22 Vivek Murthy, "We Have Become a Lonely Nation. It's Time to Fix That," *New York Times*, April 30, 2023.

23 America's Families and Living Arrangements. U.S. Census Bureau. 2022.

24 Christos Makridis, "New Gallup Data on Emotional Well-Being by Family Status," *Institute for Family Studies*, (July 25, 2022).

25 Joint Economic Committee. Long-Term Trends in Deaths of Despair. 2019.

26 Ying Chen, et al., "Marital transitions during earlier adulthood and subsequent health and well-being in mid- to late-life among female nurses: An outcome-wide analysis," *Global Epidemiology* (2023).

27 Sam Peltzman, "The Socio Political Demography of Happiness," *George J. Stigler Center for the Study of the Economy & the State* (2023).

28 Naomi Gerstel and Natalia Sarkisian, "Marriage: The Good, the Bad, and the Greedy," *Contexts* (2006).

29 Joint Economic Committee. The Space Between: Renewing the American Tradition of Civil Society. 2019.

30 Joint Economic Committee. Volunteering in America. 2017.

31 Tocqueville, *Democracy in America.*

32 Tocqueville, *Democracy in America.*

33 Gerstel and Sarkisian, "Marriage: The Good, the Bad, and the Greedy"

34 William Clinton, "Remarks to the California Democratic Party in Sacramento," *The American Presidency Project*, https://www.pres-

idency.ucsb.edu/documents/remarks-the-california-democratic-party-sacramento

35 Charles Krauthammer, "Moral Values Myth," *Washington Post*, November 12, 2004.

36 Joel Kotkin and Samuel Abrams, "The Rise of the Single Woke Female," *Real Clear Politics*, https://www.realclearpolitics.com/2023/01/17/the_rise_of_the_single_woke_female_589278.html#!

37 Lydia Saad, U.S. Women Have Become More Liberal; Men Mostly Stable," Gallup. 2024.

38 2008 Democratic Party Platform. Online by *The American Presidency Project.*

39 Trent Ollerenshaw, "The Asymmetric Polarization of Immigration Opinion in the United States," *Public Opinion Quarterly* (2023).

40 Gender Gap Public Opinion, Center for American Women and Politics, Rutgers-New Brunswick. https://cawp.rutgers.edu/gender-gap-public-opinion

41 Hani Zainulbhai, "Women, more than men, say climate change will harm them personally," Gallup. 2015.

42 "America's Abortion Quandary," Pew Research Center, Washington, D.C (May 6, 2022) https://www.pewresearch.org/religion/2022/05/06/americas-abortion-quandary/

43 "Abortion trends by gender." Gallup. 2024. https://news.gallup.com/poll/245618/abortion-trends-gender.aspx

44 Paul Ehrlich, *The Population Bomb* (New York: Ballantine Books, 1971).

45 Brenan, Megan, "Americans' Preference for Larger Families Highest Since 1971," Gallup. 2023.

46 U.S. Census Bureau, "Historical Tables. Historical Table 2: Distribution of Women Age 40-50 by Number of Children Ever Born and Marital Status: Selected Years, 1970-2022."

47 Daniel Cox, "Emerging Trends and Enduring Patterns in American Family Life," *Survey Center of American Life* (2022).

48 Nicole Maestas, Kathleen Mullen, and David Powell, "The Effect of Population Aging on Economic Growth, the Labor Force, and Productivity," *American Economic Journal: Macroeconomics* (2023).

49 Douglas Downey and Dennis Condron, "Playing Well with Others in Kindergarten: The Benefits of Siblings at Home," *Journal of Marriage and Family* (2004).

50 Lynn White, and Agnes Reidmann, "Ties Among Adult Siblings," *Social Forces (*1992).

51 Joint Economic Committee. The Consequences of Declining Fertility for Social Capital. 2022.

52 Brad Lendon, "South Korea to See Population Plummet to 1970s Levels," CNN, December 15, 2023.

53 Oren Levin-Waldman, "Income, Civic Participation and Achieving Greater Democracy. *Journal of Socio-Economics* (2013). Martin Gilens, *Affluence & Influence: Economic Inequality and Political Power in America.* Princeton University Press 2012.

54 Simon Bienstman, "Explaining the 'democratic malaise' in unequal societies: Inequality, external efficacy and political trust," *European Journal of Political Research* (2023). Carles Boix, Democracy and Redistribution. Cambridge University Press. 2003

55 Alexi Gugushvili, "Social origins of support for democracy: a study of intergenerational mobility," *International Review of Sociology* (2020). Christian Houle, "Social Mobility and Democratic Attitudes: Evidence From Latin America and Africa," *Comparative Political Studies* (2019).

56 Laurence Whitehead, *Democratization: Theory and Experience* (Oxford University Press 2002).

57 Mitchell Seligson, "The dimensions and political impact of crime on the Guatemalan population," *Family, Migration, Violence, and Environment* (2000).

58 Catalina Smulovitz, "Citizen Insecurity and Fear: Public and Private Responses in Argentina." In Hugo Frühling, Joseph Tulchin and Heather Golding (eds.), *Crime and Violence in Latin America: Citizen Security, Democracy, and the State* (2003).

59 James Madison, *The Federalist Papers*, essay number 10 (New York 1787).

60 Thomas Carothers and Andrew O'Donohue,, *Democracies Divided: The Global Challenge of Political Polarization*, (Brookings Institution Press 2019).

Chapter 7

1 Leah Ruppanner, "Gender Linked Fate Explains Lower Legal Abortion Support Among White Married Women," *PLOS One* (2019).
2 Lena Edlund and Rohini Pande, "Why Have Women Become Left-Wing? The Political Gender Gap and The Decline in Marriage," *Quarterly Journal of Economics* (2002).
3 Kimberle Crenshaw, "Demarginalizing the Intersection of Race and Sex: A Black Feminist Critique of Antidiscrimination Doctrine, Feminist Theory and Antiracist Politics," *University of Chicago Legal Forum* (1989).
4 Kimberle Crenshaw, "Demarginalizing the Intersection of Race and Sex: A Black Feminist Critique of Antidiscrimination Doctrine, Feminist Theory and Antiracist Politics," *University of Chicago Legal Forum* (1989).
5 Jeffrey Jones, "LGBTQ+ Identification in U.S. Now at 7.6%," *Gallup* (2024).
6 Jeffrey Jones, "LGBTQ+ Identification in U.S. Now at 7.6%," *Gallup* (2024).
7 Rector, Robert and Menon, Vijay, "Understanding the Hidden $1.1 Trillion Welfare System and How to Reform It." The Heritage Foundation. 2018.
8 Chatterjee, Chandrayee, "Impact of the Affordable Care Act Medicaid Expansions on Marriage and Divorce Decisions," The Center for Growth and Opportunity at Utah State University. 2021.
9 Stone, Lyman, "Affordability or Achievability? The Challenge for Family Policy in America," American Enterprise Institute, 2019.
10 Lisa Arnold and Christina Campbell, "The High Price of Being Single," the *Atlantic*, January 14, 2013.
11 Princeton Survey Research Associates International, "2016 Poverty Survey," *The American Enterprise Institute* and *the Los Angeles Times*, 2016.
12 Wilcox, Bradford, Price, Joseph, and Rachidi, Angela, "Marriage, penalized: Does social-welfare policy affect family formation?" Washington, DC: American Enterprise Institute and the Institute for Family Studies. 2016.

13 Patrick Brown, "Working-Class Americans' Views on Family Policy," *Institute for Family Studies* (2021).

14 Rebecca Traister, *All the Single Ladies: Unmarried Women and the Rise of an Independent Nation* (MarySue Rucci Books, 2016).

15 The White House, FACT SHEET: The American Families Plan, 2021.

16 Lawrence Schweinhart, *Lifetime Effects: The High/Scope Perry Preschool Study Through Age 40* (Ypsilanti: HighScope Foundation, 2005).

17 Craig Ramey, and Frances Campbell, "Preventive education for high-risk children: cognitive consequences of the Carolina Abecedarian Project," *American Journal of Mental Deficiency* (1984).

18 The White House, The American Families Plan, 2021.

19 Heckman, James, "Invest in Early Childhood Development: Reduce Deficits, Strengthen the Economy, The Heckman Equation," 2023.

20 U.S. Department of Health and Human Services, Head Start Impact Study Final Report. 2010.

21 U.S. Department of Health and Human Services, Third Grade Follow-up to the Head Start Impact Study: Final Report, 2012.

22 Dale Farran, "Effects of a statewide pre-kindergarten program on children's achievement and behavior through sixth grade," *Developmental Psychology* (2022).

23 Anya Kamenetz, "A top researcher says it's time to rethink our entire approach to preschool," NPR, February 10, 2022.

24 Kamenetz, approach to preschool.

25 Michael Baker, Jonathan Gruber, and Kevin Milligan, "The Long-Run Impacts of a Universal Child Care Program," *American Economic Journal: Economic Policy* (2019).

26 Richard Reeves, *Of Boys and Men* (Washington, D.C.: Brookings Institution Press, 2022).

27 Reeves, *Of Boys and Men.*

28 Reeves, *Of Boys and Men*

29 Reeves, *Of Boys and Men.*

30 Reeves, Richard, "Dads Matter, Period," Substack. 2022.

31 Reeves, *Of Boys and Men.*

32 Reeves, *Of Boys and Men.*

33 Joyce Benenson, *Warriors and Worriers: The Survival of the Sexes* (Oxford: Oxford University Press, 2014).

34 Benenson, *Warriors and Worriers*

35 Benenson *Warriors and Worriers*

36 Lee Gettler, "Evidence for an adolescent sensitive period to family experiences influencing adult male testosterone production," *Proceedings of the National Academy of Sciences* (2022).

37 Ohjae Gowen, "Becoming a Father, Staying a Father: An Examination of the Cumulative Wage Premium for U.S. Residential Fathers," *Social Forces* (2023).

38 Karen Benjamin Guzzo, "New Partners, More Kids: Multiple-Partner Fertility in the United States," *The Annals of the American Academy of Political and Social Science* (2014).

39 Ana Fostik, et al., "Union Instability and Fertility: An International Perspective," *European Journal of Population* (2023).

40 Dorius, Cassandra and Guzzo, Karen Benjamin, "The Long Arm of Maternal Multipartnered Fertility and Adolescent Well-being," National Center for Family & Marriage Research. 2013.

41 Juliana McGene and Valarie King, "Implications of new marriages and children for coparenting in nonresident father families," *Journal of Family Issues* (2012).

42 Patricia Schnitzer, and Bernard Ewigman, "Child Deaths Resulting from Inflicted Injuries: Household Risk Factors and Perpetrator Characteristics," *Pediatrics* (2006).

43 Susan Sorenson and Devan Spear, "New data on intimate partner violence and intimate relationships: Implications for gun laws and federal data collection," *Preventive Medicine* (2018).

44 "Nearly Half of U.S. Adults Say Dating Has Gotten Harder for Most People in the Last 10 Years," Pew Research Center, Washington, D.C. (August 20, 2020) https://www.pewresearch.org/social-trends/2020/08/20/nearly-half-of-u-s-adults-say-dating-has-gotten-harder-for-most-people-in-the-last-10-years/

Chapter 8

1 Mellisa Kearney, *The Two-Parent Privilege: How Americans Stopped Getting Married and Started Falling Behind* (Chicago: University of Chicago Press, 2023).
2 Bridgett vonHoldt, et al., "Structural variants in genes associated with human Williams-Beuren syndrome underlie stereotypical hypersociability in domestic dogs," *Science Advances* (2017).
3 Research News, "They call it puppy love, but what is it really?" Vanderbilt University (2019).
4 Ruth Feldman, "Oxytocin and social affiliation in humans," *Hormones and Behavior* (2012).
5 Hasse Walum, et al., "Genetic variation in the vasopressin receptor 1a gene (AVPR1A) associates with pair-bonding behavior in humans," *Proceedings of the National Academy of Sciences* (2008).
6 Allison Fries, et al., "Early experience in humans is associated with changes in neuropeptides critical for regulating social behavior," *Proceedings of the National Academy of Sciences* (2005).
7 Kory Floyd, "Relational and Health Correlates of Affection Deprivation," *Western Journal of Communication* (2014).
8 Noelia Breitman, "Couple age discrepancy and risk of intimate partner homicide," *Violence Victims* (2004).
9 Joseph Henrich, "The puzzle of monogamous marriage," *Philosophical Transactions of the Royal Society* (2012).
10 Henrich, "The puzzle of monogamous marriage."
11 Ezra Klein, "Ezra Klein Interviews Dan Savage," the *New York Times*. January 10, 2023.
12 "Ezra Klein Interviews Dan Savage"
13 Janet Hardy and Dossie Easton, *The Ethical Slut: A Practical Guide to Polyamory, Open Relationships, and Other Freedoms in Sex and Love* (Emeryville: Greenery Press, 1997).
14 Hardy and Easton, *The Ethical Slut.*
15 Hardy and Easton, *The Ethical Slut.*
16 Hardy and Easton, *The Ethical Slut.*

17 David Buss and Todd Shackelford, "From Vigilance to Violence: Mate Retention Tactics in Married Couples," *Journal of Personality and Social Psychology* (1997).
18 Mark Oppenheimer, "Married, With Infidelities," the *New York Times*, June 30, 2011.
19 Smith, Heather and Hawkins, Alan. "Is There a Battle of the Sexes in 'Consensual' Non-Monogamy?" Public Discourse. The Witherspoon Institute. 2019.
20 Arline Rubin and James Adams, "Outcomes of Sexually Open Marriages," *The Journal of Sex Research* (1986). Rhonda N Balzarini, "Demographic Comparison of American Individuals in Polyamorous and Monogamous Relationships," *Journal of Sex Research* (2018).
21 "Key findings on marriage and cohabitation in the U.S.," Pew Research Center, Washington, D.C. (November 6, 2019) https://www.pewresearch.org/short-reads/2019/11/06/key-findings-on-marriage-and-cohabitation-in-the-u-s/
22 Kasey Eickmeyer, "Trends in Relationship Formation and Stability in the United States: Dating, Cohabitation, Marriage, and Divorce," The Marriage Strengthening Research and Dissemination Center, 2020.
23 Sheila Kennedy and Larry Bumpass, "Cohabitation and children's living arrangements: New estimates from the United States," *Demographic Research* (2008).
24 Eickmeyer, "Trends in Relationship Formation and Stability in the United States."
25 Daniel Lichter, Sharon Sassler, and Richard Turner, "Cohabitation, Post-Conception Unions, and the Rise in Nonmarital Fertility," *Social Science Research* (2014).
26 Susan Brown, Bart Stykes and Wendy Manning, "Trends in Children's Family Instability, 1995–2010," *Journal of Marriage and Family* (2016).
27 Colleen Wynn, "Paternal Multipartner Fertility and Child Neighborhood Disorder," *Annual Meetings of the Population Association of America* (2016).
28 Wendy Manning, "Cohabitation and Child Wellbeing," *Future Child* (2015).

29 Sandi Nelson, Rebecca Clark, and Gregory Acs, "Beyond the Two-Parent Family: How Teenagers Fare in Cohabiting Couples and Blended Families," *Urban Institute* (2001).

30 Pamela Smock, "Heterosexual Cohabitation in the U.S.: Motives for Living Together among Young Men and Women," Center for Family and Demographic Research, Bowling Green State University (2006).

31 Smock, Cohabitation in the U.S

32 Hanna Rosin, "Boys on the Side," the *Atlantic*, (2012).

33 Rachel Martino, "Archives of Sexual Behavior The Role of Feminism and Gender in Endorsement of Hookup Culture among Emerging Adults," Archives of Sexual Behavior (2024).

34 David Buss, *The Evolution of Desire: Strategies of Human Mating* (New York: Basic Books, 1994).

35 Dan Kopf, "These statistics show why it's so hard to be an average man on dating apps," *Quartz*, August 15, 2017, https://qz.com/1051462/these-statistics-show-why-its-so-hard-to-be-an-average-man-on-dating-apps

36 Christian Rudder, *Dataclysm: Who We Are (When We Think No One's Looking)* (New York: Crown Books, 2014).

37 Kopf, "These statistics show…"

38 Kate Bolick, "*All the Single Ladies*," the *Atlantic* (2011).

39 David Frederick, et al., "Differences in Orgasm Frequency Among Gay, Lesbian, Bisexual, and Heterosexual Men and Women in a U.S. National Sample," *Archives of Sexual Behavior* (2017).

40 Lucy Napper, "Assessing the Personal Negative Impacts of Hooking Up Experienced by College Students: Gender Differences and Mental Health," *The Journal of Sex Research* (2015).

41 Nicholas Wolfinger and Samuel Perry, "Does a longer sexual resume affect marriage rates?" *Social Science Research* (2023).

42 Frank Newport, "Most in U.S. Want Marriage, but Its Importance Has Dropped," Gallup. 2013.

43 Matthew 5:31-33 New Revised Standard Version.

44 Matthew19:8-8 New Revised Standard Version.

45 Paul Amato and Alan Booth, *A Generation at Risk: Growing Up in an Era of Family Upheaval*, (Cambridge: Harvard University Press, 2000).

46 Amato and Booth, *A Generation at Risk*
47 Tamara Fackrell, "Wandering in the Wilderness: A Grounded Theory Study of the Divorce or Reconciliation Decision-Making Process," BYU (2012).
48 Imran Rasul, "Marriage Markets and Divorce Laws," *Journal of Law, Economics, and Organization* (2006).

Chapter 9

1 Ashton Pittman and William Pittman, "In-Depth: How Brett Favre Got $6 Million In Welfare Funds for a Volleyball Stadium," *Mississippi Free Press*, September 16, 2022.
2 Ronald Reagan, "A Time for Choosing," The American Presidency Project, https://www.presidency.ucsb.edu/people/president/ronald-reagan
3 William Clinton, "Address Before a Joint Session of Congress on Administration Goals," The American Presidency Project, https://www.presidency.ucsb.edu/documents/address-before-joint-session-congress-administration-goals
4 U.S. House of Representatives, Committee on Ways and Means Subcommittee on Human Resources, Testimony of Eloise Anderson, Wisconsin Department of Children and Families and Chairperson of the Secretaries Innovation Group, 2015.
5 Robert Moffitt, Brian Phelan, and Anne Winkler, "Welfare Rules, Incentives, and Family Structure," *The Journal of Human Resources* (2020).
6 Marianne Bitler, "The Impact of Welfare Reform on Marriage and Divorce," Working Paper, RAND corporation, (February 2004) https://www.rand.org/content/dam/rand/pubs/working_papers/2005/RAND_WR110.pdf
7 Robert Wood, et al., "Strengthening Unmarried Parents' Relationships: The Early Impacts of Building Strong Families," *Mathematica Policy Research* (2010).
8 Robert Wood, et al., "The Long-Term Effects of Building Strong Families: A Relationship Skills Education Program for Unmarried Parents," *Mathematica Policy Research* (2012).

9 JoAnn Hsueh, et al., "Early Impacts from the Supporting Healthy Marriage Evaluation," Manpower Demonstration Research Corporation (2012).

10 Erika Lundquist, et al., "A Family-Strengthening Program for Low-Income Families Final Impacts from the Supporting Healthy Marriage Evaluation," Manpower Demonstration Research Corporation (2014).

11 Fourth Amendment to the Fundamental Law of Hungary.

12 Harry Benson, "Marriage: We need to talk about Hungary," *Marriage Foundation* (2022).

13 Jennifer Lundquist, "Reinstitutionalizing families: Life course policy and marriage in the military," *Journal of Marriage and Family* (2014).

14 Family Feud: Child Allowance Edition. American Compass. 2021.

15 Lyman Stone, "Romney's 'Family Security Act' Is Pro-marriage: What the Numbers Tell Us," Institute for Family Studies (2021).

16 Amber Lapp and David Lapp, "Work-Family Policy in Trump's America" *National Review.* December 14, /2016.

17 Family Feud: Child Allowance Edition. American Compass. 2021.

18 Nicholas Eberstadt, *Men without Work* (Conshohocken: Templeton Press, 2022).

19 David Cesarini, et al., "Fortunate Families? The Effects of Wealth on Marriage and Fertility," National Bureau of Economic Research (2023).

20 Leah Brooks and Zachary Liscow, "Infrastructure Costs," *American Economic Journal: Applied Economics* (2023).

21 *Tennessee Valley Authority v. Hiram Hill* 437 U.S. 153. 1978.

22 Length of Environmental Impact Statements. Executive Office of the President. 2020.

23 David Autor, "The China Shock: Learning from Labor Market Adjustment to Large Changes in Trade," *National Bureau of Economic Research* 2016.

24 Josh Bivens, "Using standard models to benchmark the costs of globalization for American workers without a college degree," Economic Policy Institute. 2013.

25 Press Briefing by Gene Sperling, Director of the National Economic Council, Martin Bailey, Chairman, Council of Economic Advisors, Lawrence Summers, Secretary of the Treasury and Robert M. Solow,

Professor Emeritus at Massachusetts Institute of Technology. Online from The American Presidency Project.

26 "Where's the Growth? Assessing the Results of the Globalization Experiment," American Compass. 2022.

27 Oren Cass, The False Promise of Good Jobs. American Compass. 2022. https://americancompass.org/the-false-promise-of-good-jobs/

28 Michael Pettis, Bad Trade. American Compass. 2022.

29 Ruggles, "Patriarchy, Power, and Pay"

30 George Borjas, "Native Internal Migration and the Labor Market Impact of Immigration," *The Journal of Human Resources*. 2006.

31 Jerry Kammer, "The 2006 Swift Raids. Assessing the Impact of Immigration Enforcement Actions at Six Facilities," *Center for Immigration Studies*. (2009).

32 George Borjas, "Yes, Immigration Hurts American Workers," *Politico Magazine*, September/October 2016.

33 Michael Amoir, "The contribution of immigration to local labor market adjustment," *Centre for Economic Performance* (2020).

34 Cass, *The False Promise of Good Jobs*

35 Alvaro Mezza, et al., "Student Loans and Homeownership," *Journal of Labor Economics* (2020).

36 Erin Velez, Melissa Cominole, and Alexander Bentz, "Debt Burden after College: The Effect of Student Loan Debt on Graduates' Employment, Additional Schooling, Family Formation, and Home Ownership," Education Economics. 2018.

37 Brett Hollenbeck, "The Financial Consequences of Legalized Sports Gambling," Working Paper, (2024).

38 Benjamin Gurrentz, "Millennial Marriage: How Much Does Economic Security Matter to Marriage Rates for Young Adults?," Fertility and Family Statistics Branch, U.S. Census Bureau (2018).

39 Sam Bowman, John Myers, and Ben Southwood, "The housing theory of everything," Works in Progress (2021).

40 Quoctrung Bui, Matt A. V. Chaban, and Jeremy White, "40 Percent of the Buildings in Manhattan Could Not Be Built Today," *New York Times*, May 20, 2016.

41 Diana Thomas and Devon Gorry, "Regulation and the Cost of Child Care," *Mercatus Center Working Paper* (2015).
42 Thomas and Gorry, "Regulation and the Cost of Child Care"
43 Katherine Guyot and Richard Reeves, "Unpredictable work hours and volatile incomes are long-term risks for American workers," *Brookings Institution*, August 18, 2020, https://www.brookings.edu/articles/unpredictable-work-hours-and-volatile-incomes-are-long-term-risks-for-american-workers/
44 Amber Lapp and David Lapp, "Work-Family Policy in Trump's America," *Institute for Family Studies* (2016).
45 "Does part-time work offer flexibility to employed mothers?" Monthly Labor Review, U.S. Bureau of Labor and Statistics (2022).
46 Lyman Stone, "Putting Things in Order: Relationship Sequencing Preferences of American Women," *Institute for Family Studies* (2023).
47 Nicholas Wolfinger and Samuel Perry, "Does a longer sexual resume affect marriage rates?" *Social Science Research* (2023).
48 Scott Stanley, Galena Kline Rhoades, Howard Markman, "Sliding vs. deciding: Inertia and the premarital cohabitation effect," *Family Relations* (2006).

Conclusion

1 Edmond Burke, *Reflections on the Revolution in France* (New York: Penguin Classics, 1982).
2 "Mothers and work: What's 'ideal'?" Pew Research Center, Washington, D.C. (August 19, 2013) https://www.pewresearch.org/short-reads/2013/08/19/mothers-and-work-whats-ideal/
3 Robert VerBruggen, "The Real Housewives of America: Dad's Income and Mom's Work," *Institute for Family Studies* (2019).
4 "Mothers and work: What's 'ideal'?" Pew Research Center, Washington, D.C. (August 19, 2013) https://www.pewresearch.org/short-reads/2013/08/19/mothers-and-work-whats-ideal/ "Employment Characteristics of Families – 2023," Bureau of Labor Statistics. (April 24, 2024) https://www.bls.gov/news.release/pdf/famee.pdf

INDEX

ABOUT THE AUTHOR

CONN CARROLL IS THE COMMENTARY editor for the Washington Examiner. He served as a communications director in the US senate for seven years before returning to journalism. He is a graduate of the George Washington University and the Antonin Scalia Law School. He lives in northern Virginia with his wife and three children. You can follow him @conncarroll.

Made in the USA
Middletown, DE
10 May 2025

75367368R00146